Henry R. Stiles

A Supplement to the History and Genealogies of Ancient Windsor, Conn.

Containing Corrections and Additions Which Have Accrued...

Henry R. Stiles

A Supplement to the History and Genealogies of Ancient Windsor, Conn.
Containing Corrections and Additions Which Have Accrued...

ISBN/EAN: 9783744787079

Printed in Europe, USA, Canada, Australia, Japan

Cover: Foto ©ninafisch / pixelio.de

More available books at **www.hansebooks.com**

A

SUPPLEMENT

TO THE

HISTORY AND GENEALOGIES

OF

ANCIENT WINDSOR, CONN.,

CONTAINING

CORRECTIONS AND ADDITIONS

WHICH HAVE ACCRUED SINCE THE PUBLICATION OF THAT WORK.

BY HENRY R. STILES, M. D.,

WOODBRIDGE, N. J.

ALBANY :

J. MUNSELL, 78 STATE STREET.

1863.

TO

MY FRIEND,

D. WILLIAMS PATTERSON

OF WEST WINSTED, CONN.,

AN ENTHUSIASTIC, PATIENT AND ACCURATE GENEALOGIST;

A SINCERE LOVER OF THE TRUTH, WHICH IS

THE SOUL OF HISTORY;

THIS VOLUME

IS RESPECTFULLY DEDICATED.

NOTE.

Three years ago, when I published the *History and Genealogies of Ancient Windsor, Conn.*, I was induced, if not compelled, by a super-abundance of material, to give my subscribers, without additional charge, over 300 pages more than was promised them—an act of generosity which, as it is easy to see, was much more advantageous to them than to me. And when, at last, relieved from the burdens of authorship and financial cares, I felt that I certainly had fully paid (both principal and interest) *my* share of the debt of love which I owed to the old town of Windsor; and little dreamed that I should ever again put myself in harness for her historical benefit. But, unfortunately for my " sweet dream of peace," I found myself *inwrought* into old Windsor's history and interest. I could not henceforth be an uninterested looker on, and found myself still tracing out the lines of her ancient families, and that—shall I confess it—there was an indefinable charm, for me, in all that pertained to Windsor history. Many errors I detected in the printed volume— some of clerical, others of typographical origin—some evident faults of commission, and not unfrequently a fault of omission. These were to have been expected; the utmost circumspection could not have guarded entirely against them, in a work of such size, and containing so many dates, names, etc. Correspondents also constantly furnished me new suggestions, ingenious elucidations, " missing links," and " unknown quantities," which threw new light and value upon my printed page. New sources of authority also came to light, by the discovery of ancient records in unthought-of hiding places. What wonder is it, then, that the *notes* which gradually enriched the margins of my library copy of the Windsor History, soon grew so voluminous as to suggest the idea of a Supplement ? For what Genealogist or Historian, who, when he has found a new fact, or a " nugget," is not willing, like the woman in the parable, to call his friends and co-laborers together, saying, " Rejoice with me; for I have found the piece which I had lost ?" Therefore, I have compiled this Supplement; if it convicts me of shortcomings in my former work, it will, at least, assure my friends of my desire to make good any deficiencies, and to add to their pleasure and profit.

I have not blown my trumpet long and loud about this Supplement (for honestly, I was afraid of awaking the *echoes*), but have compiled it simply of the new material which has come to hand since the publication of the History.

I am under especial obligations to H. SIDNEY HAYDEN, Town Clerk of Windsor; to the Town Clerk of Windsor Locks; Mrs. HIRAM B. CASE, wife of the Town Clerk of Bloomfield; Rev. GEO. B. NEWCOMB of Bloomfield; D. WILLIAMS PATTERSON of West Winsted; CHAS. J. HOADLY and Hon. J. HAMMOND TRUMBULL of Hartford; and to SAMUEL H. PARSONS and EDWIN STEARNS of Middletown, for favors received in the compilation of this volume.

And now, as I lay down my pen from correcting the last proof of this Supplement, I feel that my " labor of love " for Ancient Windsor is *finished*. If the citizens of that venerable town have need, in the future, of the services of a historian, they need not apply to their true friend,

Woodbridge, N. J., Nov., 1862.   HENRY REED STILES, M. D.

ABBREVIATIONS USED IN THIS VOLUME.

In addition to those used in the *History of Ancient Windsor*, and which are probably familiar to its readers, we have employed the following :

E. W. C. R.—The Record of Baptisms in the 2d Church of Windsor, afterwards the 1st Church of East Windsor, and now the 1st Church of South Windsor, from 1761-1845; sometimes called the *Cook Record*, from the family by whom it was commenced and kept for many years.

R. Mss.—An ancient private record of Births, Marriages and Deaths in Wintonbury parish (now Bloomfield township); furnished to us by Eliza Mills Rundall of Seneca Falls, N. Y.

N. S. R.—The Pastoral Records of the North Society of Windsor, under the ministry of the Rev. Theodore Hinsdale, 1761-1794.

W. C. R.—The Records of the First Church of Windsor, commenced by the Rev. D. S. Rowland.   Marriages, 1777-1846; Baptisms, 1790-1855; Deaths, 1790-1857.

Wby. C. R.—The Records of the First Church of Wintonbury parish (near Bloomfield, Ct.), Births, Marriages and Deaths, 1738-1830.

Mss. Col. Rec.—Three volumes of ancient Colonial Records, recently discovered by C. J. Hoadly, State Librarian of Connecticut, and deposited in the State Library at Hartford.   These volumes contain transcripts of the Land Records, and of the Births, Marriages and Deaths of Windsor, Fairfield, Wethersfield, and some other towns, recorded by order of court, and thus forming duly authenticated and reliable records.

Bap., Baptized.

Prob., Probably.

Poss., Possibly.

Ment., Mentioned.

N. B.—Genealogists will hardly need my recommendation to examine *Trumbull's Col. Rec. of Connecticut ; Hoadly's Records of the New Haven Colony*, and *Savage's Genealogical Dictionary*, in connection with any investigations which they may make into Windsor families.   In the latter grand and valuable work, some corrections will be found for my *Windsor History*—discrepancies between the works must be settled by patient investigation—yet no one can feel sure that he has exhausted his subject unless he has compared my volume with the three works mentioned above, and which are inexhaustible treasuries of genealogical information.

SUPPLEMENT.

Page 5, line 23, for *Medforth* read *Medford.*

P. 20, l. 13, for *Elisworth* read *Ellsworth.*

P. 22, l. 41, add the same Edward Preston probably, who settled afterwards at New Haven.

P. 22, l. 42, Edward Pattison, seems not to have been a land holder at Windsor, but to have early removed to New Haven, where (according to *New Haven Col. Rec.*, ii, 18) he signed the fundamental agreement, June 4, 1639. *New Eng. His. and Gen. Reg.*, ix, 362, shows that sister Pattison, wife of Edward, had two children baptized, John, January, 1644, and Elizabeth, July 12, 1644, at New Haven. John probably died young, as Dodd's *East Haven Register*, p. 149, shows, that in 1662, Thomas Smith m. Elizabeth only child of Ed. Pattison, and gives their descendants. He also shows that Pattison d. Oct. 31, 1669. D. W. Patterson of West Winsted, Conn., in communicating the above facts concerning his ancestor, says : " I suppose your authority for saying that he was in the neighborhood of Hartford as late as 1670, is (*Conn. Col. Rec.*, ii, p. 130) the grant of land to him by the General Court at its May session, 1670, and this puzzled me when taken in connection with Dodd's record of his death in 1669. But his petition was very likely prepared for the October session in 1669, and not acted upon until May, 1670; for in *Conn. Col. Rec.*, iii, 116, is a notice from Thos. Smith (his son-in-law) that he had procured the grant of land to Edward Patterson to be laid out to himself, and the court approved it, ' he being the heire of sayd Patteson;' this last you see reconciles the whole."

P. 37, l. 9, for *Noreton* read *Norton.*

P. 39, l. 25, for *Edward* read *Thomas ;* for *David* read *Edward.*

P. 62, l. 10 to 18, the list of tax-payers here referred to "taken from an old *Book of Rates*," is as follows :

Those having a family, a horse [and] two oxen :"

John Bissell,	S. Grant (no horse),
Thos. Bissell,	T[ahan] Grant,
Sam. Bissell,	Jon. Grant,
Timo. Buckland,	S. Gibbs,
Thos. Buckland,	G. Gibbs,

Nich. Buckland,
Peter Browne,
Sam. Barber,
Mr. D. Clarke,
Ed. Chapman,
Job Drake, Jr.,
H. Denslow,
Jos. Ellsworth,
James Enno,
Ben. Eggleston,
John Fyler,
Will Filly,
Jas. Griswold,
Jos. Griswold,
Walter Gaylord,
J. Gaylord,

W. Hoskins,
J. Hosford,
D. Hayden,
Mich. Kelsey,
Jon. Loomis
T. Loomis,
D. Moore,
J. Moore,
S. Marshall,
J. Maudsly,
Jon. Osborn,
Jon. Osborn, Jr.,
John Owen,
Wl. Phelps,
Mr. Pinne,
Jos. Phelps.

" Single men."

Josias Alvord,
John Birge horse and 2 oxen
Jos. Birge, horse
T. Burnham, horse,
E. Elmer,
W. Filley,
Ephm. frory, horse,
Jon. Filley
Jon. [Tailer, h]orse and 2 oxen,
Hen. Tailer, horse,
D. Treat, horse,
Jas. Hillier, horse,

T. Eggleston, horse,
[undeci.] Moses [or Moore], horse,
Thos. Phelps, horse,
Nat. Pond, horse,
Thos. Parsons, horse,
J. Parsons, horse.
Ebns. Parsons, horse,
Jos. Sanders, horse,
T. Saxton, horse,
Wido. Fyler,
D. Wilton,
[one undecipherable]   Total, 24.

" Family, horse and 4 oxen."

Mr. J. Allyn,
J. Bissell,
Nat. Bissell,
Job Drake,
J. Ellsworth,
J. Osborn,
Jacob Drake,
Jas. Eggleston,
An. Hoskins,

Joseph Loomis,
N. Loomis,
J. Moses,
—— Newbury,
Jon. Porter, Sr.,
—— Stoughton,
Owen Tudor,
Mr. Wolcot,
H. Wolcot.   Total, 18.

S. Rockwell,
John Strong,
Nic. Sension,
Jon. Stiles,
Step. Taylor,

John Terry,
W. Thrall,
T. Thrall,
R. Watson,
N. Winchell.
[and one other which could not be deciphered.]   Total, 53.

" Family and horse."

Ben. Alvord,
Danl. Birge,
Sam. Baker,
W. Buell,
Jo. Cross,
[Rev.] Mr. Chauncy,
N. Cook,
T. Debble, Jr.,
Ebns. Debble,
Jno. Debble,

Lft. Fyler,
Zurob. Fyler,
Sam. Filley,
John Gillet, Senr.,
Jon. Gillet, Jr.,
Corn. Gillet,
Jon. Gillet,
Jos. Gaylord,
R. Hayward,
T. Hall,

N. Holcomb,
Jos. Lomas,
Ed. Messenger,
And. Moore,
Peter Mills,
Josias Owen,
Jon. Porter,
Tim. Phelps,
Abm. Phelps,

N. Pinne,
Tim. Palmer,
Hump. Prior,
Abm. Randell,
R. Strong,
Hen. Stiles,
[Rev.] Mr. Woodbridge,
S. Wilson.   Total, 37.

"Family only."

W. Adams,
T. Burnham, Jr.,
J. Colt,
W. Morton,
J. Drake, Sr.,
Jo. Denslow,
E. Elmer,
J. Elmer,

M. Filley,
Sam. Forward,
J. Hodge,
N. Palmer,
Thos. Sanders,
R. Vore,
N. Wilton.
                     Total, 15.

P. 62, l. 22, for *Daniel* read *David.*

P. 68, l. 13, add as an illustration, "Thomas Stoughton for his unnecessary withdrawing of himselfe from the publique preaching of the Word on the Lord's day, is fined 5s. *Pt. Ct. Rec.,* vol. II, April 18, 1654.

P. 75, l. 30, for *infringed* read *impinged.*

P. 113, line 2, add the following extract from the recently discovered 2d vol. of Ct. Records in *Conn. Archives :* At a Particular Court, held at Hartford, May 13, 1662. "This court orders that William Heyden of Wyndsor, shall for future cease to improve the lands at Nameleck that belongs to Spaniunk wᶜh is by the Bounds of John Bissel's Lottments. And yᵗ neither the said William nor any other shall any way hinder, or directly or indirectly prevent John Bissel's compounding with yᵉ Indian for that land."

Pp. 124 and 125. Addenda to description of *The Town House.* Mr. JABEZ H. HAYDEN of Windsor Locks, to whose surveys we are mainly indebted, as before stated, for this plan and distribution of Ancient Windsor, has, since the publication of the foregoing, sent us the following note, relative to the Palizado : "I am not quite satisfied with Matthew Grant's figures yet ; the Palizado *does not prove* exactly, though pretty near it. I am more and more confirmed in the opinion that the present 'parsonage' stands on the 'Town House lot,' which gives the north bounds of the Palizado, and there is no question about the other three sides."

P. 137, l. 9 and 10. Addenda to remarks on *Broad Street,* by J. H. Hayden : "I do not now remember the earliest date at which the present Broad Street is noticed, but it was, at first, but six rods wide where the present traveled road is. I find that when Mr. Warham and his wife Abigail (April 1, 1664), made over the dwelling house and land of John Branker, deceased, it bounded ' east by the highway on the bank against the Little Meadow, and westerly, against or by the highway *as it is appointed* to rauge;' proving that at that date the highway on the east had not been changed to its present place, and one would infer that what is now Broad street was then only appointed or set out, and not in use. Broad street was at first but six rods wide, and was probably widened by the owners on the east side, when the highway on the upland against Little Meadow (on which they built) was removed to its present location, that they might bring the street nearer their houses. When they rebuilt, they of course, placed their houses behind their barns, and facing the new Broad street."

P. 159, l. 41. This "setting in the yard," was in other words, guard or sentinel duty in the meeting house yard during divine service, a precaution quite necessary in those days of savage invasion and surprises. The following item from the records (*Windsor Rec.*, II, p. 13) explains the matter somewhat more clearly : "The townes[men] meet, and Ephraim Strong and Nathaniel Pinne demanded paye for setting in the yard, and they are allowed to be payed 2s. apiece out of ye towne-rate, and so likewise others that stand in like account with them as have set in ye yard without their ½ lb. of puder [powder] a man payed to them, but was promised 12 pence a man to each man, in lieu of puder."

P. 160, after l. 30, insert the following interesting incident, extracted from the *Remarkable Providences* of Rev. Increase Mather, a book which, from its extreme scarcity, has been almost unknown to our authors hitherto, and has only recently been made available by its re-publication in London, under the editorship of George Offer, Esq.

Mather says (p. 24 of the above London edition): "In the next place we shall take notice of some remarkable preservations which sundry in Windsor in New England have experienced; the persons concerned therein being desirous that the Lord's goodness towards them may be ever had in remembrance, wherefore a faithful hand has given me the following account: Jan. 13, 1670.—Three women, viz: the wives of Lieut. Filer, and of John Drake, and of Nathaniel Lomas, having crossed Connecticut river upon a necessary and neighborly account,* and having done the work they went for, were desirous to return to their own families, the river being at that time partly shut up with ice, old and new, and partly open. There being some pains taken aforehand to cut a way through the ice, the three women abovesaid got into a canoe, with whom also there was Nathaniel Bissell and an Indian. There was likewise another canoe with two men in it, that went before them to help them, in case they should meet with any distress, which indeed quickly came upon them, for just as they were getting out of the narrow passage between the ice, being near the middle of the river, a greater part of the upper ice came down upon them, and struck the end of their canoe, and broke it to pieces, so that it quickly sunk under them. The Indian speedily got upon the ice, but Nathaniel Bissell and the abovesaid women were left floating in the middle of the river, being cut off from all manner of human help besides what did arise from themselves, and the two men in the little canoe, which was so small that three persons durst seldom, if ever, venture in it. They were, indeed, discerned from one shore,

---

* Undoubtedly to attend a woman in confinement.

but the dangerous ice would not admit from either shore one to come near them. All things thus eircumstanced, the suddenness of the stroke and distress (which is apt to amaze men, especially when no less than life is concerned), the extreme coldness of the weather, it being a sharp season, that persons out of the water were in danger of freezing, the unaptness of persons to help themselves, being mostly women, one big with child, and near the time of her travail (who also was carried away under the ice), the other as unskilled and inactive to do anything for self-preservation as almost any could be, the waters deep, that there was no hope of footing, no passage to either shore in any eye of reason, neither with their little canoe, by reason of the ice, nor without it, the ice being thin and rotten, and full of holes. Now that all should be brought off safely without the loss of life, or wrong to health, was counted in the day of it a *remarkable Providence*. To say how it was done, is difficult, yet, something of the manner of the deliverance may be mentioned. The abovesaid Nathaniel Bissell, perceiving their danger, and being active in swimming, endeavored what might be the preservation of himself and some others; he strove to have swum to the upper ice, but the stream being too hard, he was forced downwards to the lower ice, where, by reason of the slipperiness of the ice, and disadvantage of the stream, he found it difficult getting up; at length by the good hand of Providence, being gotten upon the ice, he saw one of the women swimming down under the ice, and perceiving a hole or open place some few rods below, there he watched, and took her up as she swam along. The other two women were in the river till the two men in the little canoe came for their relief At length all of them got their heads above the water and had a little time to pause, though a long and difficult, and dangerous way to any shore, but by getting their little canoe upon the ice, and carrying one at a time over hazardous places, they did (though in a long while) get all safe to the shore from whence they came."

P. 162. At the end of the chapter, add the following from p. 223 of the above quoted work:

"July 20, 1683, a considerable flood unexpectedly arose, which proved detrimental to many in that colony [i. e., Connecticut]. But on August 13, a second and more dreadful flood came. The waters were then observed to rise twenty-six feet above their usual boundaries; the grass in the meadow, also the English grain was carried away before it; the Indian corn, by the long continuance of the waters is spoiled, so that the four river towns, viz : Windsor, Hartford, Wethersfield, Middletown are extream sufferers. They write from thence that some who had hundreds of bushels of corn in the morning, at night had not one peck left for their families to live upon."

P. 190. In regard to the Rev. Mr. Woodbridge, we have the following from Mr. John Ward Dean of Boston, in a letter to the author :

"My ancestor, Rev. Benj. Woodbridge, appears to have had opponents (and

2

adherents, too), wherever he was. After he left Windsor, he preached in Bristol, now in the state of Rhode Island, and after that in Medford, Mass. One curious circumstance concerning him was related to me recently by the Rev. Mr. Page of Cambridge. There was trouble between him and a portion of his flock at Medford, and the matter was carried before the General Court or Legislature, who ordered that the town should pay Mr. W. the amount due him, amounting to a considerable sum, and that the church should then proceed to choose a pious and learned minister for their pastor. The money was paid, and the church called together to choose a pastor, and the choice *fell upon the Rev. Benjamin Woodbridge,* the old pastor. There was some wincing, but the opponents could not deny that he was a pious and learned minister, and the General Court had not ordered the church to choose another man."

P. 202, l. 4, for *Crane* read *Crow.*

P. 208, l. 25, for *Tyler,* read *Fyler;* same on 28th line.

P. 211, after line 34, insert the following item: "December 8, 1709, liberty was granted by the town to Jonathan Ellsworth, Thomas Marshall and Thomas Moore, to erect a mill on the mill brook on the south side of the rivulet, provided it be built within two years."

P. 221, l. 35, for 1757, read 1657.

P. 225, note, for *Ebenezer,* read *Elijah;* same on page 323.

P. 252, l. 23, for *west,* read *east.*

P. 253, after l. 34 add "Zebulon Seymour, carp'r began work on meeting house, July 6, 1761, ceased Nov. 7." The "seating" of the new edifice was completed on 15 of October, and in the old record of baptisms, is the following entry: "November 22, 1761, that was the first sabbath [we] met in, our new meeting house, there was four children baptized that day."

P. 255, after l. 8, insert the following: Mr. A. S. Kellogg of Vernon, Conn., has kindly called our attention to the fact that, in the year 1760, a part of the Second Society in Windsor, was set off to help form the Society of North Bolton. He says: "Something respecting this may be found in the *Records of the Colony,* vols. VIII and IX, but most of the papers are in the State Library," *Ecclesiastical,* vol. XII. "They are under the title North Bolton, which accounts for their not having attracted your attention. My notes are very brief and incomplete, but, if I made correct abstracts, the Assembly, in May, 1750, appointed a committee upon the memorials of Benj. Stoughton and others, of Windsor, for an Ecclesiastical Society, with certain limits; and of Isaac Jones and others, of Bolton, for an Ecclesiastical Society, with certain other limits. In each case it was reported that they were "too few." February 12, 1754, Isaac Jones, Moses Thrall and John Hills of Bolton, David Smith, John Searl and Joseph Steadman of the South [or Second] Society of Windsor, and John Craw and Samuel Hills of the Parish of Ellington, petitioned for an Ecclesiastical Society. April 23, 1760, a final petition was granted, and in Oct. 1760, North Bolton was made a society, its north and west boundaries being thus defined in the resolution: (Starting from the northeast corner of Bolton) thence turning westward in the line between Bolton and Ellington, to Bolton northwest corner, and still continuing the same course into Ellington about a mile and a half and forty-two rods; thence turning and running southwardly at the west end of the second tier of lots to Hartford line; thence turning eastward in said line to Bolton or the T ditch; thence turning southwardly one mile in the line betwixt the towns of Hartford and Bolton; thence eastward to the first mentioned bounds."

These " Hartford lines" are the present boundaries of Manchester, and the T ditch is at the N. E. corner of Manchester.

The part taken from Windsor seems to have been a rhomboid, its longer sides being the present west line of Vernon, and a parallel line running from the *re-entrant* angle in the S. W. corner of the town. The line of Windsor, and afterwards of East Windsor, used to pass within 60 or 80 rods of the site of the present meeting house at Vernon Center.

P. 255, at bottom, add the following document—which explains itself—relative to the respective salaries of Messrs. Edwards and Perry.

The Rev. Mr. Edwards settled Sept., 1695.
His salary the first year 1696 was £60 & £12 for wood £72 0 0
    2 year 1697 Idem. 72 0 0
    3 year 1698, £70 & £12 for wood 82 0 0
    4 year 1699 Idem. 82 0 0
    5 year 1700. . . . . 92 0 0
    6 year 1701. . . . . 92 0 0
    7 year 1702. . . . . 92 0 0
    8 year 1703. . . . . 92 0 0
    9 year 1704. . . . . 92 0 0
  10 year 1705. . . . . 92 0 0
  11 year 1706, £100 & £12 for wood. 112 0 0
  12 year 1707, £100 & £12 for wood 112 0 0
  13 year 1708, 100 & £12 for wood 112 0 0
  14 year 1709, 90 & £12 for wood 102 0 0
  15 year 1710, 100 & £12 for wood 112 0 0
  16 year 1711, 100 & £12 for wood 112 0 0
  17 year 1712, 100 & £12 for wood 112 0 0
  18 year 1713. . . . . 120 0 0

                        £1754 0 0
                        1480 0 0

                        £274 0 0

N. B.—£274 Divided By 18 the number of years leaves £15 4 5 the sum that Mr. Edwards' salary annually exceeded Mr. Perry, for the First 18 years of their Ministry, Including all Donations, subscriptions, & additions made Mr. Perry since his settlement.

The Rev. Mr. Perry settled 11th June 1755.
His salary the first year 1756. . . . . £60 0 0
    2 year 1757. . . . . 60 0 0
    3 year 1758 . . . . 60 0 0
    4 year 1759. . . . . 75 0 0
    5 year 1760. . . . . 75 0 0
    6 year 1761. . . . . 75 0 0
    7 year 1762. . . . . 75 0 0

8 year 1763 £75 subscrip £25....................	100 0 0	
9 year 1764	75 0 0	
10 year 1765..............................	75 0 0	
11 year 1766 £75 addition £50................	125 0 0	
12 year 1767..............................	75 0 0	
13 year 1768..............................	75 0 0	
14 year 1769 £75 addition £40..............	115 0 0	
15 year 1770 £75 addition £40..............	115 0 0	
16 year 1771..............................	75 0 0	
17 year 1772 £75 addition £20..............	95 0 0	
18 year 1773..............................	75 0 0	
	£1480 0 0	

£1480 Divided By 18 leaves £82 4 5.

This document (together with a duplicate) was found among some old papers in the garret of Maj. H. W. Grant of South Windsor, Conn., by H. R. S., 1859.

P. 258, l. 23, " on the 8 Dec., 1708, it was voted to give Job Drake thirty acres of land on the east side of the sequestered land in exchange for about ¾ of an acre of land he resigns up to the town for a burying place, on the East side of the great river." 1st Book Wind. Rec., 102.

P. 262, l. 30, for *Wadworth*, read *Wadsworth*.

P. 275, l. 12, for *Gurdon* Hall, read *Gordon* Hall.

P. 278, John Aborns' epitaph should read " by a flash of *Lightling*."

P. 287, E. Pinney d. 1835. See p. 748.

P. 287, Battle of Stillwater, 1777.

P. 311, l. 12, for *Stodant* read *Stoddard*.

P. 328, l. 1, for *Elward* read *Edward*.

P. 344, these *deaths* of soldiers occurred in 1758, except that of Mumford, which was in 1760. *Cheffield* here should be *Sheffield*, and *Greenbank* should be *Greenbush*.

P. 345, l. 31, insert after " very forlornness," the words " of hope."

P. 349, l. 2, for *Fuxley*, read *Huxley*.

P. 351, l. 2, Parsons d. Oct. 1762, Cook d. Dec. 1762. All these deaths occurred in the year 1762.

P. 353, after l. 32, add, " East Windsor was declared a distinct town by the Governor and Assembly, at their session at Hartford on the second Thursday in May following."

P. 354, 355, *addenda*. Extracts from Parson Hinsdale's (North Windsor) *Church Records*. " Aug. 13, 1768, Mary and Elizabeth, daughters of David Thrall, and Jerusha, daughter of Charles Thrall, were all, at once, unhappily drowned in Pequonnock river, as they went in for their diversion," and, " no longer after than August 17, Mr. Henry Chapman, in the dusk of the evening, climbing a scaffold in a barn, fell and received a wound in his head of which, in a few hours he died. How hard God calls to a hardened people ! "

P. 358, l. 26, after the words " Society Records," add " by Henry Allyn, Clerk."

P. 367, 1. 23, for *Hon. John M.*, read *Richard.*

P. 375, note 2 on this page belongs to following page.

P. 376, note 2 on this page belongs to following page.

P. 386, after 1. 8, insert " Deo. 1775, or Jan. 1776, JOHN GILMAN (*Wby.*), d in camp, a. about 18. (*Wby. Ch. R.*)

P. 399, after 1. 7, add Lieut. SAMUEL WING, d. at Danbury, in the service, July 1777. Hinsdale's (No. Windsor) *Church Records.* See pages 429 and 825. Also " Jan. 1777, LUTHER CENTER, returning from captivity in New York d. at Wintonbury." (*Wby. Ch. R.*)

P. 400, after 1. 5, add the names of SAMUEL COY (see also page 409,) and JOEL DENSLOW (see also page 420,) both of whom died in camp, June, 1778.

P. 417, after 1. 26, add name of THOMAS BARBER in same Co. with Lemuel Drake, which see for further particulars.

P. 420, after 1. 30, add name of LEMUEL DRAKE, his services as recorded in his affidavit before pension agent (Samuel H. Parsons, of Middletown, Conn.), were as follows : About the 15th of August, 1776, he enlisted, at Windsor, under Maj. Roger Newberry, in a company of which Benj. Allen was first lieutenant, and Austin Phelps second lieutenant; remained in service until 'latter part of October, '76, when he was dismissed, being at that time at, or near, Valentine's Hill, N. Y. After his enlistment he was marched to Wethersfield, and from thence sailed to New York city, where his company was stationed in Little Dock street, near the East river, and at the time of the battle on Long Island his regiment were paraded near the wharf, but were not called into the action.

He had a second tour of duty, from August to the latter part of October, 1777. This time he was *drafted* at Windsor, in a company commanded by Jonathan Wadsworth of Hartford, captain, Phelps of Windsor, lieutenant, and Owen, ensign. This company belonged to a regiment commanded by Col. Cook of Wallingford, Lieut. Col. Woodbridge, Maj. Kent. They marched from Hartford, to Stillwater, N. Y., where he was in the battles under Gen. Gates, was present at Burgoyne's surrender at Saratoga, N. Y., marched to Albany, was there detailed as one of a guard (under Capt. Blake, Austin Phelps, lieutenant, and Reuben Wadsworth, orderly), to escort 100 prisoners to Hartford. Again, in September, 1778, he was drafted, at Windsor, to go to New London, where he served between two and three months in the militia, commanded by Capt. Allen of New London, and —— Bissell of East Windsor, sergeant, mostly on guard service.

P. 424, 1. 25, the following particulars concerning GEORGE LATIMER's services, are gathered from the same source as the above : He enlisted as wagoner in Capt. Daniel Jones' company, July 15, 1777, for three years, his term expiring July 15, 1780. He then enlisted again, at Hartford, went to Pomfret, where he was one of a company of ten men in charge of ammunition wagons, returned to Hartford, went to New York state, at Red Hook and Fishkill.

He was drafted for three months in summer of '76, was at New York at the retreat from Long Island. In or about March, 1777, was drafted for three months, and went to Whiteplains, where he was at the time Danbury was burned.

P. 425, l. 21. Additional particulars from same sources as the preceding : INCREASE MATHER enlisted at Windsor in early part of April, 1775, in the company of Captain or Major Roger Enos, Lieuts. Willys and Blodget, and Converse, sergeant, for 8 months. He then enlisted while at Roxbury, for 12 or 14 months; was there when the battle of Bunker's Hill was fought. About the middle of November he enlisted, with consent of his captain, in another company, commanded by E. F. Bissell, Capt.; Lieut. Humphreys and Ensign Richard Goodman, in Col. Jedediah Huntington's regiment, from which he was discharged January, 1777.

During this service he was on Long Island, in August, 1776, was in several skirmishes there, and was in the army in its retreat from Long Island through Westchester. From July, '76, to January, '77, he acted as sergeant.

P. 426, l. 13, insert the name of ROSWELL NOBLES born Oct. 24, 1758. He enlisted for one year, as a drummer, at Simsbury, May, 1776, in a company commanded by Capt. Noah Phelps, Lieut. Carver and Ensign Benj. Holcomb, belonging to a regiment commanded by Col. Andrew Ward, Lieut.-Col. Johnson and Major Isaac Cook; was dismissed from the service near Morristown, N. J., May, 1777.

P. 426, l. 34, insert name of AUSTIN PHELPS, see deposition above of Lemuel Drake.

P. 427, by an error of arrangement, three colored soldiers are entered under the head of the Prior family.

P. 433, after l. 22, add, in Rev. Mr. Rowland's *Records of Baptisms* in Windsor Church, the following entry occurs : " 1795, Baptisms in *new* meeting house, and *united* parishes." Then follows under this, a record of the baptism, January 4, of a daughter of Samuel Allen.

P. 438. The First Congregational Church and Society of Windsor has a Church Fund, concerning which we have not been able to learn much. It probably had its beginning in the bequest of Jane (Fooks), the widow of William Hosford of Windsor, who returned to her home in Old England after her husband's death. On the 15th of January, 1671, being the 23d year of Charles the 2d, Mrs. Hosford, described as " of Tiverton, in the county of Devon, widow," made her will, of which her son Stephen Gaylord, John Witchfield and Walter Fyler of Windsor, were appointed the executors. She devised certain moneys to Esther (or Stephen), Samuel and Sarah Gaylord, and to their children; the rent of a meadow to her sons-in law, John Hosford, and the three above named, during the life of the testator. After her demise, the meadow, comprising about 20 acres of meadow and swamp, was to go and belong to the " Old Church of Windsor " forever. (*Lands, vol. 1, p. 90, Conn. Arch.*) On 13th of Oct., 1692, complaint was made to the General Court, by petition from the Windsor Church, that they were kept out of the right and use of the aforesaid land, it being yet in the hands of her heirs, who say she is not dead. And the Court, considering that she was aged when she returned to England, and has been there 40* years or so, and not heard from lately, declared her to be *dead in law*, unless it could be *proved* that she was alive or had been heard of within 7 years past. (*Docs. in Conn. Arch.*) The land was fully confirmed to the Church, Sept. 3, 1695.

The Rev. Joseph Marsh, also, the third minister of this church, devised his property, after his wife's death, to the Windsor Church, for gospel and school purposes.

P. 439, l. 24, after *separatists* insert *alone*.

P. 451, after l. 32, insert the following item from Timothy Loomis' common-place book: " 1714, April 5. The school house was raised on t'other Hill." Taking Loomis' residence as our standpoint, we infer that he had reference to Stoney Hill, by the expression " t'other hill."

P. 480, under head of Stores, Trade, Commerce, etc., insert the following item from Timothy Loomis' common place book, as illustrative: " 1739, I sent 221 weight of tobacco to Barbadoes in the sloop, The Windsor, whereof 20 pounds was my son Timothy's."

P. 493, l. 10, for (*Windsor Locks*) read (*Suffield*).

Sheep.—In olden time there were more sheep raised than at the present day. These sheep were all turned into one large flock, and herded by a shepherd, either in some large field or in the streets.

In June, 1733, the people of Windsor voted, "that the sheep in this town shall be put in *three* flocks, that is to say on the north side of the Rivulet, to be one flock, and on the east side of the Great River to be one flock, and on the south side of the rivulet to be one flock." It was also decided that each flock could be divided if it was deemed best.

In 1735, the east side Windsor people voted that there should be put one flock on that side of the Great River, and Messrs. Lieut. Joseph Loomis, Mr. Joseph Rockwell and Mr. Abiel Abbott should be a committee " for ordering the prudentials of the flock this present year or summer." By the term " ordering the prudentials " was meant as is elsewhere seen, the hiring of a shepherd and folding the sheep.

After the Revolution, one " Old Hendricks " as he was called, a Hessian, was the shepherd. The old fellow had married a Windsor negro wench as black as a stove-pipe, and afterwards became quite disgusted with his bargain, affirming that he would cheerfully " give all of forty shillings," if he could get quit of her. He once in a crazy mood, tried to hang himself with a nice cord which he used for ditching, but was cut down in time to save his life. He became very indignant, not because his life was saved, *but because they had cut his nice ditching cord !*

---

* She went in 1655.

(Reprinted from the *Congregational Quarterly*, April, 1862.)

CHURCH COVENANT OF WINDSOR, CONN., A. D. 1647.*

[Dated Windsor, Oct. 23, 1647.]

1. We believe though God made man in an holy and blessed condition, yet by his fall he hath plunged himself and all his posterity into a miserable state. Rom. III, 23 ; v. 12.

2. Yet God hath provided a sufficient remedy in Christ for all broken hearted sinners that are loosened from their sins, and selves and world, and are enabled by faith to look to Him in Christ for mercy, inasmuch as Christ hath done and suffered for such whatever His justice requires to atonement and life; and he doth accept His merits and righteousness for them that believe in Him, and imputeth it to them for their justification, as if they had satisfied and obeyed themselves. Heb. vii, 25; Mat. xi, 28 ; xxii, 24 ; v. 4, 6 ; 1 Cor. i, 30; Rom. iv, 3. 5 ; v. 19.

3. Yet we believe that there is no other name or means to be saved from guilt and the power of sin. John, xiv, 6 ; Acts, iv, 12.

4. We believe God hath made an everlasting covenant in Christ with all penitent sinners that rest on him in Christ, never to reject, or cease to do them good. Heb. viii, 6; vii, 22; 1 Sam. xii, 22; Jer. xxxii, 40.

5. We believe this covenant to be reciprocal, obliging us to be his people, to love, fear, obey, cleave to him, and serve him with all our heart, mind and soul ; as him to be our God, to love, choose, delight in us and save and bless us in Christ; yea, as his covenant binds us to love him and his Christ for his own sake, so to love our brethren for his sake. Deut. x, 12; Hos. iii, 3 ; ii, 21 ; Deut. xxvi, 17-19; John, iv, 21.

6. We believe that God's people, besides their general covenant with God, to walk in subjection to him, and christian love to all his people, ought also

---

* For this interesting document we are indebted to the kindness of Hon. J. H. Trumbull of Hartford. Mr. T., says, " I found it a few weeks since in the MS. Note Book of one of the Deacons of that church (Matthew Grant), along with full notes of a sermon by Mr. Warham, Aug. 15, 1647 (two months before this covenant was adopted), ' on the matter and form of a church and of baptizing children.' 1 was pleased with the discovery, as the covenant is of much earlier date than any I have seen or known of in Connecticut. Mr. Warham was at the Cambridge Synod, in June, 1647 ; out of which, apparently, grew the sermon ; and the sermon prepared the way for the adoption of the Covenant. I may observe, however, that the sermon is, in great measure, a digest of Hooker's *Survey*, which Mr. W. must have not only perused, but thoroughly studied in MS. for it was not printed till the next year."

The Windsor Church was formed at Plymouth, England, in March, 1630 [there is a mistake in Sprague's notice of Warham; *Annals*, I, 10; Hawe's Note in *Eccl. Cont. Conn.*, p. 86; and Mc-Clure's *Hist. Windsor, Mass. Hist. Coll.*, 1st series, v, 166; all of whom make January, 1630, as the date, owing to a neglect of the fact that the year O. S., began with *March*, so that the "beginning of the year " would be March 1, and not January 1], by people from the counties of Devon, Dorset and Somerset; and Warham and Maverick were ordained its pastor and teacher. They arrived at Dorchester, Mass., about the 1st of June, where they first settled. But hearing from the Dutch of a valuable tract of land on the Connecticut, they concluded to remove, and went in a body in the summer of 1635; carrying their church organization and Mr. Warham with them—Maverick dying in Dorchester. This creed and covenant (for it partakes of both elements) seems to have been adopted eleven years after the settlement of Windsor. Warham died in 1670, and Cotton Mather says, he was the first minister in Connecticut who preached " with notes."   Rev. H. M. Dexter.

to join themselves into a church covenant one with another, and to enter into a particular combination, together with some of his people, to erect a particular ecclesiastical body, and kingdom, and visible family and household of God, for the managing of discipline and public ordinances of Christ in one place in a dutiful way, there to worship God and Christ, as his visible kingdom and subjects, in that place waiting on him for that blessing of his ordinances and promises of his covenaut, by holding communion with him and his people, in the doctrine and discipline of that visible kingdom, where it may be attained. Rom. xii, 4, 5, 6; 1 Cor. xii, 27, 28; Ephes. iv, 11, 12; Acts, ii, 47; Exod. xii, 43, 44, 45; Gen. xvii, 13; Isa. xxiii, 4.

7. We for ourselves, in the sense of our misery by the fall and utter helplessness elsewhere, desire to renounce all other saviours but his Christ, and to rest on God in him alone, for all happiness, and salvation from all misery; and do here bind ourselves, in the presence of men and angels, by his grace assisting us, to choose the Lord, to serve him, and to walk in all his ways, and to keep all his commandments and ordinances, and his Christ to be our king, priest and prophet, and to receive his gospel alone for the rule of our faith and manners, and to [be] subject to the whole will|of Christ so far as we shall understand it : and bind ourselves in special to all the members of this body, to walk in reverend subjection to the Lord to all our superiors, and in love, humility, wisdom, peaceableness, meekness, inoffensiveness, mercy, charity, spiritual helpfulness, watchfulness, chastity, justice, truth, self-denial, one to another, and to further the spiritual good one of another, by example, counsel, admonition, comfort, oversight, according to God, and submit or[selves] subject unto all church administration in the Lord.

FINIS.

3

A LIST

Of Natives of the Towns formerly comprised within the limits of Ancient Windsor, who have studied or graduated at Yale College.

This list, although probably by no means complete, has been compiled with the utmost care from the valuable file of catalogues in Yale College Library, and from all other attainable sources, and may be considered reliable, as far as it goes.* Many of Windsor's children have graduated at other colleges, but to trace them out would require more labor and time than we could spare.

ABBREVIATIONS. Grad., graduated; med., medical department; theo., theological department; fresh., soph., jun., sen., freshman, sophomore, junior and senior classes.

ABBE, Alanson (E. W.), grad. med. 1821.

ALLEN, John, s. of Alex. (W.), b. 1705 ; lived at N. Haven ; grad. 1729.

ALLYN, Maj. Henry, s. of Col. Matt. (W.), b. 1699 ; grad. 1721 ; d, at W., 1753. A teacher, military officer, benevolent and good.

    Dr. Samuel, s. of Sam. (W.), b. 1703; "went South," says Pres. Stiles in *itinerary*, " where he d. perhaps 1780;" grad. 1725.

ARMS, Hiram P. (W.), grad. 1824.

BAKER, Rev. Jacob, s. of Joseph (W.), b. 1710 ; licensed by Windham Assoc. May, 1739 ; never settled ; grad. 1731.

BARBER, Rev. Eldad (E. W.), grad. 1826 ; theo. 1829.

BARTLETT, David Ely (E. W.), grad. 1828. (See p. 536.)

    John Leffingwell (E. W.), grad. 1824. (See p. 536.)

    Shubael F. (E W.), grad. 1833. (See p. 536.)

BISSELL, Aaron (E. W.), fresh. in 1779. (See pp. 548, 551.)

    Benjamin (E. W.), grad. med. 1826.

    Edward (E. W.), grad. 1851. (See p. 551, l. 40.)

    Rev. Hezekiah, s. of David (W.), grad. 1733, 1st past. Wby. (See pp. 372, 553.)

    Theodore (E. W.), fresh. in 1820.

BOOTH, Chauncey (E. W.), grad. 1810.

BROCKWAY, John H. (Ell.), grad. 1820.

BUTLER, Dea. Isaac, s. of Thos. (W.), b. 1693 ; d. at Wby. ; grad. 1722.

CASE, William (E. W.), grad. 1821 ; theo. Andover, 1822–23.

CHAFFEE, Hezekiah (W.), fresh. in 1779. (See p. 567, l. 2.)

    Hezekiah B. (W.), grad. 1809. (See *Chaffee* in this Supplement.)

    Samuel G. (W.), grad. 1810. (See *Chaffee* in this Supplement.)

CLARK, Noah B. (E. W.), grad. 1833 ; law, 1834.

---

* Thirty of these names have been kindly furnished to us by RALPH D. SMITH, Esq. of New Haven, Conn.

COLT, Hon. Peter, s. of Benj., b. at E. W., 1733; grad. 1761; d. 1802; was
Assist. Commis. Genl.; removed to Paterson, N. J., and to Rome,
N. Y.

DIGGINS, John (E. W.), prob. s. of Jeremiah; grad. 1740.

Augustus (E. W.), grad. 1767; m. Nancy (dau. of Ephrm.) Pease
of Somers.

DRAKE, Richard G. (W.), grad. 1830. (See p. 585.)

EDWARDS, Rev. Jonathan (E. W.), grad. 1720. (See p. 589.)

ELLSWORTH, Hon. Henry L. (W.), grad. 1810. (See p. 602.)

Rev. John (Ell.), grad. 1785. (See pp. 289, 599.)

Joseph (E. W.), grad. 1825.

Major Martin (W.), grad. 1801. (See p. 602.)

Hon. Chief Justice Oliver (W.), ent. in 1763, remained three
years, and grad. at Princeton, N. J. (See pp. 600–602.)

Oliver, Jr. (W.), grad. 1799. (See p. 602.)

Oliver (W.), grad. 1830.

Hon. William W. (W.), grad. 1810. (See p. 602.)

FILLEY, A. B. (W.), law, 1831–32, grad. A. B. Wash. Coll.

FITCH, George (W.), grad. 1801.

GOODWIN, Rev. Hezekiah (Wby.), grad. 1761. (See p. 377.)

GRANT, Rev. John (W.), grad. 1741; ord. by Presb. of N. Y., pastor of Pres.
Ch. at Westfield, N. J., Sept., 1746; he d. there Sept. 15, 1753.

Ebenezer, s. of Sam. (E. W.), grad. 1726; b. Oct. 3, 1706; merchant. (See p. 636.)

Friend (W.), grad. 1761.

Sidney A. (E. W.), fresh. in 1806.

Roswell (E. W.), grad. 1765.

GILLET, John, s. of John (W.), grad. 1758. (See p. 629, l. 34, 38, 39.)

Horace C. (E. W.), grad. med. 1829. (See p. 630–1.)

GILLETTE, Francis (Wby.), grad. 1829. (See p. 631–2.)

GRISWOLD, Rev. Benjamin (W.). (See pp. 644–5.)

Gaylord (W.), grad. 1787. (See p. 648, l. 33.)

HALL, Junius (Ell.), grad. 1831.

HASKELL, Edward (E. W.), fresh. in 1829–30. (See p. 652.)

HOOKER, James (W.), fresh. in 1806. (See p. 667.)

HUBBARD, George (W.), grad. 1803.

John M. (W.), 1829.

JENCKS, Charles W. (E. W.), fresh. in 1822.

LOOMIS, James C. (W.), grad. 1828–30.

Osbert B. grad. 1835. (See *Loomis* in this Supplement.)

William O. grad. med. 1831.

MARSHALL, Elisha G. (W.), grad. med. 1831. (See p. 697.)

MATHER, Rev. Allyn (W.), grad. 1771. (See p. 702.)

Rev. Azariah (W.), grad. 1705. (See p. 700.)

MATHER, Dr. Charles (E. W.), grad. 1785. (See p. 702.)

Frederick E. (W.), grad. 1833. (See p. 702, l. 37.)

Rev. Nathaniel, b. 1695 (see p. 701, l. 3) ; grad. 1715 ; d. at River-
head, L. I., Mch. 20, 1748.

Nathaniel (E. W.), grad. 1810.

Oliver (W.), grad. 1799.

Oliver W. (W.), grad. 1837.

Dr. Samuel, s. of Dr. Sam. (W.) ; grad. 1726.

MILLER, Horatio (W.), grad. 1819.

MILLS, Rev. Jedidiah (Wby.), grad. 1722 (see p. 704) ; d. at Huntington, Jan.,
1776.

Rev. Gideon (W.), grad. 1737. (See p. 704.)

Rev. Ebenezer (W.), grad. 1738 ; (s. of Peter ; b. 1710 ; settled at E.
Granby, 1742 ; and Sandisfield, Mass. ; d. 1799, a. 89.)

Samuel (W.), grad. 1776.

MOORE, Dr. Abijah, grad. 1726 ; resided and d. at Middletown, 1759.

Rev. John, s. of John (W.); grad. 1741.

NEWBURY, Henry (W.), soph. in 1798.

Capt. Roger (Wby.), s. of Capt. Benj., grad. 1726. (See pp. 330,
721.)

Roger (W.), grad. 1799.

NIGHTINGALE, Joseph (prob. W.), grad. 1728.

Aaron, grad. 1758 (prob. W.)

PHELPS, Alexander (W.), grad. 1744. Tutor.

Bildad (W.), s. of Capt. Josiah, b. 1739 ; grad. 1758 ; d. Mch. 12,
1814.

Rev. Benajah, grad. 1761 ; settled at Manchester, Mch., 1780 ; d.
Nova Scotia, Feb. 10, 1795.

POTWINE, Benjamin (E. W.), med. 1813.

Lemuel S. (E. W.), grad. 1854.

Thomas S. (E. W.)

Stephen Atwater (E. W.), grad. 1833. (See p. 757, l. 35.)

PORTER, Solomon (E. W.), grad. 1775.

REED, Rev. Julius A. (E. W.), grad. 1829. (See p. 760).

Dr. Maro McLean (E. W.), grad. 1822; med. 1824. (See p. 759.)

Dr. Elijah Fitch (E. W.), honorary degree, 1824. (See p. 759.)

ROCKWELL, Eliud (W.), grad. 1766.

Rev. Matthew, s. of Dea. Sam. (E. W.), grad. 1728. (See p. 763.)

William H. (E. W.), grad. 1824.

Dr. Sidney W. (E. W.), honorary degree, 1855.

ROWLAND, Rev. Henry A. (W.), grad. 1823. (See p. 768.)

ROWLAND, William S. (W.), grad. 1836. (See p. 768, l. 25.)

SELDEN, Edward (W.), grad. 1811.

SILL, Elisha N. (W.), grad. 1820. (See p. 772.)

SILL, Horace H. (W.), fresh. 1814. (See p. 772.)

    Dr. Theodore (W.), grad. med. 1831. (See p. 773.)

SKINNER, Samuel W. (E. W.), grad. 1842.

STILES, Rev. Isaac (W.), grad. 1722. (See p. 785.)

    Rev. Abel (W.), grad. 1733. (See p. 787.)

    Ezra (E. W.), grad. 1823. (See p. 793.)

STOUGHTON, J. W. (E. W.), 1840, left in soph. year.

STRONG, Elisha B. (W.), grad. 1809.

SWEATLAND, Peter (W.), grad. 1740.

TUDOR, Rev. Samuel (E. W.), grad. 1728. (See p. 816.)

    Dr. Elihu (E. W.), grad. 1750. (See p. 816.)

VIETS, Rev. Roger, s. of Dr. John (W.), grad. 1758.

WATSON, John B. (E. W.), grad. 1814.

    Sereno (E. W.), grad. 1847.

WEBSTER, David (W ?), grad. 1741.

WILLES, Rev. Henry (E. W.), s. of Joshua; b. 1690; d. at Franklin, Conn.,
    Sept. 30, 1758; grad. 1715.

WOLCOTT, Dr. Alexander (E. W.), grad. 1731. (See pp. 832, 878.)

    Alexander (W.), grad. 1778.

    James (Ell.), in Coll. 1825.

    Gov. Oliver, s. of Gov. Roger (E. W.); grad. 1747. (See p. 833.)

    Josiah, s. of Hon. Roger (E. W.); grad. 1742. (See p. 831, l. 6.)

    Samuel (E. W.), grad. 1833.

    William, s. of Wm. (E. W.); grad. 1734. (See William[6], p. 832.)

    William (E. W.), grad. 1775. (See p. 832, l. 12.)

GENEALOGIES.

ABBE (Abby, Abbie, etc.), p. 515, l. 10, add HARRIET m. Daniel Bacon of Mass., Nov. 28, 1838. (W. C. R.)

ABBOT, p. 515, ABIEL (perhaps the one mentioned in l. 27) had a child bap. Nov. 22, 1761. (E. W. C. R.) ORREL, had child bap. Aug. 13, 1775. (E. W. C. R.)

ADAMS, p. 516, l. 7, add LEONARD m. Sally Porter, Jan. 1, 1797.

P. 516, l. 6, for *September* read *December*. (Col. Rec.)

ASHER'S wife Nancy d. Sept. 25, 1801, a. 30.

JONATHAN, m. Mindwell Phelps, March 7, 1745. (Wby. Ch. R.)

HEZEKIAH, had Lydia, bap. Sept. 22, 1751. (Wby. Ch. R.)

THOMAS, Jr.'s widow d. February, 1784. Their children : Rosanna, bap. Aug. 7, 1760; Isabel, bap. Aug. 29, 1762; Ursula, bap. Nov. 4, 1764; Thomas, bap. May 24, 1767; Annanissa, bap. July 30, 1769; Joab, bap. March 1, 1772; Abi, bap. Aug. 14, 1774; d. Aug. 26, 1775 ; Abi, bap. May 4, 1777; Hosea, bap. Feb. 17, 1780; Mary, bap. Aug. 25, 1782. (Wby. Ch. Rec.)

ALEXANDER, l. 14, add GILES m. Abigail Skinner, at W., Nov. 11, 1823. (W. C. R.)

ALVORD, l. 39. *Timothy Loomis' MSS.* (see p. 62) supplies the date of JEREMIAH'S m. to Sarah ——, as being July 4, 1711.

"ALEXANDER ALVORD hath sixe children : Abigail, b. October, 1647; John, b. Aug. 12, 1649; Mary, b. July 6, 1651; Thomas, b. Oct. 27, 1653 ; Elizabeth, b. Nov. 12, 1655 ; Benjamin, b. Feb. 11, 1657." (Col. Rec.)

P. 517, l. 3, CHARITY, wife of Jonathan, d. Sept. 9, 1776, of epidemic dysentery. (N. S. R.)

P. 517, l. 8, JONATHAN, Jr. (undoubtedly the one mentioned in l. 4), and Elizabeth, his wife, had Elizabeth, bap. March 31, 1777; d. March 30, (!) 177– (a fair specimen of Parson Hinsdale's accuracy in keeping records) ; another child bap. on same day as former; d. April ——; John bap. Aug. 2, 1777; and another son bap. Feb. 13, 1780. (N. S. R.)

P. 517, l. 8, add PERLEY m. Elihu Anderson of E. Hartford, Dec. 17, 1817.

MARY, had William Beal; Phebe Dix and Edwin Charles, bap. July 29, 1821. (W. C. R.)

JONAS, m. Thankful Cadwell of W. Hartford, June 23, 1803. (Wby. Ch. Rec.)

ALLYN, p. 523, l. 31. CHLOE, bap. Jan. 29, 1775. (N. S. R.)

P. 521, l. 33, for Feb. 1 read Feb. 7. (Col. Rec.)

"Ould Mr. Allyn d. Sept. 12, 1675." (Col. Rec.)

P. 522, l. 31, Sgt. MATTHEW,⁶ d. May 28, 1753. (Wby. Ch. R.)

P. 523, l. 10, THOMAS,¹¹ d. Nov. 17, 1781, a. 56; he had also a James, bap. March 30, 1766; Emmile, bap. April 24, 1768; Elizabeth, bap. Sept. 16, 1770; Timothy, bap. July 4, 1773, who d. June 25, 1775; his son Luke was b. 1775. (Wby. Ch. Rec.)

P. 523, l. 22, for July 1 read July 14.

P. 523, l. 23, the 3d wife Capt. SOLOMON was Sarah Burr, m. April 14, 1795; his son Sherwood d. June 11, 1799, nearly 12 yrs.; his son Solomon was bap. Sept. 17, 1757.

P. 523, l. 25, for Abiah read Abial. (Wby. C. R.)

P. 524, l. 1, JOHN and Elizabeth had Charles, bap. March 21, 1761, and Hannah, bap. Nov. 1, 1767. (N. S. R.)

P. 524, l. 11, add ELIJAH, m. Martha Stoughton (E. W.), April, 1800; SARAH, m. John Rumsey, Dec. 31, 1812; GILMAN, m. Huldah Phelps, Sept. 6, 1814; RICHARD, m. Julia Phelps, Sept. 28, 1814; REBECCA, m. Elam French (E. W.); BETSY, m. Wm. Jesto of Wethersfield, July 30, 1823; CHESTER, m. Patty Barnes, Oct. 19, 1815; HARRIET, m. Joseph Atherton of Hartford, Dec. 29, 1833; WILLIAM, m. Naomi Hayden, June 2, 1808; AMELIA, m. Griswold C. Morgan, June 1, 1831; ELIZABETH, m. Sam. J. Norton of H., April 12, 1832. (W. C. R.)

L. 14, this EPHESTIAN (prob.) had Molly, bap. Feb. 3, 1765; a child bap. July 5, 1767; another, March 18, 1770; another, March 14, 1772; another, March 24, 1776. (E. W. C. R.)

JOHN, Jr., and Lucinda, had John, bap. June 23, 1776; Jeremy, bap. May 4, 1777; Henry, bap. Feb. 13, 1780; Nabby, bap. May 30, 1784. (N. S. R.)

JOB, m. Abigail Mather, May 16, 1777; had children, Bille (?), bap. April 8, 1781; Elizabeth, bap. Nov. 14, 1786; Roxana, bap. May 1, 1791; Catharine, bap. Sept. 1, 1793; Job, bap. Aug. 29, 1796; Timothy Mather, bap. June 7, 1801. (W. C. R.)

SAMUEL, m. Jerusha ——, and had Harriet, bap. Feb., 178–; Eli, bap. July 5, 1788; Henry, bap. May 30, 1790; Richard, bap. April 15, 1792. (N. S. R.)

SAMUEL (probably the above), had Amelia, bap. Jan. 4, 1795; Samuel Wolcott, bap. Sept. 20, 1801; Samuel Wolcott, bap. March 4, 1805. (W. C. R.)

SAMUEL, Jr., had Abigail, bap. Feb. 22, 1795. (W. C. R.)

ELISHA, had Electa, Sarepta, Elisha, Rhoda, all bap. Dec. 2, 1799; Ellise, bap. Oct. 9, 1802; Chloe, bap. Oct. 14, 1804. (W. C. R.)

HENRY (2d), had Henry, bap. Nov. 24, 1799; Julia, bap. Feb. 7, 1802; Elizabeth, bap. Nov. 4, 1804; Leonard, bap. Sept. 24, 1809; Annalet, bap. July 2, 1815; Jonah, bap. Feb., 1818. (W. C. R.)

Ens. THOMAS, Jr., m. Elizabeth Burr, April 11, 1776; had Polly, bap. Oct. 5, 1777; Thomas, bap. Dec. 5, 1779; Lucy, bap. Aug. 17, 1783; d. Feb. 27, 1813; Timothy, bap. Nov. 28, 1784; Betsey, bap. Oct. 16, 1787; Chester, bap. Oct. 17, 1790 (N. B.—His wife d. May 16, 1823, a. 34, and a ch. d. May 10, 1817, a. 1); Eunice, bap. May 18, 1794. (Wby. C. R.)

FITZ JOHN, m. Deborah Phelps, Feb., 1788; had Sarah, bap. Dec. 5, 1790 ; Sidney B., bap. Nov. 15, 1795; Candace, bap. May 24, 1801; Amelia, bap. Nov. 10, 1805; Elizabeth, bap. July, 1814. (W. C. R.)

BENJAMIN, Jr. (prob. one ment. l. 5, p. 524), had Mary Rebecca, bap. Nov. 5, 1826; Julia Huntington, bap. Sept. 28, 1829. (W. C. R.)

ANN of W., m. Noah Smith of Kensington (Berlin), Jan. 21, 1736. (Edwin Stearns of Middletown, Conn.)

SOLOMON, Jr. (prob. the one ment. l. 24, p. 523), m. Lucina Gillet, March 29, 1779; had Lucina, bap. June 28, 1779; Solomon, bap. Sept. 23, 1781; Peletiah, bap. July 3, 1808 ; William H., d. Dec. 11, 1808, a. 2 yrs.; Solomon, Jr., d. Dec. 10, 1808, a. 51 ; his wife Lucina d. Oct. 13, 1803, a. abt. 50.

Marriages from Wby. Ch. Rec.—JONATHAN, Jr., m. Hannah Holcomb or Buttles of Granby, Sept. 12, 1799.

THOMAS, m. wid. Sarah Stoughton, Dec. 1, 1806. Sarah, wife of Thomas, d. June 1, 1814, a. 52.

Births from Wby. Ch. Rec.—JONATHAN, had ——, bap. Aug. 29, 1784.

ABRAM, d. Nov. 19, 1812, a. 28; had Abigail, bap. Oct. 7, 1810 ; William, bap. July 12, 1812.

AUGUSTUS, had child, who d. Oct. 2, 1823, a. 5 mos.; JONATHAN, d. Aug. 27, 1824, a. 82; one of LUKE's twins d. Nov. 12, 1792; JOHN's child d. in spring of 1792, and a son d. Jan. 17, 1794, a. 4 yrs.; JONATHAN's wife d. Jan. 20, 1793, a. 44 yrs.; his child d. Dec. 28, 1793; Lt. THOMAS' wife d. Sept. 8, 1795 ;

JONATHAN, Jr., had a child who d. infant, Dec., 1807; ELIJAH, had infant, d. May 5, 1802; another in last part of 1810; ELIJAH's wife d. Aug. 27, 1821; child d. June 13, 1816, a. 1½ ; widow SARAH, d. Sept. 17, 1819, a. 62.

SAMUEL,* Sen., came to Cambridge, Mass., from Braintree, Essex co. Eng., 1632; was brother of Col. Matthew and Dea. Thomas ; his wife was Ann ——. He removed to Connecticut, 1635, and settled in *Windsor*, where he d. and was bur. April 28, 1648, leaving widow and six children. She removed to Northampton, Mass., where she m. 2d husband, said to be William Hurlbut; among the descendants, by her first husband were many men of note. The children of Samuel and Ann Allyn were : 1, Samuel, Jr., who m. Hannah Woodford, 1659, and removed to Northampton with his mother; 2, Nehe-

---

* Notes by Edwin Stearns of Middletown, Conn.

4

miah, who m. Sarah Woodford, 1664 ; 3, John, who m. Mary Hannum and
settled in Deerfield, and had sons John and Samuel ; 4, Abigail; 5, Dea. Obediah, settled in Middletown ; 6, name not given, and perhaps a daughter.
John and Samuel, sons of John Allen, above, settled in Enfield, Conn.,
about 1700.

DEACON THOMAS,* brother of Samuel and Col. Matthew, came first to Cambridge, Mass., from England in 1632; was freeman, 1635. He removed to
Hartford with his brother Matthew, 1635; in 1650 had much difficulty with
his brother Matthew about some contracts and bonds, when several law
suits ensued, and the court ordered Matthew to pay over to Thomas his dues
and release his "specialties." Thomas Allyn was twice m. : 1st wife was
Isabella ——, who d. about 1678 ; when Mr. Allyn m. 2, Martha Gipson or
Gibson, widow of Roger Gipson of Saybrook, Conn., about 1780–1. Mr.
Gibson d. Dec. 6, 1680, leaving 3 sons and 1 daughter : 1, Samuel, a. 8 ; 2,
Jonathan, a. 6; Martha, a. 5 ; Roger, Jr., a. 1¼, who all settled in Middletown.
Thomas Allyn removed from Hartford to Middletown in 1650, "with the first
planters of Mattabeseck" where he become a prominent man of the town,
was chosen Deacon of the 1st church, March 16, 1670, was a representative
to General Court, Selectman, &c.   Having no children, he adopted his
nephew Obediah Allyn, 4th son of his then deceased brother, Samuel Allyn
of Windsor, who lived with him during minority and received a large share
of his estate.   Deacon Thomas Allyn, d. Oct. 16, 1688; his will dated Oct.
15, 1688, and proved Feb. 5, 1689.   His widow Martha (Gipson) Allyn, d.
Nov., 1702, her will was dated April 30, 1690.

COL. MATTHEW,* brother of Samuel and Thomas, was one of the original
Braintree company that emigrated to Cambridge, Mass., and afterwards
joined Rev. Mr. Hooker's company that settled the town of Hartford, and subsequently removed to *Windsor*.   Matthew Allyn was in Cambridge, Mass.,
1632, and had 45 acres divided to him at the "Common Pales (much the
largest share of any settler).   1633, had 1 acre for a cow yard, and 3 acres
planting ground granted "on Neck."   1635, he had *grants or purchased* 5
acres at "Wigwam Neck;" 6 acres at "meadow near Watertown," and 5
acres at "Charlestown Lane."   He owned 5 houses on the Town Plot of
Cambridge, 1635, lived near the meeting house and was by far the largest
landholder in Cambridge.—*Cambridge Records.*

OBEDIAH,* 4th son of Samuel and Ann Allyn of Windsor, nephew of Col.
Matthew, was adopted by his uncle Thomas Allyn of Middletown, soon after
the decease of his father (Samuel), where he resided, and after his uncle's
death inherited most of his estate.   He was admitted to the 1st Church, Middletown, by certificate from the church in Windsor, May 2d, 1669, but owned
the covenant, Nov. 9, 1668, *and was chosen Deacon* May 31, 1704, when the
church was first organized.   He m. 1, Elizabeth Sanford of Milford, Conn.,
Oct. 23, 1669, by whom he had 8 children, viz.: 1, Obediah, b. Nov. 20,
1670; 2, Thomas, b. Sept. 20, 1672 ; d. Nov. 8, 1672 ; 3, Thomas 2d, b. Sept.

14, 1673, chosen Deacon, April 6, 1727) ; 4, Mary, b. Sept. 1675 (Mrs. Beriah Wetmore) ; 5, Anna, b. Sept. 12, 1677 (Mrs. John Lane ; 2d, m. Nath. Bacon); 6, Thankful, b. Sept. 8, 1679 ; 7, Samuel, b. March 5, 1684 ; 8, John, b. Sept. 27, 1686; Mrs. Elizabeth (Sanford) Allyn, d. —— ; Dea. Obediah Allyn m· 2d wife, Mary, widow of John Wetmore and dau. of John Savage; Dea. Obediah Allyn d. April 7, 1723; Mrs. Mary (Wetmore) Allyn d. Oct. 20, 1723.

JONATHAN ALLEN and Thomas Alvord both were recommended from church in Northampton, Mass., and admitted to 1st Church Middletown, March 16, 1729; he m. Elizabeth Allen of Middletown, Oct. 20, 1726, dau. of Thomas and Hannah Allen. He resided in Middlefield Society and was Deacon of the church in that parish, May 26, 1743 ; he was a descendant of Samuel Allen, who d. in Windsor, 1648 ; Dea. Jonathan Allen's 1st wife Elizabeth, d. Oct. 19, 1762; when Mr. Allen m. wid. Rebecca Wetmore, July 6, 1763 ; he d. Dec. 23, 1783, a. 80 ; his widow Rebecca d. Feb. 6, 1791, a. 88 yrs. Children by 1st marriage : 1, Thomas, b. June 27, 1728; d. Sept. 25, 1736 ; 2, Hannah, b. April 10, 1730 ; 3, Elizabeth, b. July 30, 1734 ; d. Oct. 10, 1762 ; 4, Thankful, b. March 2, 1736 ; 5, Thomas, b. April 18, 1737 ; 6, Sarah, b. March 24, 1741 ; 7, Experience, b. Feb. 27, 1743; 8, Lucie, b. July 28, 1748.

ANDERSON, p. 526, l. 4, JOHN, had Timothy, bap. Aug. 8, 1762; a child, bap. Dec. 17, 1765; a child, bap. July 3, 1774. (E. W. C. R.)

JOHN, Jr., had child, bap. Nov. 23, 1777; a child, bap. Oct. 21, 1781; a child, bap. May 23, 1784 ; a child, bap. Aug. 6, 1786 ; a child, bap. Aug. 3, 1788; Lorrel, bap. Sept. 9, 1792; a child, bap. July 13, 1794. (E. W. C. R.)

ASA, had a child, bap. May 1, 1763; another, June 23, 1765; another, bap. Sept. 10, 1769 ; another, bap. April 9, 1775. (E. W. C. R.)

ANDROSS, ELIJAH, had Elijah, bap. Feb. 10, 1765; Mary, bap. March 9, 1766; Rebecca, bap. Jan. 3, 1768; Love, bap. April 11, 1773 ; Elizabeth, bap. Feb. 28, 1779.

SAMUEL, Jr., had Dorcas, bap. April 24, 1774 ; Samuel, bap. June 30, 1776 ; d. April 12, 1798; Levi, bap. Oct. 18, 1778; Jerusha, bap. Feb. 19, 1781; Joel, bap. June, 1787; Rebecca, bap. March, 1788.

ANDRUS, REBECCA, wife of Samuel, d. Dec. 11, 1759, a. about 38 yrs. DORCAS, m. Joseph Wadsworth of Hartford, Aug. 8, 1793.

ANDREWS, Rev. JOSIAH B., m. Mary Bissell, Aug. 17, 1801. (All of this name from Wby. Ch. Rec.)

ATWELL, p. 526, l. 9, JOSEPH's twins, b. Oct. 25, 1754; one d. Oct. 26 ; his wife d. June 4, 1765, a. about 30 ; they also had Anna, bap. Oct. 17, 1756; Ozias, bap. July 23, 1758. (Wby. Ch. Rec.)

AVERY, p. 526, after l. 7, insert ROBERT, m. Anna Barber, Feb. 6, 1780. (W. C. R.)

BAILEY, p. 526, l. 32, this SMITH was bap. May 16, 1773, and had a child, bap. June 13, 1773. (E. W. C. R.)

BAKER, p. 526, l. 18, for Oct. 17, read Oct. 14. (Col. Rec.)

P. 526, 1. 27, JOSEPH W., in W. C. R., is called " Jr."

P. 526, 1. 28, add, IRENE, m. Wm. Francis, Jr., March 1, 1818.

BALDWIN, p. 526, after 1. 33, add, THEOPHILUS, and wife Alethea, had Lydia, Samuel, Polly; Theophilus, bap, Sept., 1785; Henry, bap. March 12, 1786; Morris, bap. Nov. 13, 1792. (N. S. R.)

AMBROSE, m. Harriet Marshall, Nov. 21, 1839. (W. C. R.)

BANCROFT, p. 527, 1. 2, JOHN, d. May 2, 1686. (Col. Rec.)

P. 527, 1. 18, for Esther *Leason* read *Gleason.*

THOMAS, had children, bap. as follows: Jan. 1, 1769; Jan. 11, 1771; March 14, 1773; Sept. 19, 1778; March, 1782. (E. W. C. R.)

ANSON, had child, bap. May 27, 1792; Naomi, bap. Jan. 20, 1799; Timothy, bap. July 28, 1805. (E. W. C. R.)

SAMUEL, had children bap. as follows: June 14, 1772; April 30, 1775; April 6, 1777; June 27, 1779. (E. W. C. R.)

SAMUEL, Jr., had children bap. Nov. 2, 1806; July 24, 1808; Samuel, Oct. 7, 1810; Joseph, March 7, 1813; Harriet, May 28, 1815; Horace, April 19, 1818. (E. W. C. R.)

ABNER, had Eunice, bap. Oct. 28, 1764; also children bap. March 8, 1767; March 6, 1768; Oct. 3, 1771; and Julia, bap. June 1, 1801; possibly this last may be the child of another Abner. (E. W. C. R).

SAMUEL, had children bap. Nov. 20, 1763; Aug. 23, 1767; Sept. 24, 1769.

SAMUEL, had child, bap. May 23, 1784. (E. W. C. R.)

ELI, had children, " W——," bap. Sept. 19, 1802; May 27, 1804. (E. W. C. R.)

 BARBER, p. 528, 1. 15, THOMAS, the emigrant, d. Sept. 11, 1662; his wife d. Sept. 10, 1662. (Col. Rec.)

P. 528, 1. 19, JOHN,[2] m. Bathsheba *Coggins* of Springfield, at S., Sept. 2, 1663. (Col. Rec.)

P. 528, 1. 22, for *Mary* read *Mercy ;* date of marriage should be Dec. 17, 1663. (Col. Rec.)

P. 528, 1. 25, SAMUEL,[4] m. Mary *Coggins*, Dec. 1, 1670; he m. his 2d wife in *January.* The wife of Samuel d. May 19, 1676. (Col. Rec.)

P. 528, 1. 32, DAVID was b. 1686. (Col. Rec.)

P. 528, 1. 42, for 1698 read 1690. (Col. Rec.)

P. 529, 1. 42, the maiden christian name of 2d wife of Gideon[15] was *Mary,* and they were m. Aug. 17, 1769. (Wby. C. R.)

P. 530, last l., JAMES, d. Sept. 20, 1776. (Wby. C. R.)

P. 531, 1. 2, JAMES, the father, d. Jan. 2, 1802, a. 60; his wid. Esther, d. Dec. 12, 1805, a. 59; there was also a brother *Roger, bap.* with Oliver. (Wby. Ch. Rec.)

P. 531, 1. 4, the record of this family is more fully given in the following transcript (for which we are indebted to Mr. D. W. Patterson of West Winsted, Conn.), from an old account book of Benjamin Barber's: " Benjamin Barbur His Book, Decembr 3rd 1778, Then I was married to Mrs.

Ruth Boles. Octo^{br} 27th 1780, Then our Daughter Ruth was Born. Sept. 20, 1783, Then our Son Jonah was Born. April 12, 1797, Then Died Benjamin Barbur Aged 44 com the 6 day of august." (This identifies him as the son of Jonah Barber,[18] p. 530, which before was not fully done.) June 16, 1807, then Died Jonah our Son Aged 23 years and 9 months." (unmarried). "Benjamin Barber's accounts," says Mr. Patterson, "show him to have been a sort of universal genius, weaving, mending shoes, teaming, letting horses, drawing teeth, selling brandy and metheglin." "Ruth Barber, his daughter, married Erastus Woodford (Nov. 14, 1805, W. C. R.), settled in Winsted, and both died here a few years ago."

P. 530, l. 13, JONAH,[18] of Poquonnoc, had a Tabitha, bap. May 22, 1758. (Wby. Ch. Rec.)

P. 531, l. 17, for *Cass* read *Case*. Their children were Allyn, Ogden, James and Esther. (Wby. Ch. Rec.)

GIDEON, m. Rhoda Drake, Dec. 22, 1791, and had Maria, bap. March 1, 1795 ; Anna Gillet, bap. May 7, 1797 ; Rhoda, bap. May 24, 1801. (W. C. R.)

ABEL, m. Polly Mather, Nov. 24, 1794, and had Fanny, bap. Dec. 27, 1795 ; Rebecca, bap. July 30, 1797 ; John Mather, bap. Nov. 10, 1799. (W. C. R.)

SAMUEL, m. Hannah Olds of Suffield, Sept. 8, 1760, and had Martha, bap. June 28, 1761 ; Samuel, bap. July 25, 1762. (Wby. Ch. Rec.)

FREEMAN, m. Mabel Palmer, April 9, 1795, and had Norman, bap. July 3, 1796 ; Theodore, bap. March 18, 1798 ; Warren Marsh, bap. April 17, 1801 ; Harriet, bap. Nov. 7, 1802 ; Emily, bap. Jan. 1, 1809 ; son, bap. Oct. 13, 1811. (W. C. R.)

JERIJAH, Jr.,[23] (p. 530) had Rhoda Ann, bap. Oct. 25, 1819. After his death his widow had Nathaniel Hayden ; John Henry and Samuel Jerijah, bap. June 5, 1820. (W. C. R.)

THADDEUS, m. Patty Eggleston, Nov. 24, 1805.

ELI, had Eli Harvey, bap. March 11, 1792 ; Horace, bap. Feb., 1794 ; Laura, bap. Nov. 6, 1796 ; Jerusha, bap. July 22, 1798 ; Giles, bap. May 25, 1800 ; Orrin, bap. June 20, 1802. Abigail, bap. Sept. 30, 1804 ; Jane, bap. Oct. 9, 1808. (W. C. R.)

LUKE, had Charlotte Melvina, bap. Dec. 26, 1813.

ABNER, had Abner, bap. Dec. 27, 1795 ; Strong, bap. Nov. 10, 1799 ; John, bap. Sept. 1802 ; Ralph, bap. July 5, 1807 ; George Pierpont, bap. Nov. 5, 1809 ; Julia Ann, bap. Nov. 3, 1811. (W. C. R.)

REUBEN, had Wealthy, bap. Oct. 14, 1787 ; Luther, bap. Feb. 6, 1791 ; Elnathan, bap. Oct. 20, 1793 ; Reuben, bap. Oct. 4, 1795 ; Tirza, bap. Sept., 1804. (W. C. R.)

BENONI, m. Patty Goodwin of Hartford Nov. 11, 1790 (W. C. R.); FIDELIA, m. Alonzo Bridges of Mulford, N. Y., Sept. 22, 1824. (W. C. R.)

AARON, had Elizabeth, bap. Jan. 18, 1784; Levi, bap. Aug. 9, 1799. (W. C. R.)

ISAAC, had Martha, d. Nov. 12, 1739, a. about 5 mos. ; Amaziah, bap. Sept. 21, 1740 ; Seth, bap. Jan. 9, 1743. (Wby. Ch. Rec.)

THOMAS, had Thomas, bap. June 20, 1814 ; Sarepta, bap. June 22, 1817 ; Betsey, bap. Aug. 22, 1819. (Wby. Ch. Rec.)

' ROGER, had Erastus, bap. July 5, 1807 ; Joshua Kilborn and Mary Ann, bap. Sept. 22, 1805. (W. C. R.)

P. 529, l. 12, this NOAH and Sybil, also had Noah, bap. July 22, 1764, and child, bap. Oct. 12, 1766. (E. W. C. R.)

J. WARNER BARBER (author of Hist. Coll. of several states), bap. Oct. 6, 1816. (E. W. C. R.)

Marriages from W. C. R.—ELI, Jr., m. Clarissa Wilson, Jan. 13, 1819 ; JOHN, m. Ann Newberry, Jan. 21, 1796 ; SHUBAEL, m. Mary Denslow, July 4, 1802 ; ABIGAIL A , m. Lyman Stockbridge of H., Dec. 14, 1809 ; HORACE, m. Lucy Wilson, March 16, 1817 ; CHARITY, m. Pitts Fuller, Nov. 16, 1808 ; TRUMBULL, m. Hannah Irvin, March 27, 1815 ; ABIGAIL, m. Thomas Boardman, Aug. 22, 1799.

Marriages from Wby. Ch. Rec.—JOEL (of 1st Society in Windsor), m. Mary Drake, Nov. 23, 1758.

ESTHER, m. Aaron Foot of Northampton, N. Y., April 7, 1799.

CHARLES, m. Dolly Newbury, July 26, 1801.

ESTHER, m. Jas. Barber of Medway, Dec. 8, 1803.

JERUSHA, m. Sam. Lemons, April 24, 1808.

THOMAS, Jr., m. Hannah Hubbard, Aug. 18, 1811.

RUTH, m. —— Francis of Newington, Aug., 1815.

DAVID, Jr. (of Poquonnoc), prob. s. of David,[16] m. Jane Filley, Dec. 15, 1776.

MARY, d. March 3, 1813, a. 66 ; ASA, d. May 30, 1814 ; THOMAS, son of Thomas, d. June, 1814 ; OLIVER'S child, d. Aug. 30, 1814, a. 2¼ ; GRANDISON'S, d. Dec. 12, 1814 ; BETSEY, d. April 17, 1815, a. 20 ; THOMAS' child, d. April 21, 1816, a. 1 yr.

Widow MARTHA, d. Aug. 6, 1758, a. about 80 yrs ; MARY, d. May 7, 1786, in 80th yr.

ALLYN'S wife, d. Jan. 1, 1821, a. 42 ; his child, b. and d. April 3, 1824 ; ERASTUS, d. July 2, 1824, a. 41 ; OLIVER'S child, d. Sept., 1824 ; THOMAS, d. July 31, 1820, a. 32.

BARKER, p. 532, l. 7, SAMUEL, m. Sarah Cook, June 30, 1670. (Col. Rec.)

P. 532, l. 10, add, ETHAN, m. Sarah Denslow, March 8, 1814 (W. C. R); EPHRAIM, m. Jerusha Ellsworth, Aug. 4, 1790. (W. C. R.)

SETH, had a child, which d. May, 1766, a few hours old. (Wby. Ch. Rec.)

BARNARD, AARON, m. Lucy ——, who d. Sept. 7, 1782 ; he had children, prob. by 2d wife, bap. Hezekiah and Horace, June 5, 1785 ; Sarah, Sept. 3, 1786.

OLIVER H., m. Anna F. Moore, July 9, 1828.

BARN[E]S (all notes on this name from Wby. Ch. Rec.) Lt. EBENEZER, who, with his wife, came from New Cambridge, d. Sept. 21, 1774, a. about 55 yrs.

TIMOTHY, had Polly, bap. Dec. 15, 1774; Dorcas, bap. Feb. 16, 1777; Timothy, bap. Sept. 19, 1776; Eunice, bap. Sept. 16, 1781; ——, Aug. 31, 1783.

STEPHEN, had ——, d. Aug. 10, 1781, a. about 6 weeks.

BARNETT, ROBERT, m. Ruth ——, who d. April 1st, 1754, a. about 52 yrs.; he d. Sept. 20, ; had Joseph, bap. April 29, 1739, d. May 9, 1739; Anne, bap. April, 1740; Mary, d. July 7, 1743, a. about 16 yrs. (Wby. Ch. Rec.)

ROBERT, m. Hannah Parsons, March 16, 1758, and had Hannah, bap. July 23, 1758; Robert, bap. March 5, 1761; Jose, bap. Jan. 22, 1764, d. May 17, 1765; Sarah, bap. June 10, 1766, d. June 12; Jose, bap. June 7, 1767; Asaph Parsons, bap. Sept. 16, 1770.

JOHN, had James, bap. Aug. 4, 1751; John, bap. July 1, 1753; Rebecca, bap. Oct. 19, 1755; Mary, bap. Sept. 17, 1757; Marine, bap. Sept. 30, 1759; Samuel Holcomb, bap. Dec. 13, 1761.

BARRETT, p. 532, ZEBULON, had John, bap. Jan. 13, 1799; 2 child. bap. Nov. 17, 1805; Backus, bap. Jan., 1808. (E. W. C. R.)

BARTLETT, p. 532, l. 40, EZAZA (Isaiah), d. (prob.) July 13, 1665. (Col. Rec.)

P. 533, l. 1, the date of Benjamin's marriage should be Feb. 16, 1664, according to *Col. Rec.*

P. 533, l. 7, JEHOIDAH, m. Sarah Hillier of Windsor, July 10, 1673. Their son Joseph was b. 1684. (Col. Rec.)

P. 533, l. 36, ISAIAH, m. Abia Gillet, Dec. 3, 1663. For Sept. 11, on same l., read 12. (Col. Rec.)

P. 536, l. 1, the family of Rev. JOHN,[7] from *Wby. Ch. Rec.:* Harriet, bap. May 19, 1816; Mary, bap. June 21, 1815; Delia Jane, bap. Oct. 8, 1820; John Newton, bap. Aug. 24, 1823; Ann Eliza, bap. May 21, 1826; David Van Watrous Golden, bap. June 22, 1728.

ISAAC, m. Olive Rowel, April 29, 1772. *Children*—Olive, bap. May 30, 1773, d. Jan. 13, 1777; Jesse, bap. April 30, 1775, d. Oct. 7, 1777; Isaac, bap. Aug. 3, 1788; Olive, bap. Nov. 6, 1777; Louise, bap. June 3, 1781. (Wby. Ch. Rec.)

BASS, p. 537, insert, NATHAN, had children bap. May 6, 1764; Dec. 1, 1765; Oct. 23, 1768. (E. W. C. R.)

BAXTER, p. 537, l. 31, add, FRANCIS, Jr., had child, bap. March 7, 1790; Anne, bap. Dec. 4, 1791; child, bap. Feb. 16, 1794; another, Oct. 30, 1796. (E. W. C. R.)

BEAMOND, p. 537, l. 34, JONATHAN, had children bap. Feb. 29, 1764; Oct. 27, 1765; Oct. 11, 1767; June 18, 1769; Sept. 20, 1773; May 12, 1776; Jan. 17, 1779. (E. W. C. R.) THOMAS, m. Lydia Roberts, Jan. 18, 1753; had Thomas, bap. Oct. 21, 1753; Lydia, bap. Jan. 26, 1755; Daniel, bap. Aug. 29, 1756; Elisha, bap. June 24, 1759.

"The widow Beaman" d. Aug. 18, 1752, a. about 82 yrs. (Wby. Ch. Rec.)

BELCHER, p. 537, l. 35, see also *N. E. Hist. and Gen. Register*, xii, 178.

BELDING (Belden), p. 537, insert after l. 40, GEORGE, m. Hannah Porter, July 19, 1796, and had Harriet, bap. Aug. 13, 1797, and George, bap. Nov. 7, 1804; Sarah Augusta, bap. July 16, 1809 ; NATHAN, had Alfred Goodwin, July 16, 1848 ; Charles Edmond, bap. July 3, 1855. (W. C. R.)

CHARLOTTE, m. Lewis Burr Sturges, May 14, 1794.

BENNET, p. 538, insert after l. 9, WILLIAM, and wife Sarah, moved to Windsor, Conn., from Ipswich, Mass.

BENTON, p. 538, l. 10, ELIHU STANLY, m. Anna Filley, April 1, 1784, and had Fanny, bap. July 26, 1789 ; William Sidney, bap. April 17, 1791 ; Elizur, bap. Nov. 1, 1795; Anna Maria, bap. July 23, 1797; Henry, bap. Oct. 11, 1801. (W. C. R.)

HEPZIBAH, d. March 11, 1795.

P. 538, l. 11, THOMAS, Jr., had Jerod Bunce, bap. June 1, 1800; Mary Stanly, bap. Sept. 20, 1801; Jennet, bap. March 27, 1802; Julia, bap. June 23, 1804; Caroline Dickinson, bap. May 13, 1809. (W. C. R.)

SAMUEL, m. Fanny Benton, Nov. 17, 1814. WILLIAM, m. Chloe Loomis, Nov. 4, 1821. (W. C. R.)

BESUM, JOHN, drowned in the Great river, May 30, 1675. (Col. Rec.)

BIDWELL, p. 538 (same as Biddle), "Doctor" EPHRAIM, had children, bap. Feb. 19, 1786; 2 bap. Nov. 26, 1786 ; June 3, 1787 ; one early in 1788; Ephraim, April 5, 1789 ; Sarah, Feb. 27, 1791 ; Horace, Cynthia, Eunice and Julia, Sept. 6, 1807. (E. W. C. R.)

From Wby. Ch. Rec.—P. 538, l. 16, this JONATHAN, m. Hannah Hubbard, Aug. 6, 1740; had Mabel, bap. July 2, 1749 ; Candace, bap. June 22, 1755, d. Aug. 21, 1761; Theodosia, bap. Feb. 6, 1758 ; Mabel, bap. Feb. 1st, 1747, was "scalded with milk," and d. Sept. 19, 1748.

JONATHAN, Jr., m. Abigail Eggleston, July 18, 1771 ; he d. June 11, 1787; Jonathan, bap. Aug. 17, 1783 ; Nathaniel, bap. Aug. 7, 1786. (Wby Ch. Rec.)

NATHANIEL, m. Triphena Parsons, Feb. 11, 1810, and had Triphena, bap. July 21, d. Dec. 28, 1811 ; Nathaniel, bap. Sept. 20, 1812 ; Jonathan, bap. May 8, 1814; Cyrus, bap. Aug. 11, 1816; Cornelius, bap. Aug. 9, 1818; Lucia, bap. July 29, 1821; Cornelius, bap. Oct. 28, 1827. (Wby. Ch. Rec.)

JAMES, had Horton, bap. Sept. 20, 1812 ; Ansou Lorenzo, bap. June 11, 1815 ; Catharine, Eliza and Joseph Seymour, bap. Nov. 3, 1816 ; Julia, bap. Oct. 11, 1818 ; Sarissa, bap. Aug. 22, 1819 ; Samuel Walter, bap. Aug. 24, 1823 ; Sarah Elizabeth, bap. Aug. 6, 1826.

Marriages.—ANNA, m. Nathaniel Austin of Torringford, Sept. 27, 1775 ; HANNAH, m. Samuel Foot, March 27, 1766 ; ABIGAIL, m. Charles Seward of Torrington, March 11, 1773 ; JONATHAN, Jr., m. Anna Brown, March 16, 1800. (Wby. Ch. Rec.)

Deaths.—Widow PRUDENCE, d. Feb. 14, 1763, a. 80 yrs.; LOVICIA, wife of James, d. Sept. 16, 1821, a. 37; RACHEL, d. May 27, 1792, a. 41 yrs ; widow HANNAH, d. Feb. 26, 1794; JONATHAN, d. May 12, 1811, a. 65; JONATHAN'S youngest child was scalded to death, April 8, 1812 ; also another child d. May 11, 1814, a. 5 ; CORNELIUS, d. April 25, 1820, a 25. (Wby. Ch. Rec.)

BIRGE, p. 538, 1. 23, the name of the emigrant should be *Richard*, not *Daniel.*

P. 538, 1. 30, he was buried Sept. 29, 1651. (Col. Rec.)

P. 538, 1. 32, for *Elizabeth* read *William.* (Col. Rec.)

P. 538, 1. 33, JEREMIAH, was b. Jan. 14, 1649, according to *Col. Rec.*, which agrees with the *age* given on last line of the page.

P. 539, 1. 5, for 1651, read 1652.

P 539, 1. 12, the first Daniel b. 1680, *died* Jan. 12, 1681 (Col. Rec.), which makes next line incorrect and worthless.

P. 539, 1. 24, for *her*, read *his.* Same line, "Abigail, b. Feb. 15, 1731, m. James Spencer, 1751." In regard to this item, Mr. D. W. Patterson sends the following correction : " I have it *Esther*, m. James Spencer, and that I *know* is the right name. She was bap. in Bolton, Conn., Feb. 20, 1732, and I have in my notes that she was born Feb. 15, 1732. That date is not from record, but from the mouth of her son, Jeremiah Spencer, now (1860) living in Torringford, in 91st year ; but some six months later I saw him again, and he then said that she was born *the same day that George Washington was*, which was Feb. 11, 1732." "Abigail, above referred to, was bap. at Bolton, Feb. 8, 1730. James Spencer, m. Esther Birge, Nov. 21, 1751."

P. 539, 1. 27, Hinsdale's *N. S. R.* says, JEREMIAH, d. Sept. 15, 1776, of epidemic dysentery.

P. 539, 1. 32, for 1713, read 1763. The Bolton Church Records show that this Capt. Jonathan died at Stamford, Conn., Nov., 1776, " by wounds received at the battle of White Plains " — instead of being killed in that battle, as stated in the text. It is said that it was a musket shot wound in his arm which caused his death. His widow m. Deacon Amasa Loomis. See p. 682.

P. 539, 1. 40, *Harris*, in the bap. record of N. S., is called *Horace*, which is probably the correct name.

JOSEPH, had Jeremy, b. Sept. 22, 1686 ; MARY, wife of Joseph, d. April 11, 1690. (Col. Rec.)

BISSELL, p. 540, JOHN, Jr.,[2] and THOMAS,[3] were the subjects of the following marvelous deliverance, as related by Increase Mather, in his *Essay for the Recording of Illustrious Providences, etc.*, published in 1684 : " Remarkable also was the deliverance which John and Thomas Bissell of Windsor, aforesaid (see p. 8 of this Supplement), did at another time receive. John Bissell, on a morning, about break of day, taking nails out of a great barrel, wherein was a considerable quantity of gunpowder and bullets, having a candle in his hand, the powder took fire. Thomas Bissell was then putting on his clothes, standing by a window, which, though well fastened, was by the force of the powder carried away at least four rods ; the partition wall from another room was broken to pieces ; the roof of the house opened and slipt off the plates about five feet down ; also the great girt of the house at one end

. 5

broke out so far, that it drew from the summer to the end most of its tenant. The woman of the house being sick, and another woman under it in bed, yet did the divine Providence so order things as that no one received any hurt, excepting John Bissell, who fell through two floors into a cellar, his shoes being taken from his feet, and found at twenty feet distance, his hands and his face being very much scorched, without any other wound in his body."

P. 541, Mr. A. S. Kellogg of Vernon, Conn., sends the following note : " I am satisfied that you have *not* ' given the right fathers ' to the families of the *John Bissells*. Of the three Johns named in your foot note, I think it was the *first* (John,[6] b. 1661) who had the family you assign to John.[14] At any rate, the Coventry settler, whom you call ' John 3rd,[6] ' was the son of your John,[14] p. 543, l. 1 (*White Memorials*, p. 30). 'For your *third* John, son of Thomas,[3] see Trumbull's *Col. Rec. of Conn.*, III, p. 450. Of your *second* John, son of Samuel,[4] I can say nothing. It is *possible* that he is the one who had the family of John.[14] Your Lt. John,[16] was an influential citizen of Bolton, where he d. March 8, 1771, a. 87, ' one of the first settlers.' He cannot, therefore, be son of Capt. John of Coventry, for he was *older*. It is very probable that he *was* the son of Abigail Filley, and the grandson of Samuel.[4]" The Bissell genealogist would do well to consult the *Hartford Probate Records*.

P. 541, l. 30, Col. Rec., verify the date of Hannah's birth ; consequently strike out the interrogation point.

P. 541, l. 33, Mindwell, b. Oct. 23. (Col. Rec.)

P. 541, l. 34, Jonathan was b. March 30, 1664; d. Sept. 22, 1672. (Col. Rec.)

P. 541, l. 38, David, b. 1681. (Col. Rec.)

P. 542, l. 17, for 20, read 26; for Dec. 3, read 8. (Col. Rec.)

P. 542, l. 18, for 18, read 1. THOMAS,[10] also had Eunice, b. March 30, 1686, and Nathaniel, b. April 14, 1690. (Col. Rec.)

P. 542, l. 19, for Aug. 3, read 23. (Col. Rec.)

P. 542, l. 22, Isaac, " son of Thos., Sen.," b. Sept. 22, 1682 (Col. Rec.); examine Luke, page 541, l. 24.

P. 542, near foot, widow of Thos. Loomis of *Hatfield*. (Col. Rec.)

P. 543, l. 25, DANIEL'S[19] wife Jerusha, d. Feb. 19, 1780. (N. S. R.)

P. 544, l. 1, the 11th of Nov. is given as the date of Daniel's death ("worn out with age and infirmity"), by N. S. R.

P. 544, l. 11, JOSIAH,[21] can this be the one mentioned by Rev. Hinsdale, in N. S. R., "Dec. 21, 1776, died Josiah Bissell, Esq., of the small pox, at Reading. A Pillar is fallen ! A year of great mortality "?

P. 544, JOSIAH,[21] m. on 11th of Aug. (Wby. C. R.)

For obituary notice of the wife of John, Esq., see *Connecticut Courant*, No. 322, Feb. 26, 1771.

P. 545, l. 15, Aurelia, d. Sept. 21, 1777. (N. S. R.)

P. 545, l. 41, JABEZ,[38] m. Dorcas ——— ; also had Jonathan Marsh, bap. March 21, 1762. (N. S. R.)

P. 547, l. 1, the obituary of JOSIAH,[44] belongs to his son Josiah.[66] Edward son of Josiah[44] was bap. Jan. 27, 1793; his son Richard was bap. Sept. 26, 1796. (N. S. R.) His dau. Mary Mather, bap. Oct. 1, 1809. (W. C. R.) See also Reilly's *Sketches of Rochester, N. Y.*

HENRY BISSELL or BASSELL came from Windsor with his wife "Content," to Middletown Upper Houses (now the town of Cromwell), about 1736. He m. Content Cole, Aug. 26, 1736, by Rev. Wm. Russell of Middletown, and had seven children. He d. suddenly while in church, March 30, 1777, in 79th year. His widow d. Dec. 11, 1794, in 85th year. Mr. Bassell removed to the Middletown Townplot (now city), 1745, when he purchased the lot of the late Rev. Mr. Noadiah Russell, on Meeting House Square, 1745, rebuilt the house and kept tavern until his death. Children : Mary, b. Upper Houses, May 16, 1737, d. May 19, 1740; Henry, b. Feb. 16, 1739; Charles, b. Dec. 25, 1740; Content, b. April 25, 1743; David, b. Sept. 11, 1744; John, b. at Middletown, Nov. 1, 1748; Thomas, b. Feb. 5, 1752. (From E. Stearns, Middletown, Conn.)

DELIVERANCE BISSELL. The 1st Ch. in Middletown, Conn., voted, Aug. 22, 1708, to dismiss Deliverance Bissell (alias Warner), a member of this ch., with her dau. Ruth Bissell (alias Warner), to *Windsor Scantic Church.* (From E. Stearns, Middletown, Conn.)

DAVID (I think No. 62, page 550), is credited in E. W. C. R., with a child bap. Sept. 15, 1771.

ELI ([71]), is called in E. W. C. R., "Lieut." In same Rec. his dau. Electa, is called Rebecca.

EPAPHRAS,[73] according to E. W. C. R., had child bap. Oct. 11, 1795, and one bap. June 5, 1808. His s. Theodore, was bap. June 10, 1804; Sidney, bap. in *March* instead of May, and dau. Frances, bap. Oct. 6, 1799.

TIMOTHY had child bap. May 27, 1781. (E. W. C. R.)

MATTHEW had Ami bap. [Sep. or Aug.] 12, 1762; Achsa bap. March 25, 1764, and children bap. Feb. 12, 1769; Jan. 30, 1774. (E. W. C. R.)

P. 547, l. 36, HANNAH, wife of Ebenezer,[50] d. June 14.

P. 550, l. 1, Elizabeth Backus was of E. W.

P. 551, l. 26, SOPHIA, dau. of Aaron,[72] m. Eli Haskell, July 29, 1809, and Susan, her sister, m. the same Eli Haskell, Sept. 1, 1819. See also p. 652.

P. 551, l. 39, EDWARD,[75] d. in Toledo, O., Nov. 9, 1861, a. 64. The following obituary, by an old and prominent citizen, was published in the *Toledo Blade,* of the 11th:

"We first knew the deceased in the fall of 1817, in Geneseo, Livingston county and state of New York, to which place he came from the city of New York a young man 20 years of age, to commence business as a merchant. By those who knew him he was thought to be a young man of more than ordinary promise, full of vitality, of good habits, great industry, and having entire confidence of a successful life.

"He continued in Geneseo until the spring of 1828, when he removed to

Lockport and engaged in the business of milling, having erected one of the most extensive mills at that time in Western New York. As a merchant and miller he was very successful, and as a man of integrity we never heard the least charge against him. Indeed, we know and are sure he stood deservedly high, and by his great industry and energy, guided by intelligence, succeeded in accumulating quite a large property, sufficient even at this time to satisfy most men's ambition, but not so with him, having set his mark very high.

"In the spring of 1833, when the tide of emigration began to set west, he with another gentleman made a western tour, and among many places visited came to this point, then known as Port Lawrence and Vistula, containing at that time less than 100 inhabitants; and so impressed was he with the commercial importance and value of this point, that he made a large purchase. of real estate in what is now known as Upper and Lower Toledo, and soon began to make liberal expenditures in various improvements. From the first he seemed to consider this place as his home, where he expected and intended to stake his all and to spend his days.

In 1836, associated with a few others, he began to make the Erie and Kalamazoo Rail Road to Adrian, 33 miles, at a cost of $300,000. The road was so far completed in July, 1837, as to commence the running of cars with horses, and at a time when not a barrel of flour or pork came over the road for the first year, but the same was in daily use to carry provisions to Adrian to feed the population of Southern Michigan. It was this road that in after years proved to be the lever that finally settled public opinion in favor of Toledo as the only commercial point of any great value at the south end of Lake Erie, and we now see and know that the final results of making this road at a time when all knew that as an investment 'it would not pay, has been to concentrate at this point six important railroads, costing not less than $50,000,000, and perhaps it may be said with truth, also, the 700 miles of canal, the business of which, connected with Lake Erie, is done at this point.

We think that these are no common monuments to the credit of EDWARD BISSELL, being the logical results of the opening of the road to Adrian, for which the people of Toledo are more indebted to him than to any ten other men. He lived long enough to see that his early opinions were confirmed, but not long enough to enjoy all the benefits that he anticipated. The commercial storm that swept over the whole country in the spring of 1837, carried him with others upon the breakers, and of course left him at the mercy of the wreckers; since which he has been most laborious to remedy the losses of that destructive year, and it gives us unfeigned pleasure to hear that he did succeed in some measure in leaving his family with such means as in the end, if taken care of, will prove a very rich inheritance."

His son Henry, is now Sergeant-Major of the 111th Ohio volunteer regiment in the civil rebellion. His dau. Julia W., is now the wife of Asa Backus of Norwich, Conn. His son, Edward, Jr., m. Miss Secor of Toledo, Dec. 25, 1862.

P. 552, l. 12, is this Jonathan the same as the " John Humphrey " bap. Nov. 16, 1800, of the W. C. R.?

P. 552, l. 10, add to this family the name of Eli, who d. Sept. 15, 1777. (N. S. R.)

P. 552, l. 33, the 2d wife of Ozias, was *Sarah Hoffman*, whom he m. when he was upwards of 80 years old, Elizabeth Kilbourne was the wife of Ozias, Jr.

P. 552, l. 34, Russell d. in Missouri, in 1807.

P. 552, l. 37, Daniel, was a Brigadier-General in the U. S. A., for many years, and d. near St. Louis more than 20 years ago.

P. 553, l. 9, George also had five sons, four of whom are in Iowa, and one a resident of St. Louis, Mo.

The above items relative to the Ozias Bissell branch are furnished by Lewis Bissell of St. Louis, Mo., a grandson of Ozias Bissell, Sr.

P. 553, l. 14, Elijah, and Kezia, had Laura, bap. Dec. 14, 1783. (N. S. R.)

P. 553, l. 20, Rev. Hezekiah's family from *W by Ch. Rec.* In addition to those named, Mary, bap. Sept. 6, 1747; Wealthy Ann, bap. March 19, 1752; Mary, bap. Oct. 8, 1758. Also the following record by Rev. Mr. B., *Records of Wby. Church:* "Novr. 9, (1757), at abot. 2 o clock in ye morning, dyed with the Canker fever, or the Throat Distemper my Eldest Daughter, Mary Bissell, aged Ten years, one month & Twenty Seven Days. She dyed on ye 12th Day of her Sick^s. Novr. 21st at abot half an hour after Eleven at night Dyed my other and only Daughter Wealthann Bissell, with the same Distemper, aged Five years seven months and Eighteen Days. She dyed on ye 14th Day of her Sick^s."

His first son Hezekiah, d. July 12, 1742. (Wby. Ch. Rec.)

P. 553, l. 26, *Harry* should be *Henry;* his wife was of W., and the W. C. R., give Nov. 28, as the date of their marriage.

P. 553, l. 28, 1823 should be 1827.

P. 553, l. 40, should be entirely erased, as an incorrect version of line 3, on page 550.

Josiah, had Mary Strong, bap. Nov. 16, 1800. (W. C. R.) Query—Is this identical with Mary M., line 9, page 547?

Ebenezer, had John Devotion, bap. Oct. 20, 1782. (W. C. R.) Query—Is this the John M. D., line 5, page 546? Probable.

Jacob, m. Esther ——, and had Ralph, bap. Sept. 27, 1789; infant dau. Jerusha, d. Sept. 18, 1777. (N. S. R.)

Fitch, m. Livia ——, and had Fitch, bap. Aug. 21, 1791; Cyrus, bap. July 21, 1793. (In the record of this birth the name of the mother is Livia Drusilla.) (N. S. R.)

Fitch, m. Fanny Loomis, April 3, 1815. (W. C. R.)

Ebenezer Fitch, had Eunice, bap. June 29, 1800. (W. C. R.)

Jonathan, had Sally Wolcott, bap. Aug. 31, 1794. (W. C. R.)

Joseph, had Tulla ——; had Aurelia, bap. Oct. 17, 1784. (N. S. R.)

JOSEPH and Sally ——, (possibly and probably intended for, and the correct name of Joseph's wife, instead of Tulla, as above) had Wolcott, bap. Feb. 19, 1786. (N. S. R.)

JOSEPH and Polly (same as Sally above, 1 think), had Joseph, bap. Feb. 27, 1791. (N. S. R.)

JEMIMA, m. John Crossett, May 27, 1800., N. S. R.

From East Windsor Records.—NOADIAH (probably Maj. N.-p. 550, l. 2), m. Sybil Enos of Hartland, Vt., at Hartford, July 13, 1794; who d. June, 1796; he then m. Betsy Shuttleworth of Dedham, Mass., Jan. 27, 1797; he was probably the Noadiah who had dau. Eliza, bap. Oct. 11, 1795, as recorded in E. W. C. R. AURELIA, m. Wm. Henry Mather of Suffield Jan. 1, 1824. MARY, m. Amos Daniels of Ludlow, Mass., Nov. 10, 1823. MARY, m. Timothy Smith of Amherst, Mass., June 7, 1827. ELEANOR, m. Jonah Rice of Hartford, April 24, 1832. DOLLY, m. Rufus Russel of Sunderland, Mass., Dec. 8, 1823. JANE MELISSA, m. Wm. Green, April 29, 1824. BETSY, m. James Pelton, Feb. 23, 1834. JEMIMA S., m. Chauncey C. Sexton, Nov. 28, 1839. HANNAH AMELIA, m. John C. D. Carpenter, Oct. 4, 1842. ADELIA, m. Francis W. Shepard of Northampton, Mass., April 29, 1844. CORNELIA M., m. Chas. H. Talcott of Glastenbury, Jan. 8, 1851.

ELIZABETH, d. April 29, 1849.

S. W. Graveyard.—EBENEZER's child, d. July 6, 1728 ; and son d. Dec. 28, 1757; the wife of Thomas, ELIZABETH, d. April 6, 1742. NATHANIEL, d. March 6, 1752. ESTHER, d. July 31, 1741. NOAH, s. of Noah, d. March 25, 1775. Wid. ESTHER, buried July 31, 1747. Wid. MARY, d. March 9, 1753. SARAH, buried Sept. 15, 1776. PEGGY, buried Nov. 20, 1835.

From Wby. Ch.· Rec.—JONATHAN, had Jonathan, bap. Feb. 10, 1745. ·
Dea. HEZEKIAH, d. Jan. 14, 1802, a. 59 ; had Juliana, bap. April 1, 1792. NANCY, m. Asher Adams of Boston, Feb. 23, 1800.

BLANCHARD, p. 554, l. 31, SIMON, m. Eunice Squire, Oct. 29, 1823.

P. 554, l. 29, for 1795, réad 1793.

P. 554, l. 34, for 1852, read 1832.

URSULA, m. Luke Adams, Feb. 19, 1819. (W. C. R.)

ADELISSA, m. Luman Squires, Feb. 18, 1817. (W. C. R.)

SARAH, had child bap. Aug. 3, 1766. (E W. C. R.)

BLISS, p. 555, STOUGHTON (probably son of Peletiah, line 10), had child, bap. May 20, 1787; Jan. 24, 1790 ; Peletiah, bap. April 22, 1792 ; Reuben, bap. . Feb. 7, 1795; Reuben, bap. March 17, 1799. (E. W. C. R.)

BLODGET, p. 555, l. 35, CEPHAS, then of E. W., m. Huldah Gaylord of W., Sept. 27, 1814. (W. C. R.) See also page 556, line 28.

BOLES, p. 557, l. 20, "Record of SAMUEL BOLES and Familys Births and Deaths. March 19th, 1710, Samuel Boles was born. Oct. 28, 1719, Ruth Boles, his wife, was born. August 12th, 1747, Mary, their Daughter, was born. April 3d, 1753, Ruth, their Daughter, was born. July 31st, 1750, Elizabeth, their Daughter, was born. Sept. 13th, 1762, Samuel Boles departed this life, aged 52. April 7th, 1792, Ruth, his wife, departed this life aged 73. Nov. 2d, 1737, Elizabeth, his daughter, departed this life aged 47. June 16th 1810, Mary, his daughter, departed this life —— 63. June 11th, 1831, Ruth, their Daughter, died 78 (she was the wife of Benjamin Barber, page 531, and probably the Widow Ruth Rockwell noticed on page 767, line 3). Thus ended the Family of Samuel Boles." (Furnished by D. W. Patterson of W. Winsted, Conn.)

BOOTH, p. 557. l. 37, AARON, Jr. (E. W.), m. Ann Nash (of Wby.) Oct. 22, 1773; and d. Aug. 18, 1774, aged a few wks.; David, bap. April 21, 1776; Levi, bap. April 26, 1778 ; Russell, bap. Sept. 23, 1781. The children given to his father (beginning with Chloe) must also belong to him, he probably having removed to E. W. again. (Wby. Ch. Rec.)

BOWERS, p. 558, l. 8, insert STEPHEN, m. Wealthy Loomis, Nov. 16, 1780. (W. C. R.)

JOHN (Bower), had by wife Catherine, Mary Ann, b. Feb. 17, 1765; 2 child. bap. Nov. 14, 1766 ; 2 child. bap. Feb. 15, 1769; Aug. 4, 1771 ; July 25, 1773; a John (probably same), had child. bap. Sept. 15, 1782; Nov. 19, 1797. AZEL, had child. bap. Aug. 21, 1768; Aug. 25, 1771 (all above from E. W. C. R.).

BRADLEY, p. 558, after l. 25, insert ALMOND (E. W.), m. Pamelia Spencer, April 15, 1816. (W. C. R.)

BRANKER, p. 558, insert, Mr. JOHN, d May 27, 1662. (Col. Rec.)

BROOKS, p. 558, l. 33, for 20, read 25. In l. 36, for 1665, read 1665-6.

BROWN, p. 558, l. 40, for *Salem*, read *Plymouth*.

The following from Wby. Ch. Rec.—P. 559, l. 27, JONATHAN,[3] d. Aug. 26, 1747; and his wid. Miudwell, d. March 1, 1767, a. about 92.

P. 559, l. 40, The wife of BENJAMIN,[6] (Hannah) d. Aug. 25, 1759, a. perhaps 38 yrs. He m. 2, wid. Mary Brown of W. Hartford, June 12, 1760. He had by his first wife, in addition to those mentioned in the book, the following: Joseph, bap. May 27, 1753; Kezia, bap. Jan. 11, 1756; Aaron, bap. Dec. 10, 1758. By his 2d wife he had Louis, bap. March 29, 1761; Moses, bap. Feb. 5, 1764; who d. May 22, 1775. His dau. Hannah seems to have been b. in 1745.

P. 560, l. 9, for 1787, read 1737.

P. 560, l. 26, inasmuch as Justus was bap. after his father's death, the Jonathan on this line is evidently the son of some other Jonathan, than Jonathan, Jr.[12]

P. 560, l. 28, for *Eli*, read *Levi*.

P. 560, l. 11, Isaac,[8] also had the following : Isaac, bap. April 27; d. Oct. 26, 1740; Martha, bap. July 25, 1742; d. June 23, 1775 ; Isaac, bap. June 11, 1738; d. Jan. 22, 1739 ; Isaac, bap. July 25, 1743; d. Oct. 8, 1743; Mindwell, bap. Sept. 23, 1744. Martha (wife of Isaac,[8]) d. Aug. 12, 1772, a. about 68 yrs.; Isaac himself d. Sept. 8, 1775.

BENJAMIN, had Moses, bap. Nov. 4, 1781; Nabby, bap. Nov. 24, 1799 ; Miles,

Mary and William, bap. May 21, 1809 ; David, bap. June, 1812 ; Orrin, bap. July 10, 1814 ; Rosa Abigail, bap. Sept. 22, 1816 ; Lucy Elizabeth, bap. July 4, 1819 ; Fanny Lucinda, bap. May 4, 1823 ; William, bap. Aug. 6, 1826.

BENJAMIN, Jr. (perhaps the above), had Rockee, bap. Oct. 6, 1771 ; Benjamin, bap. Oct. 13, 1776.

EBENEZER, m. Susanna Pierce, Dec. 19, 1776 ; had Ebenezer, bap. Sept. 7, 1777 ; Hezekiah, bap. May 19, 1781 ; Susy, bap. July 23, 1786.

TITUS (of Poq.), had Aaron, bap. March 29, 1761 ; Abigail, bap. Oct. 2, 1763.

EZRA (of Poq.), m. Chloe Hoskins, Oct. 13, 1757 ; had Sarah, bap. April 12, 1758 ; Chloe, bap. March 4, 1759 ; Sarah, bap. March 29, 1761 ; Ezra, bap. May 29, 1763 ; Rhoda, bap. June 23, 1765 ; Isaac, bap. May 31, 1767 ; Loanna, bap. July 16, 1769 ; Hannah, bap. Oct. 25, 1772.

EZRA (perhaps the above), had —— bap. Aug. 31, 1783 ; Ursula, bap. Feb. 26, 1775 ; Polly, bap. April 26, 1778.

ALPHEUS, m. Miriam Burr, Oct. 9, 1771 ; he d. Sept. 3, 1821, a. 72 ; Charlotte, bap. Jan. 26, 1772 ; Alpheus, d. Nov. 2, 1779, a. about 20 months ; Miriam, bap. Nov. 4, 1781.

MOSES, had Sidney and Steward, bap. May 21, 1809 ; James, bap. Aug. 18, 1811 ; Elizabeth, bap. May 21, 1815.

JOSEPH, had ——; d. Nov. 23, 1705, a. about 6 months.

JOSEPH, Jr., had Luther Rogers, bap. Sept. 21, 1817 ; Mary Ann, bap. June 18, 1820 ; Almira, bap. Oct. 1824 ; Albert Stow, bap. June 22, 1828 ; had a child d. in 1829, a. 2 yrs.; also one Nov. 22, 1822, a. 15 hours.

STEPHEN, m. Ruth Mahala —— who d. (and an infant also), Feb. 4, 1811, a. 29 ; had Ruth and Stephen, bap. Sept. 28, 1806.

CORNELIUS (probably son of Dea. Cornelius, p. 559), had Cornelius, bap. Jan. 6, 1740 ; Stephen, bap. Feb. 17, 1742.

EPHRAIM, had Ephraim, bap. Oct. 22, 1738.

JOEL LOOMIS, m. Wealthyann Burr, Sept. 21, 1800, is probably same Loomis who had Anna, Salome, Sherman and Edwin, bap. June 1, 1814 ; d. June 4.

JOHN, Jr. (of Poq.), m. Hannah Owen, March 2, 1758.

URIAH, m. Chloe Clark of Poquonnoc, June 4, 1778.

SAMUEL, m. Sena ——, who d. March, 1782.

EBENEZER, m. Ruth Pinney of Simsbury, Feb. 16, 1800.

HEZEKIAH, m. Eunice Burr, Dec. 29, 1803.

AMY, m. Reuben Judd, Jr., of Hartford, Oct. 31, 1773.

SAMUEL, m. Lois Segar, April 10, 1806.

ANNA, m. Philip Putnam, Nov. 30, 1806.

LUCINDA M., m. Harry Webster of Simsbury, March 8, 1809.

BENJAMIN, m. Mrs. Theda Filley, Nov. 10, 1809.

JERUSHA, m. Calvin Hammon of Jericho, Oct. 6, 1773.

CALVIN, m. Sylvia Parsons, July 27, 1815.

SUSAN, m. Fred. Wilson of Hartland, Oct. 19, 1815.

ANNE m. —— Smith, Oct. 12, 1824.

CHLOE, m. Francis Barnard of Scotland, Oct. 8, 1778.

MARY, m. John C. Smith of Wallingford, Oct. 25, 1824.

HARRIET (wid. of Sam.), m. Oliver Baker of Springfield, Nov. 7, 1826.

ELIZABETH, (of Poq.) m. Joel Loomis of Torrington, June 4, 1752.

WEATHY ANN, m. Edwin Bissell of Wallingford, Sept. 22, 1828.

Deaths.—ABIGAIL (wife of Benjamin), d. Jan. 31, 1809, a. 57. Wid. HANNAH, d. March 23, 1802, in 81st yr. SAMUEL, d. Feb. 2, 1803, a. about 60. STEPHEN, had an infant, d. Jan. 2, 1808. SAMUEL's child, d. April 30, 1807, a. 6 mos. ANNIE, d. April 19, 1801, a. 19. SAMUEL, d. Dec. 30, 1823. LUCIA, d. June 29, 1828, a. 5. HANNAH, d. Oct. 19, 1825, a. 80. WILLIAM, d. Oct. 24, 1825, a. 23. JOSEPH, Sen'r's wife d. March 7, 1825. EBENEZER, d. June 30, 1796, a 46. An infant of PHILIP, d. June 30, 1796. MICAH's idiot child, d. Dec. 14, 1796, a. 27. BENJAMIN, d. Nov. 15, 1799. ENOCH, d. Jan. 19, 1801, a 27. Wid. SUSANNAH, d. Sept. 14, 1813. ELI's child, d. Sept. 25, 1814, a. 13 mos. LOOMIS (perhaps), d. Feb. 1818.

P. 560, l. 31, STEPHEN, m. Ruth M. Loomis, Sept. 20, 1801; and STEPHEN, (probably the same) m. Ruth Dean of Simsbury, Nov. 20, 1809.

EPHRAIM, and Mary (probably the same as Ephraim and Mercy), had son Joab, bap. Feb. 15, 1767. (N. S. R.)

JOAB, had William, bap. Oct. 23, 1803. (W. C. R.)

WILLIAM, had Mary, bap. Aug. 2, 1801. (W. C. R.)

JOHN, m. Ruby Palmer, Sept. 30, 1798.

EUNICE, m. John Robeson, Aug. 4, 1800.

BUCKLAND, p. 562, l. 13, Mary, b. Dec. 13.

P. 562, l. 15, Hannah, d. Dec. 23, 1676.

P. 562, l. 27, Hannah, d. Sept. 15, 1674; "b. ye first day."

P. 562, l. 28, John d. also Dec. 7.

A Thomas, m. Hannah (dau. of Nathl.) Cook, Oct. 21, 1675. (All above from Col. Rec.)

BUEL, p. 563, l. 15, Sarah, b. in Nov. (Col. Rec.) BENONI, had Elnathan before March 11, 1744. (Wby. Ch. Rec.) Peter, m. Martha Coggens, "both of Windsor," March 31, 1670. (Col. Rec.)

BULL, Capt. MANNING, had a child which d. Feb. 7, 1769, a. few hours; Daniel, bap. Feb. 18, 1770. (Wby. Ch. Rec.)

BURNHAM (page 564) insert ABNER, bad child. bap. Aug. 20, 1780; Feb. 24, 1782; May 23, 1784; Feb. 19, 1786; Nov. 18, 1787; Oct. 4, 1789; Matthew Rockwell, bap. July 24, 1791; El—, bap. Sept. 8, 1793; Emily, bap. June 20, 1796; Abner, bap. Jan. 19, 1798; W——, bap. Sept. 8, 1799. (E. W. C. R.)

ELIJAH, had child, bap. June 13, 1773. (E. W. C. R.) —— Burnham, had child. bap. Nov. 1773; Feb. 6, 1774; May 14, 1780. (E. W. C. R.)

" WILLIAM, son of Thos. Burnam and Elizabeth, dau. of Nathaniel Lomas, were m. June 28, 1671." (Col. Rec.)

6

Daniel, had child. bap. Aug. 13, 1775. (E. W. C. R.)

Stephen, had child bap. July 17, 1796; June 21, 1801; and Wells, bap. March 16, 1794. (E. W. C. R.) Charles, had child bap. Sept. 11, 1775. Silas, m. Hannah Morton of E. Hartford, Sept. 3, 1747. (Wby. Ch. Rec.)

BURLISON, Daniel, had Esther, bap. Dec. 8, 1751; d. Feb. 9, 1752. Job, had Abigail, bap. May 4, 1755. (Wby. Ch. Rec.)

BURR, p. 564, Abraham, had Henry and Abraham, bap. Aug. 5, 1804; William, bap. Oct. 29, 1809. Titus, m. Elizabeth Wilson, Sept. 1814. (W. C. R.) Isaac (probably Dr. Isaac, live 26), had. child. bap. May 29, 1792; Sept 28, 1794; Jerusha, Horace, Orrin, bap. Feb. 1, 1801. (E. W. C. R.) Solomon, m. Deborah Watson, Nov. 27, 1754. Samuel's (line 32) first child b. Oct. 4, 1753. (R. MSS.)

All following from Wby. Ch. Rec.—P. 564, l. 13, Stephen and Sarah's children were Clarre, d. Sept. 6, 1775, a. 2¼ yrs.; Eunice, d. Sept. 12, 1775, in 7th year; Eunice, bap. Oct. 13, 1776; d. Sept. 5, 1777; Clare, bap. April 4, 1779.

P. 564, l. 15, Nathaniel, Jr., had Horace, bap. March 29, 1767; Elijah, bap. April 17, 1768; Bissell, bap. Jan. 26, 1772; Nathan, bap. Feb. 25, 1776.

Nathaniel m. Hannah Loomis, July 8, 1740, had Hannah, bap. Nov. 8, 1741; Nathaniel, bap. June 19, 1743; Isaiah, bap. Sept. 8, 1745; Anna, bap. March 8, 1747; Eunice, bap. July 16, 1749; Salem, bap. June 14, 1752; Miriam, bap. July 21, 1754; Freelove, bap. July 11, 1756.

See also under head of Phelps, Shubael.

Adonijah had Adonijah, bap. Jan. 21, 1750; Zabina, bap. Dec. 15, 1751; Asa, bap. Nov. 11, 1753; Roger, bap. Nov. 9, 1755; Beersheba, bap. Oct. 2, 1757.

Gideon m. Eunice Loomis, Nov. 11, 1742; she d. Aug. 30, 1746, a. about 26 yrs.; had Eunice, "an abortive child;" bap. June 17, 1743, "in his house;" d. same day; Eunice, bap. Oct. 14, 1744; Sarah, bap. Sept. 7, 1746; Gideon, bap. Nov. 20; d. Nov. 30, 1749; Gideon, bap. Dec. 9, 1750; Elizabeth, bap. May 20, 1753; Hannah, bap. June 8, 1755; Ozias, bap. Dec. 4, 1757; Phena, bap. Oct. 26, 1760; Moses, bap. April 3, 1763.

Noadiau, Jr. (p. 564, l. 39), m. Abigail Pease, May 17, 1757; had Abigail, who d. March 5 or 7, 1777, in 18th yr.; Noadiah, bap. May 18, 1760; Hannah, bap. July 5, 1761; Joseph, bap. Oct. 9, 1763; Thede, bap. April 28, 1765; Rachel and Rhoda, twins, bap. March 16, 1766; Abi, bap. March 27, 1768; Kezia, bap. May 7, 1769; Abraham, bap. July 15, 1770; Lois, bap. July 14, 1771; Asena, bap. Nov. 8, 1772; d. Sept. 23, 1775; Noah, bap. July 17, 1774; d. Sept. 22, 1775; Noah, bap. June 2, 1776; Martin, bap. Aug. 2, 1778; Abigail, bap. Oct. 10, 1779.

Noadiah Jr. m. Hannah Rowley, Jan. 20, 1780; had Wealthyann, bap. Sept. 24, 1780; Titus, bap. Aug. 31, 1783. *Wby. Ch. Rec.* in 1785, say "some time last spring, Noadiah Burr, Jr., had a child scalded to death; " Noadiah had Erastus and Oliver, bap. Aug. 19, 1778.

EBENEZER m. Hepzibah Brown, Jan. 10, 1740, had Ebenezer, bap. Aug. 8, 1741; Oliver, bap. Feb. 27, 1743 ; Lucy, bap. June 30, 1745 ; Daniel, bap. March 8, 1747; Aaron, bap. Oct. 28, 1750.

SAMUEL (p. 564, l. 32), his wife Christian, d. Jan. 27, 1782; had ——, bap. Sept. 23, 1764; Mary, bap. August, 1765 ; Samuel, bap. Nov. 15, 1761; Kitta, bap. Aug. 5, 1764; Peletiah, bap. July 24, 1768.

SAMUEL JR. m. Clarissa Barber of Windsor South, Oct. 15, 1792, who d. Nov. 24, 1795, a. about 23, and had Peletiah Watson, bap. June 17, 1798 ; Clarissa, bap. July 6, 1800; Pamela, bap. Oct. 7, 1804 ; Samuel, who d. Oct. 3, 1804, a. about 2 yrs. ; Samuel, bap. July 3, 1808.

AMOS m. Anne Rowel, Dec. 30, 1761 ; he d. July 19, 1775, in 65th yr. ; Amos, bap. April 22, 1764 ; Eunice, Thomas and Timothy, bap. Nov. 4, 1792; Timothy, bap. June 30, 1799 ; Nathan, bap. Aug. 3, 1800 ; Laura, bap. Aug. 8, 1802.

ISAIAH m. Eunice Rowel, May 10, 1773; he d. April 27, 1779, in 34th yr. ; had ——; d. Nov. 30, 1773, about 2 hrs. old; Joab, bap. Jan. 8, 1775 ; Irum, bap. Feb. 16, 1777; Isaiah, bap. July 18, 1779.

ISAAC had Rockee (Roxa?), bap. Aug. 6, 1780 ; Deborah, bap. Oct. 17, 1784; Chester, bap. June 16, 1787.

JOHN, JR. m. Tabitha Loomis, Dec. 17, 1747; had John, bap. Aug. 5, 1750.

SALMON (see l. 36, p. 564) had Salmon, bap. March 21, 1756; Elizabeth, bap. March 26, 1758 ; Salmon, bap. March 30, 1769; Theodore, bap. Oct. 9, 1763.

ALPHEUS had Anne, bap. Jan. 29, 1775 ; Alpheus, bap. Feb. 8, 1778.

SALEM, m. Ann Cole, Feb. 17, 1780 ; ELEANOR, m. Amariah Watson of New Hartford, Dec. 5, 1776.

NOAH m. Lucy Cadwell, Nov. 28, 1799 ; his child d. May 3, 1809 ; HANNAH, m. Luther Barber of Norfolk, Oct. 15, 1761.

ISAAC, m. wid. Tabitha Filley, Aug. 13, 1800 ; ANNA, m. Edmund Brown of Norfolk, May 9, 1761.

SAMUEL's son, Samuel Jr. d. Oct. 21, 1816, a. 4; HANNAH, d. June 11, 1804, a. 43 ; EBENEZER, d. May 3, 1811, a. 70 ; SAMUEL, d. Aug. 13, 1817, a. 87 ; SAMUEL's wife, d. May, 1817; JOHN, d. May 5, 1741, a. about 71 ; NOADIAH, d. Feb. 12, 1762, a. about 60; NOADIAH, d. June 28, 1793, a. 61; JOHN, d. Sept. 25, 1769, in 74th yr. ; Wid. DEBORAH, d. June 27, 1792, in 70th year ; SAMUEL JR. d. Sept. 16, 1814, a. 53; Wid. BURR, d. Sept. 4, 1767, in 93d year; THEODORE, d. Feb. 23, 1796, a. 33 ; TITUS, d. Jan. 26, 1799, in 62d yr.; NATHANIEL, d. May 5, 1772, a. about 66 yrs. ; JOSEPH, d. Jan. 29, 1812 ; LINUS, d. Sept. 2, 1775, a. perhaps 43 ; AMOS' son d. Aug. 20, 1794, a. 3 yrs. ; MARTIN's child, d. October, 1809, a. 9 mos. ; Samuel's wife Sarah, d. Feb. 25, 1806, a. 76; wid. HANNAH, d. Dec. 16, 1777, in 75th yr. ; wid. ABIGAIL, d. May 15, 1814, a. 76; wid. RUTH, d. Dec. 9, 1814, a. 74; STEPHEN, JR., d. April 3, 1682 ; RHODA, d. Oct. 23, 1722, a. 50 ; ISAAC d. May 13, 1822, a. 63; ISAAC's wife, d. March 13, 1799, a. 42.

BUTLER, p. 565, RICHARD m. Mary Griswold, Oct. 19, 1817 ; had son Josiah, bap. Sept. 7.

L. 24, Josiah, d. October, 1799. R. MSS., 1755. (Wby. Ch. Rec.)

L. 19, *Wby. Ch. Rec.* makes dates of Samuel's child one year later, viz : Jerusha's death, and births of Jerusha 2d, Abigail and Zachariah 1st and 2d. Also gives'd. of Zech. 1st as Sept. 24, 1754, a. 18 mos.; d. of Zech. 2d, April 1, 1759, a. 3 yrs. and about 7 mos.

THOMAS JR. and his wife Abigail moved to Windsor from Ipswich, Mass.

BOTTOLPH, DAVID, had David, bap. June 5, 1740; Elijah, bap. May 16, 1742. NATHANIEL, m. Anne Gillet, Dec. 27, 1770; had Lucy and Lucretia, bap. June 13, 1773 ; the former d. 1783 ; Luerne, bap. May 3, 1778 ; d. Sept. 1, 1779 ; Anne, bap. Aug. 21, 1780; d. same day ; Nathaniel, bap. Sept. 9, 1781 ; d. Oct. 10, 1785. (Wby. Ch. Rec.)

Dea. Isaac, m. Sarah, who d. Jan. 12, 1753, a. 54. (Wby. Ch. Rec.)

Joseph d. March 8, 1797, in 20th yr. ; Anna, d. Dec. 27, 1792, a. about 40. (Wby. Ch. Rec.)

CADWELL. *All the following from Wby. Ch. Rec.*—P. 565, 1. 32, THOMAS m. Mary Porter, Dec. 20, 1752, and had —— b. May 16, 1753. (R. MSS.)

MATTHEW had Matthew, bap. June 12, 1748 ; Elizabeth, bap. March 11, 1750 ; Anne, bap. Jan. 5, 1752 ; Peletiah, bap. July 7, 1754; Theoda, bap. Dec. 5, 1756; Hulda, bap. Aug. 19, 1759 ; John, bap. Jan. 3, 1762; Lois, bap. March 18, 1764 ; Elizabeth, bap. Aug. 1765 ; Justus, bap. Aug. 25, 1775. Rosanna, wife of Matthew, d. June 26, 1787. Perhaps mother of the above family.

MATTHEW, Jr., m. Joanna Marshall, Feb. 12, 1767, he d. Aug. 1, 1773, in 48th yr. Had Matthew, bap. May 24, 1767 ; Justus, bap. May 7, 1769, d. Oct. 28, 1775 ; Abijah, bap. March 18, 1770 ; George, bap. May 2, 1773 ; Elizabeth, who d. instantly while at dinner, Nov. 3, 1764, in 15 yr. ; Joanna, bap. May 8, 1774, who d. Oct. 13 or 14, 1775 ; Justus, bap. April 19, 1776, who d. Sept. 30, 1777, a. 15 mos.

JAMES, who d. Aug. 29, 1771, in 75th yr., had James, bap. Dec. 26, 1742.

JAMES, Jr., m. Mary Foot, Nov. 19, 1767, and had Aaron, bap. Nov. 6, 1768; Mary, bap. Nov. 11, 1770 ; Rhoda, bap. Feb. 7, 1773 ; James, bap. July 30, 1775 ; Martin, bap. Feb. 15, 1778.

MOSES, had Lois, d. Aug. 23, 1741, a. about 5 yrs ; Timothy, d. Feb. 18, 1738, a. about 6 yrs. ; Olive, bap. Nov. 25, 1739, d. Aug. 20, 1741 ; Timothy, bap. Sept. 6, d. Sept. 20, 1741.

SAMUEL, Jr., had child d. Nov. 27, 1828, a. about 2 days ; also —— d. Dec. 10, 1828, a. 6 yrs.

PELETIAH, m. Lucy Foot, Nov. 7, 1776, who d. Aug. 9, 1781, a. 24 yrs. He d. Sept., 1817. Had Peletiah, bap. Dec. 7, 1777; Levi, bap. Feb. 17, 1780 ; by 2d wife, Orris and Lucy, bap. Nov. 19, 1786; Erastus, bap. Sept. 2, 1787 ; Sylvia, bap. March 6, 1796.

ALLYN, m. Nancy Latimer, May 7, 1810, had Nancy Amelia, Edward Latimer, Sidney, Elizabeth, Julia Ann, Levi Hayden, Anson, Allyn.

THEODORE, had ——, d. Sept. 24, 1785; a son who d. Nov. 1, 1799, a. 6 yrs.

THEODORUS (prob. same as above), had Roxy (adult), bap. June 17, 1821; Lovicia, Huldah, Esther, Theodorus and Mary, bap. July 29, 1821; Marcia Jannet, bap. Aug. 10, 1823; Edward S. bap. July 16, 1826. HULDAH, m. Norman W. Moses of Simsbury, Nov. 23, 1831. ABIJAH (see l. 27, previous page), m. Eunice Allyn, May 9, 1793, had an infant d. March 30, 1794, and his wife d. March 31, 1794, a. 26 yrs. AARON, m. Chloe Ford, Aug. 24, 1794. LEVI, m. Roxy Brown, Oct. 7, 1799, who d. Sept. 2, 1803, a. 25. THEODORE, m. Roxy Parsons, Oct. 25, 1704. ORRIN, m. Harriet Pettibone, Oct. 12, 1815. ROXY, m. Jonathan Bodwell of Farmington, Oct. 14, 1828. MELISSA, m. William Watson of Torringford, Jan. 30, 1828. SARAH, m. Jedidiah Olcott of New Hartford, Oct. 3, 1759. CIREY, m. Hezekiah Goodwin, Aug. 3, 1815. ORRIN, had child which d. Oct. 23, 1826, a 1 yr. THEODORE, d. June 9, 1826, a. 44. Maj. MATTHEW's wife Mary, d. Nov. 2, 1804, a. 46. The wid. ELIZABETH, d. Oct. 10, 1775, a. perhaps 45 yrs. The WID. d. April 24, 1822. ANNE, d. Dec 15, 1778, in 27th yr. JAMES, d. Dec. 16, 1811.

CALVIN's child d. Dec. 30, 1812, in 7th yr. CALVIN himself d. Nov. 30, 1813, a 27.

ROGER had Rhoda, who d. April 20, 1813, a. 4; also, child d. Dec. 30, 1815, a. 27, and child d. April 5, 1816, a. 3 weeks. IRA's child, d. April 26, 1817, infant; JUSTUS, d. Dec. 29, 1815, a. 7 yrs.

CARTER, p. 566, l. 9, read May 10, 1653. (Col. Rec.)

CARVER, p. 566, insert BENJAMIN had Chloe, bap. Sept. 25, 1763, and 3 children bap. Oct. 11, 1772. (E. W. C. R.)

CASE, p. 566, TITUS had Rebecca, bap. May 8, 1791; Sarah, bap. Feb. 2, 1794; Titus Vesper, bap. Nov. 13, 1796; Francis, bap. Oct. 21, 1798. (W. C. R.)

All following from Wby. Ch. Rec.—SAMUEL, Jr., m. Violet Burr, April 7, 1757, and had Violet, bap. Jan. 28, 1759; Eunice, bap. Jan. 16, 1763; Louis, bap. Feb. 1, 1767; Peletiah, bap. Sept. 4, 1768; Samuel, bap. Sept. 23, 1770, d. Aug. 23, 1775; Russell, bap. June 13, 1773.

Dea. SAMUEL, d. Sept. 23, 1768, in 73d yr., his wife Eunice, d. Sept. 1, 1775, in 72 yr.; Mary, of Samuel, d. Sept. 8, 1775, a. about 10 yrs; Perlee, of Samuel, d. Sept. 9, 1775, in 6th yr.

REUBEN m. Ruth Goodrich, July 9, 1747. Ruth, wife of Dea. Reuben (prob. same), d. Jan. 23, 1782, in 65th yr.; had Reuben bap. May 15, 1748. William Robe, bap. April 8, 1750, d. Nov. 30, 1828, a. 78; Ashbel, bap. June 21, 1752; Elihu, bap. March 3, 1754; Darius, bap. July 17, 1757; Ruth, bap. Nov. 18, 1759; Huldah, bap. Oct. 3, 1762; Allin, bap. May 20, 1764; Lucy, bap. Oct. 4, 1767; Anne, bap. April 25, 1771; Susy, bap. March 12, 1775; Susanna, bap. Sept. 21, 1777. Reuben, Jr., had ——, bap. April 16, 1780; Lucy, bap. Aug. 25, 1782.

ASHBEL had Chloe, bap. Sept. 17, 1775; Ashbel, bap. June 21, 1778; Timothy, bap. Feb. 19, 1781; ——, bap. Aug. 31, 1783.

WILLIAM ROBE, m. Hulda Loomis, Feb. 3, 1775, and had William, bap. Aug. 27, 1775; Hulda, bap. Nov. 23, 1777: Abiah, bap. Oct. 3, 1779; Ruth, bap. Aug. 25, 1782; Horace, bap. Aug. 29, 1784.

GEORGE, m. Rhoda Pirce, Dec. 19, 1776, she d. April 11, 1779, in 20th yr.; a George (prob. this one), d. May 5, 1793, middle aged; child ——, d. Feb. 12, 1778, a. about 7 days; George, bap. Aug. 6, 1780; Robert, Rhoda, bap. Sept. 1784; Lydia, bap. July 23, 1786.

ELIHU, m. Freelove Burr, May 7, 1777; had Freelove, bap. Feb. 19, 1781. JAMES, had Hepzibah, bap. Aug. 6, 1780.

DARIUS, m. Hepzibah Foot, Oct. 21, 1779.

HEZEKIAH, m. Susanna Adams, Dec. 25, 1805; had a child d. June 17, 1815. ROBERT's wife d. June 28, 1817, a. 32; child d. infant, July 24, 1817. BENJAMIN, d. Aug. 21, 1818. JOSHUA, d. Feb. 15, 1764, a. about 68 yrs. JOSHUA, d. Aug. 4, 1778, a. about 50 yrs. PELETIAH's child d. Nov. 16, 1801, a. 1 yr.; and his infant d. April 10, 1795. RUSSEL, d. Jan. 27, 1802, middle aged. Wid. MARY, d. Sept. 19, 1803, a. 78. HEZEKIAH's wife d. Oct. 9, 1804, a. 27. ALEXANDER, son of Joshua, Jr., d. May 12, 1763, a. about 6¼ yrs. ELIZABETH, wife of Oliver, d. July 13, 1772, a. perhaps 25 yrs. Wid. ANNA, d. March 28, 1811, a. 84. NATHANIEL, d. Dec. 15, 1763, a. about 26. BENJAMIN, d. Feb. 19, 1798, in 88th yr. The wid. of AMMI, d. May 9, 1773, a. 74 yrs. SAMUEL, d. Aug. 27, 1775, a. about 40 yrs. Wid. of LOIS, d. Feb. 16, 1799, a. 66.

P. 566, l. 20, for William, read James. (Col. Rec.)

NATHANIEL, m. Miriam ——, who d. Sept. 24 (N. S.), 1752, a. about 45 yrs; he d. June 5, 1753, a. perhaps 50 yrs.; had Nathaniel, bap. Feb. 18, 1738; Silas, bap. Aug. 3, 1740; Nathaniel, bap. Feb. 1, 1761.

Hannah, wife of Nathaniel, d. June 3, 1761, a. about 22 yrs. Nathaniel, of Nathaniel, d. Nov. 13, 1762, a. 21 mos.

BENJAMIN, m. Hannah Drake, Nov. 10, 1743; she d. July 9, 1760, a. about 52 yrs.; had Zenas, bap. June 5, 1748.

BENJAMIN, m. wid. Mary Loomis of Simsbury, June 13, 1763; had Benjamin, bap. Oct. 12, 1766.

HANNAH, bap. June 2, 1765; Rebecca, bap. April 30, 1769.

ZENAS, m. Mary Loomis, March 2, 1769; had Morton, bap. Sept. 17, 1769; Zenas, bap. Sept. 29, 1771; Shadrack, bap. Dec. 5, 1773; Polly, bap. Sept. 15, 1776, d. Oct. 15, 1778; Nathaniel, bap. April 29, 1776; Zenas' son, d. Oct. 14, 1795, in 17th yr.

JOSHUA, Jr., had Oliver, bap. May 22, 1749; Elisha, bap. Oct. 7, 1750; George, bap. Feb. 9, 1752; Mary, bap. Jan. 26, 1755; Alexander, bap. Nov. 14, 1756; Rhoda, bap. Oct. 29, 1758; Lydia, bap. Jan. 11, 1761; Sabara, bap. Aug. 22, 1762; Rosetta, bap. Aug. 19, 1764; Mabel, bap. May 11, 1766; Alexander, bap. March 6, 1768.

CALEB, m. Christian Burr, April 11, 1771; had Christian, bap. March 22, 1772; Joanna, hap. March 12, 1775, d. Sept. 26 or 27, 1775; son d. Oct. 13, 1796, a. 2 yrs.

JONAH, had Jonah, bap. Aug. 30, 1741.

SARAH, m. Hez. Richards of West Hartford, May 8, 1755. EUNICE, m. Elisha Lawrence of Kenington, May 13, 1756.

NEWTON, m. Laura Roberts, Nov. 26, 1812. Richard's wife had a child bap. Dec. 5, 1779. (E. W. C. R.)

CASS, p. 566, insert NATHANIEL (Wby.), d. June 5, 1753; his wife d. Sept. 13, 1752. (R. MSS.).

CHAFFEE, p. 567, l. 2, HEZEKIAH, Jr., had Abigail Sherwood, bap. July 8, 1787; Hezekiah Bradley, bap. June 28, 1789.

HEZEKIAH and Charlotte had Samuel Griswold, bap. Jan. 15, 1792; who m. Rebecca Phelps, April 13, 1815. (W. C. R.)

HEZEKIAH, Jr., m. Abigail Talcott, Dec. 25, 1814. (W. C. R.)

P. 567, l. 2, John, m. Mary Rowland, March 1, 1795.

RUFUS, m. Lovicia Francis, June 26, 1811.

BILLINGS, m. Charlotte Hoskins, Aug. 27, 1814.

CHAMBERLAIN, p. 567, OLIVER (line 8), had also children bap. April 17, 1768; Jan 24, 1771; Jan. 15, 1775; June–Oct. 1777; Dec. 26, 1779. (E. W. C. R.)

CHANDLER, p. 567, l. 13, ISAAC, had Roger, bap. Sept. 24, 1797; Mary Ann, bap. June 29, 1800; Edward, bap. Sept. 19, 1802; Martha Allyn, bap. Oct. 6, 1804; a dau. bap. June 7, 1807; Agnes Lucinda, bap. July 16, 1809; Isaac, bap. June 28, 1812. (W. C. R.)

JOHN, had Lois, bap. Nov. 29, 1795; Lester, bap. May 20, 1798.

CHAUNCEY, p. 567, l. 20, Abigail, b. Oct. 14, 1677. (Col. Rec.)

CHAPMAN, p. 567, l. 40, Mary, b. 1664, d. June 30, 1665. (Col. Rec.) Also for Mary, b. Oct. 22 (or 7), 1654, read, b. Oct. 27, 1665. Elizabeth of Windsor, m. Joseph Strickland of Hartford, Dec. 11, 1684. (Col. Rec.)

P. 568, l. 26, TAYLOR, m. Roxana Drake, Nov. 28, 1791.

Wid Mary, d. April 9, 1792, a. 75. (Wby. Ch. Rec.)

CHAPIN, p. 568, l. 28, ELIPHALET also had 2 children bap. Oct. 21, 1781; one bap. May 23, 1784; and one Oct. 5, 1788. (E. W. C. R.)

P. 568, l. 33, JOSEPH, was b. June 22, 1718; d. May 6, 1803; m. Jane Allen Wolcot, who was b. Aug. 16, 1719, and who d. Feb. 3, 1788. Their children were: Jane, b. Aug. 27, 1746; d. July 23, 1769; Solomon, b. Aug. 19, 1749; d. July 21, 1813, at Sodus, N. Y.; Irena, b. March 11, 1752; Gideon, b. April 16, 1754; Tryphena, b. May 29, 1756; m. Asahel Stiles, aud d. April 21, 1831 (being the paternal grandmother of H. R. Stiles, the compiler of this work); Joseph, b. Oct. 28, 1759; Thankful, b. July 3, 1761; d. Oct. 30, 1761; Abigail, b. March 9, 1763. (Stiles Family Record.)

CHESTER, m. Mary Ely, June, 1815. (W. C. R.)

CHAPPEL, p. 569, insert after Chapin, ADNER BROWN, m. Huldah Osborn, Jan. 1, 1797.

CLARK, p. 569, Hosea's first child, b. May 20, 1753.

From Wby. Ch. Rec.—P. 570, l. 22, this JOHN, had in addition to those mentioned in text the following: Wealthyann, bap April 17, 1763; Roswell, bap. May 19, 1765; Hannah, bap. Feb. 20, 1767; d. same day; Hannah, bap. June 12, 1768; Abiah, bap. Sept. 28, 1770; Isaac, bap. July 12, 1772; d. July 16, 1772; Isaac, bap. April 17, 1774.

HOSEA, m. Mary Skinner, Oct. 5 (N. S.), 1752; she d. of small pox, Feb. 14, 1777, a. about 52 yrs.; also a dau. Mary, d. on 27th of same disease, a. about 22 yrs.: had Abraham, bap. May 27, 1753; Mary, bap. May 4, 1775; Ira, bap. March 13, 1757; Roger, bap. June 3, 1759; Charity, bap. June 21, 1761; Amos, bap. Sept. 4, 1763; Sarah, bap. May 18, 1766; Charlotte, bap. July 9, 1769; Joel, bap. April 30, 1786.

HOSEA, m. Hannah Hoskins, Oct. 4, 1778; had Molly, bap. Aug. 6, 1780; Elihu, bap. Aug. 25, 1782.

P. 570, l. 25, this BENONI, had also ——; d. March 16, 1760, a. but a few weeks; Nance, bap. April 1, 1770; Sybil, bap. May 17, 1772; William, bap. June 19, 1774; Kezia, bap. Aug. 23, 1776; Lucy, bap. Sept. 19, 1779.

P. 570, l. 26, for *Elias*, read *Silas*.

P. 570, l. 24, EZEKIEL also had Oliver and Ezekiel, bap. Feb. 4, 1750.

SOLOMON, had Mary, bap. May 28, 1738.

SOLOMON, Jr. m. Anne Ashley of Hartford, Jan. 11, 1747-8; June 24, 1754, d. a dau. of Solomon, a. but a few hours; Anne, wife of Solomon, d. Dec. 15, 1738, a. about 38; Solomon, d. May 6, 1776, a. about 51 yrs. Children, Ann, bap. May 10, 1752; Solomon, bap. June 7, 1752; Hulda, bap. May 25, 1755; Asahel, bap. May 31, 1767; George, bap. Dec. 4, 1757; Hittie, bap. March 23, 1760; Eunice, bap. June 13, 1762; Jemme, bap. Nov. 25, 1764; Rockee, bap. Feb. 24, 1771.

ROSWELL, m. Rhoda Wilson, Aug. 5, 1793; he d. Feb. 26, 1813; had Roswell, d. Feb. 15, 1802, a. 5 yrs.; Judson and Roswell, bap. June 14, 1801; Rhoda, bap. —— 2, 1803; Roswell, bap. June 21, 1807.

NATHANIEL, had Elkaneh, bap. June 4, 1738.

ABRAHAM, had Sophia and Fanny, and Abraham Moore, bap. Oct. 25, 1801; Selden Pratt, bap. Oct. 9, 1803.

JOSIAH, m. Deliverence Eggleston, Sept. 6, 1751; had Deliverance, bap. Dec. 22, 1751.

ISAAC (of Scantic), had Ann, bap. Aug. 26, 1753.

JOHN, d. Aug. 27, 1784.

ROGER, d. March 30, 1822, a. 62; Roger's wife had a child by former husband; Nancy Judd, bap. Oct. 6, 1799; had ——, inf. d. Oct. 1786.

Capt. SOLOMON, d. March 5, 1767, in the 69th yr.

MOSES, m. Uslae [Ursula?] Phelps of Poquonnoc, Oct. 30, 1781.

GEORGE, m. Charity Clark, Aug. 15, 1779.

JOHN, m. Sarah Bak—, July 22, 1787.

IRA, m. Beda Barnes, Oct. 10, 1779; had still-born child, Nov. 15, 1793; his wife d. Jan. 22, 1800.

CLARK, HOOKER, m. Ruth Rowley, Jan. 18, 1810.

HANNAH, m. William Webber, Aug. 7, 1794.

DEBORAH, m. John Giles of Charlemont, Feb. 12, 1797.

Lt. IRA, m. Eliza Chaucer, Feb. 5, 1801.

Wid. KEZIA, d. Feb. 6, 1804, a. 75. GILES, son of Solomon, d. May 22, 1804, a. 13. HOSEA's child, d. Feb. 14, 1808, a. 2 yrs. ASADEL's wife, d. April 5, 1808. SAMUEL's child, d. April 18, 1828, a. 1½ yrs. JAMES's child, d. Jan. 13, 1800, a. 4 mos. ABRAHAM, Jr., d. Sept. 28, 1801, a. 15. yrs. ASADEL, had an inf. d. Dec. 12, 1796 ; and child, d. Feb. 11, 1800, a. 6 mos. BENONI's son still-born, May 14, 1797. HOSEA, d. Jan. 7, 1799, in 67th yr. HOSEA, d. June 17, 1813, a 34. HOSEA's wife Sarah, d. May 23, 1813, a. 34; and also an inf. Mrs. ANNA, d. Feb. 19, 1820, a. 61. Wid. Anna, d. May 24, 1812.

P. 570, Abigail, dau. of Ezekiel and Elizabeth, bap. Nov. 15, 1761. (N. S. R.)

STEPHEN, m. Roxana Mather, Oct. 6, 1802; Horace, m. Eunice Allyn, April 28, 1814 (W. C. R.); Delia, m. Noah A. Phelps of H., April 7, 1822; Grove, m. Mercy Griffin, Jan. 13, 1791 ; Cornelia, m. Isaac Roberts of W. Springfield, March 3, 1834.

P. 570, l. 36, for *Julia Fox*, read *Julia Ann Fox.*

SAMUEL, had children bap. Aug. 12, 1770 ; May 3, 1772. (E. W. C. R.)

CLEVELAND, p. 571, insert HOSMER, was bap. Dec. 11, 1791, and had Cynthia, bap. early in 1792. (E. W. C. R.)

COHOON, p. 571, l. 23, Capt. NATHAN, had Reuben and another child, bap. July 4, 1802 ; John, bap. March 24, 1805 ; Lucina, bap. Nov. 8, 1806. (E. W. C. R.)

COLLINS, p. 571, add EBENEZER, m. Roxanna Moses, Feb. 3, 1806; LOVISA, m. Erastus Hoskius, Bennington, Vt., Sept. 10, 1835. (W. C. R.)

COLT, p. 571, ALLA, dau. of Jabez and Sysil (Cecil ?), bap. Dec. 2, 1787. (W. C. R.)

COLTON. *All from W by. Ch. Rec.*—SAMUEL, m. Lois Brown, April 8, 1779; had Mary, d. Dec. 20, 1786 ; Moses and Polly, bap. Oct. 13, 1793 ; Anna, bap. Oct. 30, 1796; Orinda, bap. June 17, 1798 ; Leicester, bap. May 29, 1803.

SAMUEL, Jr., m. Patty Filley, Nov. 10, 1805; children, Samuel Hunt, Sidney Brown, Simeon Edwards and Horatio.

ANN (of Windsor), m. Sam. Humphrey of Hartford, Sept. 10, 1819.

LOIS, m. Erastus Roberts of Granby, Nov. 24, 1803.

MOSES, had Abraham Moses, bap. Sept. 10, 1820 ; Eunice Celestia, bap. March 23, 1822; Miranda, bap. Feb. 8, 1824.

SAMUEL, d. Oct. 22, 1823, a. 67; GEORGE, d. May 24, 1829, a 1 day.

7

COLYER, JOSEPH, d. Nov. 28, 1767, a. about 71 yrs., The wid. —— Colyer (prob. Joseph's), d. May 7, 1786, in 85th yr.   (Wby. Ch. Rec.)

COMINGS, p. 571, insert GEORGE, had child bap. June 16, 1776, also, Oct. 12, 1776, and March 18, 1781.   (E. W. C. R.)

COOK.   *From Col. Rec.*—P. 572, l. 5 and 6, for *April*, read *August*. On this and next line, for *b.*, read *bap.*

P. 572, l. 18, for June 26, read 28.

P. 572, l. 19, Lydia did *not* d. Oct. 24, but *May* 23, 1676, in 24th yr. ; Hannah, b. Sept. 21.

From Wby. Ch. Rec.—P. 572, l. 35, RICHARD[4], d. Dec. 5, 1760, a. perhaps 55 ; his wid. d. March 29, 1762, a. about 60.

P. 573, l. 32, JOEL, m. Sarah Pinney, April 7, 1754.

P. 573, l. 36, Elisha, b. June, *and d.* July 9, 1766.   For *Nama*, read *Ami*. After Nama (or Ami) insert an infant son who d. Dec. 7, 1786.

REUBEN, m. 1, Thankful Hodge, Nov. 8, 1744; she d. June 17, 1758, a. about 31 yrs. ; he m. 2, Mehitabel ——, who was bap. July 31, 1763, a. about 22 yrs. ; *child*, ——, d. April 5, 1756, a. about 4 weeks ; Timothy and Richard, bap. on same day as his 2d wife.   On July 1, 1759, was bap. Shubael (bound to David Filley), the son of Reuben ; Alexander, bap. Nov. 5, 1752 ; Darius, bap. March 25, 1753 ; Ebenezer, bap. June 1, 1755 ; Jerusha, d. Nov. 7, 1757, a. a few days ; Benjamin, bap. March 29, 1759 ; Jerusha, bap. June 21, 1761.

ELI, m. Rachel Russell, Dec. 21, 1777.

JOB, m. Ruth Pierce, Dec. 16, 1719.

ELISHA, m. Susanna Rowley, Jan. 16, 1800.

SEMANTHA P., m. Jas. M. Barnet of Bridgewater, Jan. 17, 1803.

MARTHA, dau. of Thos, d. Nov. 8, 1683.   (Col. Rec.)

From Wby. Ch. Rec.—NORMAN's child, d. Nov. 7, 1823, a. 7 weeks ; ELDAD, d. Oct. 6, 1825, a. 5 yrs. ; MARIAH, d. April 25, 1826, a. 16 yrs. ; JOEL, d. Dec. 4, 1801, a. about 38 ; JOEL, d. Oct. 25, 1808 a. over 60 ; ORRIN, had child, d. Feb. 10, 1808, a. about 2 ; MIRA, d. Feb. 15, 1808, a. 13.

ELISHA, had still-born infant, Oct. 4, 1803, and child d. April 22, 1807, a. about 6 yrs.; JOEL's child, d. March 17, 1792; Ensign JOEL's (l. 32, p. 573 ?) ; SARAH, d. Jan. 27, 1793 ; JOB's infant, d. April 19, 1792; PINNEY (see l. 32, p. 573), had child, d. Sept., 1793, and one d. Feb., 1799; he d. May, 1799 ; JOEL, d. Feb. 1794 ; JOEL, Jr.'s child d. Jan. 18, 1797, a. 6 mos.

MORRIS, m. Percy Goodwin, May 6, 1819.

P. 573, ELISHA, m. Hannah Bigelow, Nov. 27, 1794.

P. 573, l. 37 : this is probably the same Roswell who m. Lucina Cook, March 10, 1812.

JOSIAH, m. Chloe Cook, Feb. 14, 1793; DELIA, m. Samuel Pollentine of Eastbury, Sept. 18, 1828 (W. C. R.); ABIGAIL, m. Horace Daniels, Nov. 24, 1803 ; LUCINDA, m. Sam. Mitchell, Jan. 3, 1806 ; RHODA, m. Geo. Wright, June 8, 1809.

P. 573, l. 28, this BENJAMIN is same as Benj. (E. W.), l. 4, p. 574, and his son Oliver should be transferred to page 574.

OLIVER (prob. the one above referred to, see l. 28, p. 573), had Abigail, bap. May 30, 1801; Mary, bap. May 15, 1803; Oliver, bap. April 7, 1805 ; Frances, bap. June 25, 1808 ; Elihu, bap. Sept. 30, 1810. (E. W. C. R.)

NOAH, had Rhoda, bap. Aug. 21, 1791. (W. C. R.)

SHUBAEL, m. Lucy Westland, Jan. 5, 1783, and had Elihu, bap. Sept. 7, 1783; Silas, bap. June 7, 1790 ; Levi, bap. July 16, 1786; Elijah, bap. Oct. 28, 1792; Lucina, bap. Sept. 7, 1794 ; Deborah, bap. Nov. 1787.

DANIEL, m. Huldah Barber, March 16, 1784.

ELIAKIM (possibly the one ment. in l. 6, p. 573), had Lucy, bap. Jan. 9, 1794; John, Nov. 13, 1796 ; John, bap. Nov. 4, 1798. (E. W. C. R.)

COOLEY, p. 574, l. 30, SAMUEL, m. Mary Clark, Oct. 24, 1711.

EUNICE of Windsor, m. Amasa Johnson of Middletown, March 16, 1767, and had Eunice, b. Jan. 9, 1768; Mabel, b. Dec. 17, 1769 ; Lois, b. Sept. 25, 1771 ; Daniel, b. March 7, 1773. (Edwin Stearns, Middletown, Conn.)

CHARLES, l. 31, also had child, bap. Sept. 27, 1812, and Henry Baker, bap. May 22, 1814. (E. W. C. R.)

WILLIAM, m. Lucinda Evans of E. Hartford, June 11, 1799. (Wby. Ch. Rec.)

CORNISH, p. 574, l. 38, for *Gahiel*, read *Gabriel.*

COY, p. 575, l. 2, URIAH, m. Anna ——, they had a child Silas, bap. July 22, 1764. (N. S. R.)

P. 575, l. 3, SAMUEL, m. Sarah ——.

P. 575, after l. 4, insert SILAS, and Deborah had Ed[ward], bap. May, 1762. (N. S. R.)

CRANE, p. 575, line 9, DAVID, m. Jan. 7, 1779, Jerusha (dau. of David) Smith (p. 775), who lived in the E. W. part of North Bolton. It was doubtless their son John who d. 1799. CURTIS Crane (l. 10), d. at New Albany, Ind., Feb. 25, 1862, a. 80.

P. 575, l. 11, AARON (E. W.), m. Mary Barber of 1st. Soc. W. (at Wby.). June 16, 1778. (Wby. Ch. Rec.)

CRESEA (or Cresey), p. 575, l. 25, BENJAMIN, m. Wealthy Gillet, April 5, 1787 ; infant dau. d. May 20, 1792 ; his wife d. April 22, 1793. (Wby. Ch. Rec.)

CROSBY, p. 575, insert SIMON, had children, Dec. 23, 1781 ; Dec. 15, 1782; Feb. 6, and April 3, 1785; Sept. 30, 1787 ; Edward, bap. Aug. 1, 1790 ; Betsy, June 24, 1792 ; Hepzibah, May 31, 1795. (E. W. C. R.)

Elisha, had two children, bap. Jan. 4, 1829. (E. W. C. R.)

CROCKER, p. 575, l. 26, ELIHU, was an apprentice to Taylor Chapman.

CULVER, p. 576, l. 17, William, had also children bap. Jan. 28, 1781 ; Jan. 18, 1783. (E. W. C. R.)

DART, p. 576, insert, the wid. (mother-in-law to Joseph Colyer), d. April 8, 1753, a. about 85.

DAVIS, p. 576, REBECCA, had Daniel, bap. March 7, 1762. (E. W. C. R.)

DENSLOW, p. 577, l. 11, NICHOLAS, d. March 8, 1666. (Col. Rec.)

P. 577, l. 13 and 14, *Susannah* is the right name. (Col. Rec.)

P. 577, l. 18, JOHN, m. *Jan.* 1653; Mary, his wife, d. Aug. 29, 1684. (Col. Rec.)

P. 577, l. 20, for *Deborah*, read *Rebecca*. (Col. Rec.)

SAMUEL, m. Patience Gibbs, Dec. 2, 1686. HANNAH, dau. of Hannah, b. Nov. 14, 1690. "OLD WIDOW DENSLO," d. Aug. 14, 1669, prob. wife of Nicholas, the Emigrant. (Col. Rec.)

SUSANNAH, d. Aug. 26, 1683. (Col. Rec.)

P. 577, l. 30, this SAMUEL and Hannah, his wife, of North Windsor, had Hannah, bap. Nov. 15, 1761; Leavit, bap. May 20, 1764, d. Sept. 22, 1777; Lovisa, bap. Dec. 7, 1766; Alpheus, bap. June 19, 1769, d. Sept. 16, 1777; Thaddeus, bap. July 28, 1771. (N. S. R.)

P. 578, l. 4, add to the family of MARTIN and Lois, the following children : Thaddeus, bap. July 30, 1775 ; Lois, bap. Aug. 2, 1777 ; Anne, bap. Oct. 26, 1782; Carlos, bap. May 4, 1786; Almanga, bap. Oct. 19, 1788. (N. S. R.) '

ALPHEUS (can this be Thaddeus ?), son of Martin, d. Oct. 25, 1776.

ELIJAH and Lydia. had Elijah, bap. Feb. 10, 1765; Violetta, bap. March 17, 1766; Pamela, bap. May 7, 1774; Elihu, bap. May 11, 1778. (N. S. R.)

ELIJAH and Elizabeth, had Justus, bap. Sept. 20, 1778. (W. C. R.)

ELIJAH, m. Susannah Brown, Jan. 21, 1792.

ELIZA, m. Ephraim Harris, Jan. 27, 1831. (W. C. R.)

SUSAN, m. George Murphy, Nov. 23, 1820.

ANNA, m. Chester Loomis of Coventry, Conn., Sept. 1, 1804.

MELISSA, m. Richard Starr of H., Feb. 18, 1810.

SARAH, dau. of wid. Sarah, d. May, 1778.

JOEL, d. in camp, June 28, 1778 (N. S. R.); insert his name also in p. 420.

OLIVER, d. June 28, 1777. (N. S. R.)

GAYLORD (prob. identical with Joseph Gaylord of line 5), had Sarah and Oliver, bap. Aug. 31, 1794; Anna, bap. Nov. 10, 1799, and Olive, bap. July 3, 1803. (W. C. R.)

DEMING, SAMUEL, m. Jerusha Butler, November, 1765.

DEXTER, p. 578, l. 33, AZUBA, m. W. *Conant* Abernethy, May 20.

P. 578, l. 36 (W. C. R.), read *Winchester* instead of *Winsted*.

P. 579, l. 22 and 23, for *N. Y.*, read *Ohio*.

DIBBLE, p. 581, l. 6, DANIEL, m. Ruth Phelps, December, 1787.

All following from Col. Rec.—P. 581, l. 9, Thomas, Sr., m. Elizabeth *Hayden* of Hadley, June 25, 1683; she d. Sept. 25, 1689.

P. 581, l. 10, for Sept. 26, read 21.

P. 581, l. 11, for Dec. 17, read Dec. 7.

P. 581, l. 14, Israel had a son, who d. Dec. 1, 1679.

P. 581, l. 18, Mary Wakefield, wife of Ebenezer,[2] was of, and m. at New Haven.

P. 581, l. 27, Martha, b. 1669-70 ; d. June 13 following.

P. 581, 1. 32, for *Elizabeth* read *Mindwell*.

P. 581, l. 34, Thomas,[4] m. *Mary* Tucker, Oct. 10, 1672.

P. 581, l. 37, Mary, b. 1680; d. April 9, 1685.

DIGGENS, p. 580, l. 6, OLIVER, m. Mehitable Porter, Sept. 20, 1758 (Wby. Ch. Rec.), and had also Luke, bap. May 9, 1762; Russell, bap. Dec. 11, 1763, and children bap. Nov. 3, 1765; Sept. 20, 1767; Oct. 21, 1770; Sept. 13, 1772; Aug. 14, 1774; April, 1777; June 20, 1779; Oct. 14, 1781. (E. W. C. R.)

DOOR (DUER?), p. 581, insert Polly had child, bap. Aug. 22, 1779. (E. W. C. R.)

DORCHESTER, p. 581, l. 13, JOHN, b. 1644; became inhabitant of Springfield; m. Sarah (dau. of Samuel) Gaylord, Nov. 29, 1671. (Col. Rec.)

DRAKE, p. 583, l. 34, wid. Mary, d. Sept. 6. (Col. Rec.)

P. 583, l. 36, Joseph, d. May 22, 1664; prob. identical. (Col. Rec.)

P. 583, l. 43, Ruth, b. Dec. 1. (Col. Rec.)

P. 584, l. 3, for Lt. JOB,[2] read Lt. Job.[3]

P. 584, l. 5, Job, b. "in Oct." (Col. Rec.)

P. 584, l. 8, JOB,[4] "Sr." d. Sept. 16, 1689. Col. Rec. give him (Job son of John) two additional children, viz: Jeremy, b. Sept. 1, 1684 (prob. Jeremiah, E. W., p. 586), and Josia, b. Jan. 23, 1681.

P. 584, l. 23, JACOB,[8] d. Jan. 20, 1762. (Wby. Ch. Rec.)

P. 584, l. 36, Hezekiah, b. 1721–2; d. Oct. 7, 1763; m. Mary Filley, June 1747. (Wby. Ch. Rec.)

P. 585, l. 1, Jacob,[14] d. Sept. 11, 1771. (Wby. Ch. Rec.)

P. 585, l. 4, John, b. 1739; d. Oct. 28, 1741. (Wby. Ch. Rec.)

P. 585, l. 10, Sgt. ENOCH,[16] m. Sybil Griswold, Aug. 25, 1763; had also Sarah, bap. Dec. 7, 1755; Sybil, bap. Dec. 6, 1767; Enoch, bap. March 25, 1770; d. March 2, 1772; Enoch, bap. Oct. 4, 1772; Enoch,[16] d. Jan. 9, 1782; his son Joseph, d. 1751. (Wby. Ch. Rec.)

P. 585, l. 13, NOAH's[17] child, b. September, 1745; d. Oct. 25 in same year; he also had the following children bap.: Hannah, Oct. 26, 1746; Ira, Dec. 3; d. Dec. 9, 1749; Moses, June 9, 1751; Noah, Sept. 11, 1757; Annise, Feb. 7, 1762; Lucy, May 26, 1764. (Wby. Ch. Rec.)

P. 585, l. 16, for *Kelly*, read *Kelsy*.

P. 585, l. 17, for *Damara*, read *Damaris*. (Wby. Ch. Rec.)

Also to this family add Lucy, bap. Dec. 22, 1754. (Wby. Ch. Rec.)

P. 585, l. 18, JACOB, Jr.,[19] m. Rhoda Drake, April 12, 1764. (Wby. Ch. Rec.)

P. 585, l. 19, AARON,[20] m. *Chloe* Gillet; he also had Sarah, bap. Aug. 24, 1760; Lydia had Levi, bap. June 16, 1745; Mary, bap. Oct. 25, 1747. (Wby. Ch. Rec.)

P. 586, l. 25, JOB 3d, had Sabrina, bap. June 23, 1776. (Wby. Ch. Rec.) EBENEZER, m. Mehitable Cook, Feb. 23, 1764; he d. May 4, 1776; *child bap.*, Ebenezer and Hezekiah, July 19, 1767; Isaac, Feb. 6, 1769; James Wood,

Aug. 26, 1770 ; Lyman and Clarissa, twins, July 19, 1772 ; Ira, April 30, 1775. (Wby. Ch. Rec.)

P. 587, l. 7, LORY, m. Amelia Mills, Feb. 26, 1784, and had Amelia, bap. June 4, 1786. (W. C. R) He m. 2d, Sally Clark, Nov. 27, 1794, and had Samuel, bap. Sept. 13, 1798 ; Rhoda, bap. ——. (W. C. R.)

P. 587, l. 25, LEMUEL and Esther had Esther, bap. Oct. 4, 1795 ; Edward, bap. Feb. 5, 1797 ; Abigail, bap. June 16, 1799 ; Lemuel, bap. April 17, 1801; James, bap. Aug. 14, 1803 ; Matilda, bap. Sept. 22, 1805. (W. C. R.).

PHINEHAS, Jr. (son of Phinehas[12], p. 584, l. 39), had Anna, bap. March 5, 1781 ; Frederic, bap. July 27, 1783 ; Susanna, bap. Aug. 29, 1791 ; dau. bap. April 30, 1792 ; Francis, bap. July 13, 1794. (W. C. R.)

ELIHU, had Gustin, bap. Oct. 14, 1787 ; Elihu, bap. Oct. 9, 1791 ; James, bap. July 13, 1794; Guy, bap. March 12, 1797 ; Mary, bap. June 16, 1799 ; Mary Moore, bap. May 24, 1801 ; Lucy, bap. Dec. 11, 1803. (W. C. R.)

P. 587, l. 15, for March 6, read March 1. (W. C. R.)

From Wby. Ch. Rec.—HEPZIBAH, m. Russell Dewey of Molbury, May 26, 1802; Wid. SIBEL, m. Elisha Rose of Granville, April 17, 1777; Clarence, m. Theo. Wadsworth of Hartford, April 11, 1793 ; HANNAH, m. David Scheeld, perhaps of New Canaan, Sept. 15, 1776.

From W. C. R.—JAMES, m. Sally Simmons, April 17, 1799; WILLIAM m. Lulu Westland, November 29, 1807 ; BILDAD, m. Keziah Loomis, February, 1809 ; had Delia, bap. Aug. 5, 1810; Eleanor, bap. June 12, 1814 ; AUGUSTINE, m. Abigail Hayden, March 19, 1812 ; SARAH, m. Norton Wright of Massachusetts, May 14, 1818 ; JAMES, m. Roxanna Miller, Jan. 17, 1819 ; DAVID, m. Patty Wilson, Nov. 3, 1791; ABIGAIL, m. Wm. How-land, Nov. 15, 1829 ; LOVISA, m. Wm. B. Reed of Granby, Ct., Sept. 20, 1830.

JOSEPH, m. Lois Pierce, Nov. 19, 1772 ; had Joseph, bap. Feb. 29, 1773. (Wby. Ch. Rec.)

ELIJAH, d. May 6, 1783. Wid. SARAH, d. Sept. 3, 1794, in 87th yr. (Wby. Ch. Rec.)

The wid. ELIZABETH, m. John Elderkin of New London, March 1, 1660. (Col. Rec.)

ELIZABETH, had Job, bap. July 27, 1760.

JOHN, son of John, m. Mary Watson, March 20, 1671. (Col. Rec.)

HEPZIBAH, m. Timothy Munross of New Canaan, March 17, 1774. (Wby Ch. Rec.)

The following from E. W. C. R.—ELIZUR, had child, bap. Oct. 11, 1833. AMASA's wife (see page 586, line 23), had Tho—, bap. Oct. 13, 1799. Wid. LUCY, had child bap. May 19, 1811. Wid. ABIGAIL, had child, bap. Nov. 16, 1771. FRANCIS (poss. the one ment. in line 24, page 586), wife and dau. Eliza W., bap. Feb. 12, 1804, and dau. Elizabeth, bap. May 11, 1806. REU-BEN (prob. son Joseph, see line 11, page 586), had children bap. Sept. 13, 1767 ; Dec. 24, 1769 ; Nov. 1776.

EBENEZER, Jr. (line 19, page 586), had child, bap. Nov. 4, 1764.

ABIEL, bad children bap. Jan. 3, 1779; Nov. 25, 1781; Feb. 6, 1785; Dec. 30, 1786 : Abiel, bap. May 1, 1791; child, bap. Nov. 17, 1773; Owen, bap. Sept. 24, 1796.

JONATHAN, had Noadiah, bap. Aug. 19, 1764; and child, bap. April 30, 1769.

JOEL, had Eli, bap. April 21, 1765 ; and child bap. Feb. 15, 1767; Oct. 1, 1769. (E. W. C. R.)

GIOEON (prob. the one ment. in line 31, page 587), had child, bap. Jan. 16, 1763 ; Dorson, bap. March 18, 1764; child, bap. Nov. 16, 1766. (E. W. C. R.)

DRISCOLL, p. 587, insert FLURANCE (?), m. Mary Webster, April 24, 1674; "both of Windsor." (Col. Rec.)

DUSET, p. 587, after l. 39, insert PHILEMON, m. Martha Wing, Jan. 1779.

EATON, p. 587, add SYLVESTER, m. Charlotte Selden, April 20, 1820. RHODA, m. Sam Soper of Sandisfield, Nov. 30, 1828. (W. C. R.)

P. 588, l. 2, insert a child, bap. March 18, 1781. (E. W. C. R.)

EDWARDS, p. 590, insert RODOLPHUS, and his dau. Sally, bap. Dec. 19, 1790. (E. W. C. R.)

EGGLESTON, p. 590, l. 28, Mary, b. 1641; d. Dec. 8, 1657. (Col. Rec.)

P. 591, l. 8, strike out "(or Shadrake)." (Col. Rec.)

P. 591, l. 11, For Sarah,* read *Abigail.* The * belongs to Samuel,² previous page.

P. 591, l. 15, James⁵, d. Dec. 22, 1746. (Wby. Ch. Rec.)

P. 591, l. 19, In the list of children of John,⁶ insert Hester, b. March 14, 1682-3. (Col. Rec.)

P. 592, l. 1, for "about 1735," read *Jan.* 30, 1753. (Wby. Col. Rec.)

P. 592, l. 21, JOHN, Jr. (15 ?), m. Martha ——, who d. in childbed, July 29, 1752, a. about 18 yrs. and 8 mos. (Wby. Ch. Rec.)

P. 593, l. 12, NATHANIEL,²² d. Jan. 11, 1796, in 94th yr.; his dau. Abigail, bap. Dec. 8, 1751; son Nathaniel, bap. Aug. 15, 1745 ; Samuel,³⁴½ bap. Dec. 9, 1746. (Wby. Ch. Rec.)

P. 593, l. 17, DANIEL,²³ m. 1, Elizabeth ——; who d. Feb. 18, 1741, a. about 30; Mary, his 2d wife, d. May 6, 1776; his son Isaac, was bap. April 20, 1746; dau. Anne, bap. Jan. 17, 1751; Hannah, bap. Aug. 22, 1746. (Wby. Ch. Rec.)

P. 594, l. 15, THOMAS, m. Ann Clark, March 26, 1778.

P. 594, l. the last, SAMUEL, 34½ m. Dorcas Loomis, Aug. 9, 1770.

P. 595, l. 2, for "about 1770," read Jan. 10, 1771.

P. 595, l. 39, ELIJAH,⁴⁰ according to W. C. R., m. 16th April, instead of 3d.

P. 595, l. 6, correction ELIHU,⁴¹ m. Kezia Hoskins, Dec. 21, 1801. (W. C. R.)

P. 596, l. 11, W. C. R. give Harriet *Goodrich* as name of Joseph's⁴² wife— supplies the date, Oct. 14, 1802.

P. 596, l. 13, W. C. R. probably give the proper name and date, viz : James Francis, bap. July 3, 1803.

P. 596, l. 15, Fanny, was bap. July 5, 1807. (W. C. R.)

P. 596, l. 16, Ann, bap. Sept. 22, 1805. (W. C. R.)

P. 597, l. 35-39, add to Jonathan's children Dille and James, bap. Sept. 16, 1770; Susy, bap. Feb. 26, and d. May 6, 1775; Dorme, bap. Jan. 12, 1772 ; Susy, bap. Feb. 9, 1777.

Orrin, had children bap.: James, Sept. 18, 1814; Delia, July 3, 1817.

Nathaniel, son of Nathaniel,[21] (?) bap. Feb. 4, 1739 ; d. Nov. 20, 1741.

Samuel, had children bap.: Nabbe, April 3, 1774; Oliver, June 3, 1781 ; Aurelia, Aug. 22, 1783. Samuel, had Roxy, who d. Jan. 15, 1786.

John, had Timothy, bap. March 19, 1741 ; d. Feb. 26, 1742; also Timothy, Sarah, David, bap. Aug. 19, 1759.

Mary, had Polly, bap. July 27, 1760. Daniel, had Sarah, bap. Jan. 30, 1780. Jonathan, had John, bap. May 21, 1738.

Samuel, had Samuel, bap. April 21, 1776 ; Chloe, bap. Sept. 13, 1778.

Elisha, had Rachel, bap. Sept. 8, 1751; Jose, bap. March 3, 1754.

Daniel, Jr., had children bap. viz : Daniel, Nov. 13, 1763; Elizabeth, May 25, 1766; Horace, Dec. 2, 1770; Frederick, Nov. 13, 1774.

John, m. Martha Clark, Jan. 29, 1752.

John, Jr., m. Sarah Stannard, Aug. 31, 1753; had ———, bap. Oct. 1753. " The wife of John of Wby " perhaps a first wife of this same John. d. July 29, 1752 (R. MSS.) ; Sarah, wife of John (perhaps the same), d. Jan. 1, 1762.

Isaac, d. at Lake George, Oct. 26, 1754. Wid. Mary, d. Nov. 2, 1766, in 98th yr. Wid. Constant, d. Dec. 2, 1769, in 65th yr. Isaac, d. Oct. 1811. James, d. about 1758, a. about 26. Mahala, d. July 10, 1818, a. 25. Eliza-beth, d. Dec. 25, 9820, a. 65. Samuel, son of Samuel, d. Feb. 9, 1771, a. about 4 weeks. Wid. Abigail, d. Sept. 30, 1801, a. 93. Mary, d. Oct. 9, 1797, a. 81. Wid. Hester, d. Jan. 1757, in 92d yr. James, d. about 1758, a. about 26. *Foregoing on this page from Wby. Ch. Rec.*

Jonathan, m. Amelia Denslow, June 1, 1793. Mary, m. Ezekiel Brown, July 19, 1805. Abigail, m. Nathaniel Hooker of West Hartford, Dec. 26, 1805. (W. C. R.)

Joseph, son of Thomas, bap. Aug. 11, 1782. (W. C. R.)

The following is kindly furnished by *Edwin Stearns* of Middletown, Conn.: Samuel Eggleston (or Eagleston) son of Begat Eagleston of Windsor, was b. in England, emigrated to New England with his parents 1630, was first at Dorchester, Mass., afterwards removed 1635 to Windsor, Conn., with Rev. Mr. Warham and his company, subsequently resided in Hartford, and there m. Sarah, d. of Nicholas Disbrough of Wethersfield, 1661. He finally settled in Middletown, Conn., and bought house and lot May 18, 1663, of Wm. Smith on " Meeting House Square," where he resided until 1689, Jan. 18, when he sold the property to Rev. Noadiah Russell for £70. He was admitted to the 1st Church on a certificate from church in Windsor (and Obediah Allen was admitted from Windsor same day). He d. February, 1691, estate £105. His will was dated Dec. 26, 1686 ; names 7 children then living. Inventory, dated March 6, 1691. Children : 1, Samuel, Jr., b. March 6, 1663; 2, Thomas, b. June 4, 1667; d. Aug. 27, 1667 ; 3, Joseph, b. Jan. 24, 1668 ; d. Jan. 31, 1668;

4, Sarah, b. Oct. 26, 1670; 5, Susanna, b. May 9, 1674; Mrs. Job Payne; 6, Nicholas, b. Dec. 23, 1676; 7, Mary, b. ———, 1678; Mrs. Jacob Everts, Guilford; 8, Mercy, b. July 27, 1679; Mrs. Samuel Miller; 9, Ebenezer, b. July 7, 1689 (b. 1684-5), was 6 years old when his father died.

Corrections furnished by Elijah Eggleston of Hartford, Conn.—P. 590, l. 22, Begat's 1st wife, *name unknown,* his *second* wife *is said to have been* Sarah Talcott of Hartford, Ct.

P. 590, l. 34, James,[5] (according to Savage) b. 1656, was killed at Deerfield, Mass., Sept. 18, 1675.

P. 590, l. 37, Hester's birth in 1682-3, being over two years after her father's death, seems to be somewhat incorrect.

P. 591, l. 25, for *Grace -Moore* (?), read *Grace Hoskins,* b. July 26, 1666. See p. 668 of Windsor Hist.

P. 591. Note—This Mrs. Olivia (Eggleston) Phelps, was dau. of *Elihu* Eggleston, a merchant tailor of Hartford, Ct., who d. there April 10, 1803, in 59th yr., a most devoted christian. Dea. *Jacob* of Middletown, Ct., was said to be his brother. The *mother* of Mrs. Olivia (E.) Phelps was Elizabeth Olcott.

P. 592, l. 29, THOMAS,[17] was never married. The children assigned him must, therefore, be given to *Jedidiah,*[18] as will be seen by comparison. Thomas,[32] was b. Sept. 26, 1741.

P. 592, l. 39, Joseph's birth, for 1775, read 1757.

P. 593, l. 17, DANIEL,[23] m. *Mary Rockwell.*

P. 594, l. 22, Jedidiah's birth, for 1764, read 1768.

P. 594, l. 34, EBER,[33] for "was a Revolutionary soldier," etc., read "*a soldier of the war of* 1812-15."

P. 594, this old brick house was built in 1760, not in 1670.

P. 596, l. 4, Mrs. Mary Ann (Eggleston) Marsh, d. Aug. 7, 1849, a. 51.

P. 596, l. 5, Kesia (Hoskins) Eggleston, was b. about 1783. ELIHU and his second wife Eleanor, both d. in Marblehead, Mass. Their son Henry, b. July 12, 1809, in Salem, Mass., is now living in Manchester, N. H., and has 3 children. Their dau. Eleanor, b. in Salem, Feb. 4, 1811, m. Aaron Woods of Hillsborough, N. H., and has 9 children. Their dau. Mary Ann, b. in Salem, Sept. 21, 1814, m. Cyrus Whitmore, and lives in Hoosick, N. H.; have had 8 children. Their dau. Lucy, b. Oct. 25, 1817, d. at South Boston, Mass., Sept. 7, 1819; Charles, b. at South Boston, April 7, 1820, m. Lucina (dau. of William) Eggleston of Burke, Vt. (a descendant of Begat, the settler), lived in Hillsborough, N. H., where he d. Nov. 23, 1849. Children: Mary Ann, and Charles Byram, both d. young.

P. 596, l. 11, JOSEPH,[42] his dau. *Delia,* m. a *widower,* ——— Bancroft, who had 3 children. Fanny, d. 1862.

ELLSWORTH, p. 599, l. 15, for Oct. 1, read Oct 5. Next line read March 3, 1690-1.

8

P. 599, l. 29, JOHN⁴, m. Esther White of *Hatfield*. His son Daniel, d. 1782 (page 279)

HENRY, who d. June 23, 1824, a. 44; had Jonathan, who d. March 15, 1816, a. 4 mos. The Wid. Ellsworth (prob. wife of above), had Oliver Chaffee, Harriet Lucinda, and James Brown, bap. May 15, 1825. (*Wby. Ch. Rec.*)

P. 600. Note—The following has been received from ex-Governor William W. Ellsworth of Hartford, Conn., who says that he finds it in his father's (Chief Justice Ellsworth) Bible, and mostly in his own handwriting:

DAVID, b. June 28, 1669, had DAVID, b. July 17, 1709 (for his d. see p. 605, l. 9, Windsor Hist.), who m. Jemima Leavitt, b. Nov. 9, 1721. Their children were DAVID, b. March 7, 1742, (see Windsor Hist., p. 605, l. 1); OLIVER, b. April 29, 1745; MARTIN, b. Jan. 12, 1750; JEMIMA, March 13, 1754. After Mr. E.'s d. his wid. m. Capt. Ebenezer Grant of E. W.

OLIVER ELLSWORTH, b. April 29, 1745, and Abigail Wolcott, b. Feb. 8, 1755, were *married* Dec. 10th, 1772. Mr. Ellsworth, d. Nov. 6, 1807; Mrs. Ellsworth, d. Aug. 4, 1818. Their children: NABBY, b. Aug. 16, 1774; OLIVER, b. Oct. 22, 1776, d. a. 2 yrs.; OLIVER, b. April 27, 1781 ; MARTIN, b. April 17, 1783; BILLY, b. June 21, 1785, d. same year; FANNY, b. Aug. 31, 1786 ; DELIA, b. Jan 23, 1789 ; WILLIAM WOLCOTT and HENRY (twins), b. Nov. 10, 1791. All of whom are now dead, except William W. and Fanny.

P. 601, last line of note, MARTIN (son of Chief Justice), had Oliver, bap. September, 1810 ; Samuel Wolcott, bap. May 31, 1812 ; Abigail Wolcott, bap. May 22, 1814; Frederick, bap. Sept. 1, 1816 ; Delia Williams, bap. September, 1819 ; Ellery Sophia, bap. Dec. 26, 1823 ; Henry Martin, bap. Sept. 16, 1827. (W. C. R.)

P. 601, last line of note, HENRY (son of Chief Justice), had Ann Maria, bap. April 14, 1809 ; Henry William, bap. May 22, 1814 ; Edward Augustus, bap. April 10, 1818. (W. C. R.)

P. 602, l. 3, Hinsdale in N. S. R., says, " d. March 18, (1777) Hannah, wife of GILES Ellsworth, of a complication of maladies ! "

HEZEKIAH, m. Laurana Loomis, July 21, 1793, had Hezekiah, bap. Nov. 9, 1794 ; Laura, bap. Feb. 7, 1796 ; Nathan, bap. April 15, 1798 ; Eunice, bap. Sept. 21, 1800 ; Betsey and Fanny, bap. Nov. 16, 1808. (W. C. R.)

JONATHAN, Jr., m. Jerusha ——; had Grove, bap. June 2, 1765; Hannah, bap. Aug. 9, 1767 ; Jerusha, bap. Aug. 19, 1770; James, bap. Nov. 22, 1772; Jonathan, bap. June 11, 1775; Charles, bap. Jan. 17, 1779; Allen, bap. July 13, 1782 ; Elizabeth, bap. Feb. 9, 1785 ; Abigail, bap. April 14, 1793. (N. S. R.)

DAVID, m. Phebe ——, and had Jemima, bap. Feb. 13, 1780 ; David, bap. 1782 ; Phebe, bap. June 5, 1784 ; Lyman, bap. May 4, 1786 ; Mercy, bap. Jan. 27, 1788 ; Erastus, bap. June 6, 1790. (N. S. R.) The father from the date of bap. of his son Lyman is called " Lieut." DAVID, had Leavitt, bap. Nov. 17, 1799. (W. C. R.) Col. SAMUEL, had Sophia, Samuel and Emma, bap. Oct. 12, 1845. (W. C. R.) Giles, m. Helen Hayden, Oct. 12, 1808; George, m. Hester Pinney of Simsbury, Ct., Dec. 22, 1808; Fanny, m. Joseph Wood, May 10, 1809; Allyn, m. Hannah Wilson, Sept. 21, 1811; Ellen S., m. George W. Strong of Rutland, Vt, May 14, 1845. (W. C. R.) Abigail W., m. David A. Hall of Washington, Dec. 25, 1838. (W. C. R.) Elizabeth, m. Horace W. House, May 29, 1817; Delia, m. Thomas Scott Williams, Jan. 7, 1812; Abigail, m. Lester Pease, March, 1813; Jonathan, m. Harriet Barber, Feb. 2, 1825. (W. C. R.) Samuel W., m. Eleanor Drake, Nov. 27, 1834. (W. C. R.) Giles Jr., m. Hannah Burr, Feb. 1, 1767. (N. S. R.) Henry, m. —— Brown, Sept. 19, 1805; Alexander of Windsor, m. Chloe Pinney of Simsbury, April 9, 1806.

Jonathan, d. April 17, 1761. (N. S. R.)

From documents furnished by Josiah Ellsworth, of East Windsor, Conn., we glean the following corrections and additions:

P. 600, l. 9, for dau. of *John*, read of *Job;* next l., for *Oct.* 13, 1721, read *Dec.* 12, 1721.

P. 604, l. 5, Josiah,[22] m. Lucretia (dau. of Jeremiah) Lord of E. W., who was b. Jan. 23, 1791.

P. 604, l. 6, Lucretia Maria, m. *Rev.* Moses Stoddard. Children—Ellsworth B., b. May 19, 1842: Berthier, b. Aug. 29, 1845, d. Jan. 29, 1846.

P. 604, l. 8, Emma *A.* Bucklaud was b. Feb. 15, 1847.

P. 604, l. 9, Emily *Sophia*, m. Albert *M.* Allen. Children—Josiah A., b. Dec. 21, 1850; Celia Ann, b. Jan. 17, 1854; Alonzo A.; Avin Lord.

P. 604, l. 10, Ann *Amelia*, m. *Rev.* Lorenzo Bolles. Children—Celia Ann, b. Aug. 16, 1846, d. Apl. 1852; Lucretia Mary, b. Dec. 1, 1850.

P. 604, l. 11, Rhoda *Calista*, d. *May* 24, 1836.

P. 604, l. 12, for Julia R., read Julia *Rosette*.

P. 604, l. 23, Josiah *Orton*,[25] m. Lucy *S.* Mills. Children—Mason P., b. Mch. 16, 1847; Ellen Maria, b. Mch. 12, 1853; Althea L., b. Feb. 10, 1858.

P. 604, l. 24, Edgar *Lord*,[26] has children, Herbert E., b. Nov. 30, 1853; Willie H., b. July 30, 1855; Edward E., b. May 23, 1857.

P. 604, l. 25, John N. *Maffit*,[27] has children, Uriah Clough, b. May 6, 1851; John O., b. May 19, 1853; Angeline, b. Oct. 6, 1856.

P. 604, l. 26, Flavius Josephus,[28] has children, Flavella Jane, b. Dec. 29, 1853; Calista Ann, b. Dec. 28, 1856; Josephus F., b. June 3, d. June 11, 1858; Sarah Elizabeth, b. June 11, 1860; Flavius Josiah, b. June 23, 1862.

ELMER. *The following from E. W. C. R.*—Eliphalet, had Anne, bap. June 20, 1762; Naomi, bap. Nov. 6, 1763; he also had children bap. Dec. 8, 1765; March 6, 1768; Aug. 5, 1770; March 28, 1773; May 10, 1778; January, 1781; May 11, 1783, and Mabel, bap. March 20, 1803; possibly this last may have been a grand dau.

Joseph (probably the one mentioned on p. 607, l. 7), had children, bap. Nov. 29, 1761; Sarah, bap. April 8, 1764; Feb. 1, 1767; April 16, 1769; Joseph (possibly same), had children, bap. Sept. 1, 1782; April 27, 1783;

JOSEPH, had children, bap. April 21, 1782; Nov. 18, 1787; and Orrin, bap. Nov. 17, 1793.

SAMUEL (possibly Samuel 3d, p. 606, l. 8, or Samuel, l. 2, same page), had children, bap. Aug. 11, 1782; April 24, 1785; Nov. 29, 1789; Feb. 10, 1793.

TIMOTHY (probably same as mentioned on p. 606, l. 12), had children, bap. March 26, 1765; July 18, 1773; Aug. 15, 1779.

ALEXANDER (probably same one mentioned p. 606, l. 12), had children, bap. Jan. 28, 1781; Oct. 6, 1782.

ROSWELL, had children, bap. Oct. 17, 1778; April 22, 1781; Aug. 31, 1783; June 25, 1786; Feb. 8, 1789; July 31, 1791; Esther, Aug. 11, 1793; Huldah, June 11, 1797.

STEPHEN, had children, bap. November, 1779; Sept. 7, 1783.

JUSTIN, had Theodo, Nov. 19, 1803.

ELY, p. 605, insert DANIEL of Windsor, m. Roxy Allyn, Nov. 18, 1805.

P. 608, insert after line 11, DANIEL and Hannah had Daniel, bap. May, 1784; Marcy, bap. Feb. 20, 1785. (N. S. R)

ENOS, p. 607, l. 22, for 1686, read 1686-7.

P. 607, l. 24, JOHN[2], m. Mary (dau. of Ebenezer) Dibble, "he in his 27th, she in her 17th yr." (Col. Rec.)

P. 607, add JUSTUS, m. Clarissa Porter of E. W., Sept. 1799.

JONATHAN, d. Sept. 5, 1821, a. 52 (Wby. Ch. Rec.); PAOLI, d. Sept. 2, 1829, a. 33 (Wby. Ch. Rec.); Samuel's wife, d. Sept. 2, 1796, a. 48; JONATHAN ALEXIS, d. Oct. 27, 1819, a. 2 yrs.

JONATHAN, had two children, bap. April 24, 1785. (E. W. C. R.)

FAIRCHILD, insert p. 608, JOY, had children, bap. Dec. 14, 1777; Feb. 1780. (E. W. C. R.)

FENTON, p. 609, insert, Mary was bap. July 28, 1771. (E. W. C. R.)

FILER, p 609, l. 12 (Col. Rec.), add to record of this marriage that Elizabeth Dolman "came from England." The marriage was in 1670.

P. 609, l. 14, ZERRUBABEL was b. Dec. 23.

P. 609, l. 24, ZERRUBABEL,[3] Jr., d. Jan. 29, 1761; "the wid. Rachel," prob. his wife, d. Jan. 28, 1768, a. about 71. (Wby. Ch. Rec.)

P. 609, l. 28, JEREMIAH, d. Feb. 1776, a. about 62 (Wby. Ch. Rec.); which also give Annis for Annie, and Ormon for Norman, as in line 32; also, the m. of his son Paris (line 31), to Abigail Allyn, Aug. 15, 1777.

P. 609, l. 34, ROGER, d. Jan. 18, 1777. He m. wid. Tryphena Allin, April 7, 1760, who d. Feb. 25, 1825, a. 79. His son Allyn was b. 1763. (Wby. Ch. Rec.)

P. 609, l. 36, SILAS, m. Cateran Drake, Sept. 10, 1747. His son Silas (prob.), m. Lucy Drake, Feb. 4, 1779. (Wby. Ch. Rec.)

P. 609, l. 40, STEPHEN, m. Polly Collier, July 28, 1778. (Wby. Ch. Rec.)

RACHEL (perhaps same as l. 24), m. James Stephens, Nov. 30, 1741. (Wby.) Ch. Rec.)

ELIZABETH (wife of John), d. March 17, 1683–4. (Col. Rec.)

JERUSHA (dau. of wid. Fyler), d. June 14, 1781, a. about 12. (Wby. Ch. Rec.)

P. 609, add NAOMI, had Levi, Horace and Polly, bap. Aug 5, 1792. (W.C. R. THOMAS, d. Dec. 1778. (N. S. R.)

FILLEY, p. 610, l. 15, Samuel, b. 1673, d. Oct. 7, 1679. Next line, Josiah[3] b. *June.* Next line, Mary b. *Sept.* Also " Nouember 10, '67, Samuell, sonn of Samuell ffilly dyed by drowning in a well." (Col. Rec.) Line 31, Lt. Jonathan,[5] d. Mch. 11, 1774 ; line 41, Samuel,[8] m. Jerusha *Drake, Aug.* 13, 1739; had also Sarah, bap. Aug. 22, 1742, d. Mch. 29, 1794; Dorothy, bap. Nov. 20, 1748 ; also lost an abortive child a few hours old, Aug. 2, 1747. His son, Moses, was bap. Feb. 9, 1752. (Wby. Ch. Rec.)

P. 611, l. 8, JOSEPH,[11] d. July 17, 1775; his dau. Abigail b. 1746, " had 6 fingers on each hand, and 6 toes on each foot." He had also Daniel, bap. Nov. 27, 1757. (Wby. Ch. Rec.)

P. 611, l. 14, this Kesiah is probably the one who m. David Jones, of Somers, July 18, 1782.

P. 611, l. 16, DAVID,[13] m. Lydia *Center, of Hartford, July* 25, 1775, the wid. Lydia (perhaps same) d. Dec. 28, 1799, a. 65. (Wby. Ch. Rec.)

P. 611, l. 20, the R. MSS. makes Hezekiah, b. " Sat., Feb. 11th."

P. 611, l. 22, Lenda, d. Mch. 18, 1761. (R. MSS.) Same line R. MSS. gives " Sunday, Jan. 3rd " as date of Jonathan's birth. (R. MSS.)

Jonathan (Wby.) b. Mch. 27, 1805. (R. MSS.)

P. 611, l. 26, Amanda, was bap. Oct. 26, 1783. (W. C. R.)

P. 611, l. 28, Nathan, was bap. Aug. 9, 1790. (W. C. R,)

P. 611, l. 37, Jerusha, d. Sept. 11, 1795, a. 8. (Wby. Ch. Rec.)

P. 611, l. 39, AARON,[17] m. *Mindwell* Brown, who d. Dec. 2, 1792, in her 48 yr.; he d. Oct 28, 1808, a. 67. Third wife d. Jan. 22, 1805, a. 58. Elizabeth, wife of Aaron, (prob. the 2d wife) d. Dec. 7, 1781. (Wby. Ch. Rec.)

P. 611, l. 43, MOSES[18] had a child who d: July 10, 1799, a. 1¼ yrs.; his son Pera d. by fall from tree, April 6, 1795. (Wby. Ch. Rec.)

P. 612, l. 3, for *Mariah, Elizar*, read *Maria Eliza;* also add the name of Susan E.

P. 612, l. 9, JOSEPH,[20] d. Nov. 23, 1808. (Wby. Ch. Rec)

P. 612, l. 10, LUKE,[21] m. on May 25, 1799; he d. *Sept.* 11, 1812; she d. June 5, 1815. (Wby. Ch. Rec.)

P. 612, line 12, TIMOTHY,[22] had inf. s. d. Aug. 21, 1798, a. 3 days, and one d. Feb. 9, 1809, a. 15 mo. (Wby. Ch. Rec.)

P. 612, l. 15, DAVID,[23] m. on Jan. 19, 1797. (Wby. Ch. Rec.)

P. 612, l. 24, ELIJAH[24] m. on Mch. 28, 1802. (Wby. Ch. Rec.)

P. 612, l. 30, OLIVER, resided in Bloomfield, over 40 years before his death, over 6 miles from Cook's Hill in W. His eldest son, Oliver D., was born in 1806, instead of 1805, as in the text.

P. 612, l. 32, HULDAH, bap. Aug. 2, 1801; and liue 34, Emily m., May 2, 1816. (Wby. Ch. Rec.)

P. 612, l. 33, SUSANNAH m *Joab* Loomis, and had 4 children.

P. 612, l. 33, *Jacob* read *Job*.

P. 612, l. 41, HARLOW, d. April 10, 1804.

P. 613, l. 1, GURDON,[28] m. on May 29, 1794.

P. 613, l. 40, date of m. of Horace[34] is Oct. 25, 1808.

P. 614, l. 6, THOMAS, m. Charlotte *M.* Barber, Nov. 12, 1833. (W. C. R.)

P. 615, l 30, WALTER, who died at the tender age of 7 years, it is needless to say, *was not* "a tanner and currier," which business, however, was pursued by his brother Walter, mentioned on the next line.

P. 616, HORACE HAYUEN, m. Irene *W.* Francis, Oct. 28, 1842 (W. C. R.), which also gives the following date of bap. of his children *not* agreeing with our printed record : Joseph Baker, bap. Oct. 31, 1846 ; Henry Francis, bap. Aug. 1850 ; Mary D. Reed.

P. 617, l. 19, date of Horace's marriage is Dec. 26, 1808.

ALVIN had Elizabeth Waters, bap. Oct. 21, 1798 ; George Gray, bap. June 15, 1800; Mary Mumford, bap. Dec. 9, 1804. (W. C. R.)

SILVANUS, had Jemima, bap. May 1, 1791; July 7, 1793; Sophia, bap. Mch. 13, 1796; Fan. Oct. 15, 1797; Sally, bap. June 29, 1800. (E. W. C. R.)

ALLEN, had Laurinda Thorp, bap. Feb. 16, 1806. (W. C. R.)

ABIJAH, had Agnes, bap. Oct. 30, 1785. (W. C. R.)

DEBORAH, m. John Sackett of Wethersfield, Dec. 1, 1686. (Col. Rec.)

JONAH, d. Oct. 21, 1823, a. 60; his wife d. Feb. 4, 1818, a. 54. JONAH, Jr., had Linda, bap. Mch. 18, 1761.

From Wby. Ch. Rec.—JONATHAN (perhaps Lt. Jonathan[6]) had Jonathan, bap. Aug. 17, 1740; Margaret, bap. Aug. 7, 1743; Kezia, bap. Sept. 19, 1748.

JOSEPH, Jr., m. Charity Munsell, June (or July) 1772, had Joseph, bap. Nov. 21, 1773. •

BARNABY (perhaps and prob. same as on line 34, p. 612), had Walter Fields, bap. Aug. 10, 1823.

GURDON, had Gurdon, bap. June 25, 1809.

DAVID, had Dianthe, bap. Sept. 25, 1808; DAVID, had Nathan Gilbert, bap. July 23, 1809 ; SARAH, dau. of Joseph, had Isaac William, bap. Jan. 26, 1772; SARAH, dau. of Samuel, had Henry, bap. Aug. 19, 1764; TIMOTHY, m. Sophia Cadwell of Farmington, April 20, 1817. TIMOTHY (evidently No. 22, and prob. same as just mentioned) d. Apl. 26, 1826, a. 75. DAVID, m. Sarah Gillet, Jan. 23, 1809. DIANTHE, of W., m. Lyman Allis, Nov. 23, 1816. BEULAH (prob. same as on line 40), m. Alpheus Ingham, Apl. 3, 1817. JOSEPH, m. Chloe Burr, May 30, 1799, who d. Sept. 21, 1807 in 36 yr. (perhaps the same JOSEPH, who m. Abigail Burr 2d, Mch. 21,1808. SARAH, m. Henry Mumford of Hartwood, July 5, 1772. MARY, of 1st Soc. Windsor, m. Lent Mott, of Winchester, Jan. 1, 1760. DAVID HASKELL, m. Nancy Loomis, Mch. 2, 1828. EMILY, m. Hector Miller of Avon, Aug. 30, 1830. HARRISON, d.

Apl. 14, 1852, a. nearly 15. DANIEL, s. of Joseph, d. Mch. 22, 1758, a. 4 mo. HEZEKIAH, d. June 18, 1803, a. 45. ELIZABETH, d. Oct. 5, 1818 a. 96. KATHERINE, d. May 31, 1815, a. 47. Wid. SARAH, d. Feb. 10, 1806, a. 71.

FISH, p. 618, insert Jonathan had Eber, Albert and Miriam, bap. Jan. 4, 1829. (W. C. R.)

FITCH, p. 618, JOHN, of Hartford, m. Ann Hiller, wid, of Windsor, Dec. 9, 1656. Mrs. ANN d. Jan. 20, 1686. (Col. Rec.)

P. 619, l. 2, JOHN[4] m. 1766.

P. 619, l. 18, JEREMIAH, son of Rev. James, settled first at Lebanon, and then at Coventry, of which he was one of the earliest settlers.

P. 620, l. 6, JOHN[2] is here incorrectly given as the son of Rev. James. The *real* John, son of Rev. James, by his 2d wife Priscilla Mason, was b. Jan. 1667-8, m. Elizabeth Waterman, July 10, 1695, and had *children* Elizabeth, Miriam, Priscilla and John, and settled at *Windham*, where he d. May 24, 1743, being one of the earliest settlers, the second clerk, a magistrate, judge of probate, and a very prominent man in the town.

Furnished by Wm. L. Weaver of Willimantic, Ct., from the record, which except the death, is in John Mason's own hand writing : l. 3, JAMES, Jr.,[1] had a 2d wife, Mrs. Alice (Bradford) Adams, wid. of Rev. Wm., and dau. of Maj. Wm. Bradford of Plymouth, Mass., where he m. May 8, 1687. He was one of the earliest and principal settlers of Canterbury, where he d. Nov. 10, 1727. Children by 2d wife, Abigail, Ebenezer, Daniel, John, Bridget, Jerusha, William, Jabez.

P. 620, l. 7, for 1776 read 1676.

P. 620, l. 17, for *Ebenezer* read *Eleazer*, who settled in Windham, Ct.

P. 621, l. 14 and 15, Anna Theresa, James Lodwick, David Yeomans and John Moore, children of JAMES,[9] bap. Oct. 4, 1781. (W. C. R.)

P. 621, l. 25, Ens. JOSEPH (prob. same as this Joseph, Jr.) d. Mch. 6, 1807, a. 76. (Wby. Ch. Rec.)

P. 621, l. 26, for *Olef*, read *Olive* (Wby. Ch. Rec.); also his son Alexander d. Oct. 1770.

Same line, LUTHER, had Mary Amanda, bap. Nov. 13, 1814. and his brother JUSTUS lost an. inf. Jan. 3, 1808 ; another child, Nov. 1809; another, Mch. 18, 1811, and his wife, Aug. 1821. (Wby. Ch. Rec.)

SUSAN of Windsor, m. William Everett of Canton, Aug. 25, 1817. SAMUEL, m. Martha Rowell, Apl. 25, 1754, " ye groome was yn, as far as l could learn more yn 70 years old, and ye bride near 80 ; neither of which had been married before."—*Rev. Hez. Bissell.*

The wid. PRUDENCE, d. Aug. 9, 1813, a. 79. JOHN (pensioner), d. Oct. 14, 1825. (Wby. Ch. Rec.)

P. 621, l. 27, JOSEPH's gravestone, discovered by the author of this history in the graveyard of the old Pres. Ch. of Woodbridge, N. J., has the following inscription : " Sacred to the memory of Mr. Joseph Fitch, Junr., son to Mr. Joseph and Mrs. Prudence Fitch of Windsor, in the county of Hartford, in

Connecticut, who died Sept. ye 16th, 1791, aged 26 years and 26 days. He was the 6th eldest son of the same name who descended from Thomas Fitch, of Braintree, Eugland."

JOHN FIELD, had child. bap. Feb. 2, 1789; Julia bap. Sept. 6, 1792. (E. W. C. R.) This would indicate an error in record of his birth, (page 618.) DAVID T. m. Eunice Barber, Aug. 2, 1790.

JOSEPH FITCH's wife, d. Sept. 4, 1748; Joseph Fitch's wife, d. Oct. 10, 1771; Joseph Fitch's wife, d. Oct. 16, 1786; Joseph, d. Mch. 29, 1789, a. 89; John, son of John, son of Joseph, born Feb. 12, 1706.

FLINT, p. 621, l. 31, ARCHELAUS, had child. bap. Oct. 19, 1766, Sept. 10, 1768, Dec. 18, 1774, May 4, 1777, May 31, 1779, Aug. 19, 1781. (E. W. C. R.)

JAMES had Fradivi or Fradiri (?) bap. July 8, 1798; one bap. Feb. 16, 1800; Mary, bap. Nov. 19, 1803; Charlotte, May 11, 1806; Car[oline?], June 29, 1819. (E. W. C. R.)

FORWARD, p. 621, last l., SAMUEL, d. Sept. 16, 1684; next page, first line, his wife d. June 22, 1685. (Col. Rec.)

FOSDICK, p. 622, insert, WILLIAM had William and Dorothy, bap. May 9, 1762 ; Lawrence, Sept. 18, 1763 ; Sarah, Feb. 24, 1765; child. bap. Feb. 8, 1767; June 25, 1769 ; June 21, 1772; Nov. 20, 1774; May 5, 1776; May, 4 1777 ; July 30, 1780. (W. C. R)

FOSTER, p. 622, l. 13, ABEL (prob. son of Abel), d. Dec. 14, 1828, a. 57. ANN B. wife of Erastus, d. Aug. 30, 1832, a. 27.

SOPHRONIA, dau. of Rev. Daniel, bap. by Rev. Mr. Rowland, Oct. 17, 1784. JOHN (prob. one ment. l. 11, p. 622) had child. bap. Aug. 29, 1773 ; July 9, 1775 ; June; Oct. 1777 ; Jan. 31, 1779. (E. W. C. R.)

Rev. DANIEL m. Mrs. Elizabeth Hayden, Aug. 20, 1778.

THOMAS, l., p. 622, had Annie, bap. Feb. 17, 1765 ; Feb. 25, 1767 ; Oct. 3, 1771. (E. W. C. R.)

THOMAS, p. 622, l. 36, had child bap. Feb. 12, 1769. (E. W. C. R.)

PELETIAH (undoubtedly same as ment. l. 40, p. 622) had children bap. May 19, 1763 ; Prudence bap. Sept. 16, 1764; July 14, 1764; Sept. 27, 1767; Aug. 9, 1769 ; Feb. 19, 1775. (E. W. C. R.)

FOWLER, p. 623, l. 13, for 1654 read 1655. (Col. Rec.)

FRANCIS, p. 623, l. 19, the W. C. R. gives Sept. 2, as date of Wm.'s marriage. The same authority gives Sept. 18, 1785, as the date of their dau. Louisa's baptism. And also adds to them child., Sally, bap. July 22, 1798, and Anna, bap. July 4, 1802. (W. C. R.)

FULLER, p. 623, insert CALEB came to Middletown, Ct., from E. Windsor, by letter from ch. there, May 12, 1777. He had a family of children.— Stearn's Mem. He had had a child bap. in E. W., Mch. 30, 1766. (E. W. C. R.)

GAYLORD, p. 624, l. 3, WILLIAM, Jr. m. 2, Elizabeth Drake, Feb. 9, 1653, abe is ment. in his will ; line 5, for *Jan.* read *June.* Joseph, son of Wm. (poss. same as Josiah in text) d. May 16, 1667. (Col. Rec.)

P. 624, l. 9, for Aug. 19 read Aug. 7; l. 15, for Aug. 9, read Aug. 19; l. 17, for 1653, read 1654. (Col. Rec.)

P. 624, l. 19, John[4] m. in 1655. The Col. Rec. seems to be equally good authority for 1653 or '55.

P. 624, l. 23, John[5] m. Dec. 13. (Col. Rec.)

P. 624, l. 24, for June read Jan. (Col. Rec.)

P. 624, l. 27, Nathaniel,[6] had Hezekiah, b. Apl. 23, 1679. (Col. Rec.)

P. 624, l. 33, Joseph[7], wife Sarah, was of Farmington. (Col. Rec.)

P. 625, l. 12, Eliakim[12], Hinsdale in N. S. R., says, "Elizabeth, wife of Eliakim Gaylord, d. Sept. 21, 1776, of ye fatal dysentery," and of the same disease, "widow Elizabeth Gaylord d., Sept 2, 1776."

P. 625, l. 33. "Died, in Hopewell, N. Y., on Wednesday, Feb. 8, 1860, Rev. Flavel Stebbins Gaylord, in the 65th year of his age. He was a son of Rev. Nathaniel Gaylord, who was pastor of the Cong. Church in Hartford, Conn., more than fifty years. He was born August 22d, 1795, and graduated at Williams College, Mass., in 1816, and from the Andover Theological Seminary in 1822. His first settlement in the ministry of the Presbyterian Church was in Gorham, N. Y., where he continued ten years. He then taught the Academy in Prattsburgh, N. Y., nine years, preaching also, as there was occasion, in the vicinity; after which he was again settled in the ministry seven years in Naples, N. Y. For the last seven years he has had charge of the church in Hopewell. During his ministry of almost forty years, he has been most highly respected. He preached for the last time on Sunday, January 22d, and was the next day prostrated by paralysis, and continued in a disabled and doubtful state till February 8th, when he rapidly sunk to his rest. —*N. Y. Evangelist.*

P. 625, l. 35, for 1773, read 1783. This Flavia, m. Samuel Hale, Jr., of Suffield, April 28, 1806.

P. 625, l. 36, Eleazer, m. Hannah Haskell ; had Frances, bap. Aug. 11, 1822 ; Eleazer, May 30, 1823 ; Ebenezer, bap. June 30, 1826; Flavel, bap. Sept. 16, 1827. (W. C. R.)

Mary, m. Benj. Loomis, Jr., Feb. 21, 1805. Elijah, m. Margaret Taylor dau. of Ruth, dau. of John, son of John Stiles the ancestor. (Pres. Stiles MSS.) Betsey, m. Luke Fish, Nov. 10, 1803.

From Col. Rec.—The wife of Samuel, d. May 2, 1680. Samuel, son of Nathaniel, d. June 21, 1690. John (see John[5]?), had Thomas and Joseph, b. June 20, 1690.

From Wby. Ch. Rec.—Ethemur of W., m. Lydia Pettibone, Dec. 4, 1800 ; John, of W., m. Sarah Pinney of Simsbury, June 6, 1804.

John, m. Mary ——, had John, bap. Aug. 2, 1777 ; Betsey, bap. Dec. 11, 1792. (N. S. R.)

9

For obituary notice of Dea. WM. GAYLORD'S wife see *Conn. Courant*, No. 213, Dec. 25, 1770.

JOSEPH, d. March 19, 1761. (N. S. R.)

ALEXANDER (prob. the one on l. 27, p. 626), had four children bap. April 23, 1820. (E W. C. R.)

GIBBS, p. 627, l. 23, Miriam, who m. Josiah Bissell, was b. Dec. 2, 1681. (Col. Rec.)

P. 628, STEPHEN and Charity, had Samuel, Rufus and Charity, bap. March, 1765; Levi, bap. May 27, 1778, d. 28th June following; Benjamin (a. 14), bap. Aug. 17, 1783. (N. S. R.)

STEPHEN, had children bap. Nov. 29, 1778; Sept. 1779; Sept. 17, 1780; 3 bap. Sept. 6, 1789; Feb. 21, 1790; Feb. 10, 1793, and Elizabeth, April 20, 1794. (E. W. C. R.)

BENJAMIN and Charlotte, had Levi, bap. Nov. 11, 1792.

JAMES, m. Almena Colgrove, Feb. 8, 1813.

GILLET, p. 628, l. 27, NATHAN, Sr., d. Sept. 15, 1689; his dau. Rebecca, d. July 13, 1655; his son Nathan, Jr., b. Aug. 17; his son Benjamin, d. July 13, 1655. (Col. Rec.)

P. 629, 1 16, CORNELIUS, Jr., d. Sept. 5, 1746; his son CORNELIUS, b. 1693; d. Oct. 23, 1758, a. about 67 yrs.

P. 629, l. 20, this STEPHEN had also Asaph, bap. Feb. 15, 1741; d. Oct. 1741; Stephen, bap. Oct. 24, 1742; d. July 14, 1745; Anne, bap. Aug. 4, 1745; his first son Stephen, d. Oct. 23, 1741. (Wby. Ch. Rec.)

P. 630, l. 38, FRANCIS B. m. W. A. Baker, Dec. 7, 1840. ELIZABETH GRIS-WOLD Gillett and her sister EUNICE, bap. Sept. 30, 1798. (W. C. R.)

P. 631, l. 3, JONATHAN, Jr.[2] had also Jonathan, b. Oct. 15, 1685. (Col. Rec.)

P. 631, l. 12, JONAH, had Rebecca, bap. March 26, 1738; Tryphena, bap. Aug. 17, 1740; Simeon, bap. Oct. 23, 1743; Mercy, bap. Feb. 24, 1746; Lucy, bap. Jan. 20, 1751. (Wby. Ch. Rec.)

P. 631, l. 19, for *Lovie* read *Lois.*

P. 631, l. 21, JOEL[3], had also Joel, bap. Oct. 3, d. Oct. 4, 1738; Abner, bap. Dec. 6, 1741; Moses, bap. Nov. 27, 1743. (Wby. Ch. Rec.)

P. 632, l. 7, for Nov. 2, read Nov. 20. (Col. Rec.)

P. 632, l. 8, Jonathan, b. 1669, d. June 3, 1686. (Col. Rec.)

P. 632, l. 12, for *Barker* read *Barber.* (Col. Rec.)

P. 633, l. 1, Thos. b. 1676; is prob. same one who d. Feb. 28, 1762, in 87th yr.

P. 633, l. 9, for 1776 read 1676; Joanna, b. 1680; d. Aug. 11, 1683; next l. for 1682 read 1683, and for *June* 28 read *Oct.* 15. (Col. Rec.)

P. 633, l. 15, JONATHAN, had also Ruth, bap. Aug. 5, 1739. (Wby. Ch. Rec.)

P. 633, l. 17, it was prob. this SIMEON who m. Rebecca Audrus, May 20, 1762, and had Rebecca, bap. Sept. 4, 1762. (Wby. Ch. Rec.)

P. 633, l. 18, it was prob. this STEPHEN who m. Ruth Case, Apl. 30, 1778, and had Ruth, bap. June 7, 1779 ; Rachel, bap. Sept. 23,1781 ; Stephen, bap. Aug. 31, 1783. (Wby. Ch. Rec.)

P. 633, l. 18, it was prob. this THOMAS who m. Hannah Drake, Sept. 12, 1776, and had Hannah, bap. June 15, 1777; Thomas, bap. Aug. 29, 1779 ; Jesse, bap. June 3, 1781. (Wby. Ch. Rec.)

P. 633, l. 20, AMOS, m. Susannah Webster, Feb. 23, 1764, who d. Feb. 24, 1820, a. 77; had Susannah, bap. Dec. 30, 1764, d. Dec. 22, 1770; Huldah, bap. May 3, 1767; Rockee, bap. Mch. 19, 1769 ; Susannah, bap. July 28, 1771; Amos, bap. Mch. 13, 1774 ; Jonathan, bap. Feb. 23, 1777; Mary, bap. June 13, 1779. (Wby. Ch. Rec.)

P. 633, l. 20, JONATHAN, 3d, had also Rosanna, bap. Oct. 18, 1741 ; Abigail, bap. Mch. 30, 1746, d. Feb. 25, 1752 ; Stephen, d. same day, a. about 3 yr. 8 mo.; Thomas, bap. Oct. 9, 1747; Stephen, bap. May 13, 1753; Abigail, bap. Nov. 2, 1755; Lucina bap. Apl. 9, 1757 ; Asa, bap. Sept. 16, 1759. (Wby. Ch. Rec.)

P. 633, l. 21, Lt. JONATHAN (prob. same) m. 1, Abigail ——, who d. Apl. 23, 1758, a. 39 yr., 6 mo.; m. 2, wid. Rachel Goodrich, Apl. 26, 1759; she d. Aug. 11, 1798, a. 61 ; Nov. 29, 1761, bap. Rachel and Ruth, twins ; Ruth d. Oct. 1, and Rachel d. Oct. 4, 1776. (Wby. Ch. Rec.)

P. 633, l. 26, add to Almerin's family Charlotte, bap. July 26, 1807. (W. C. R.)

JONAH, Jr., m. Sarah Goodrich, Nov. 9, 1752; Sarah, bap. July 1, 1753 ; Levi, bap. Oct. 13, 1754 ; Jonah, bap. April 17, 1757 ; Aaron, bap. Jan. 14, 1759 ; George, bap. Dec. 28, 1760; Elizabeth, bap. April 3, 1763. *Capt.* JONAH (prob. the same) had Chloe, bap. May 13, 1770 ; Nance, bap. Sune 20, 1773. (Wby. Ch. Rec.)

JONAH, Jr., m. Wid. Eunice Whiton, Jan. 30, 1787; Jonah, bap. Oct. 20, 1793, also Elizabeth, Susannah, Dana, Chloe, Polly, Sally,'Nancy, bap. Aug. 30, 1795. (Wby. Ch. Rec.)

AMOS, Jr., m. Mitty Hubbard, Mch. 9, 1797, and had Mitty, died ; January 30, 1823, a. 24; Amos Hubbard, Fanny, Clarissa, William Augustus, bap. Apl. 22, 1810. (Wby. Ch. Rec.)

From Col. Rec.—Josia, m. *Hannah* Taintor, June 30, 1676 ; their dau. Johanna, b. 1680, d. Aug. 11, 1683 ; Elizabeth, b. 1682-3. John, had Mercy, b. Jan. 31, 1682. Mercy, m. George Norton of Southfield (Suffield ?), June 14, 1683. Wid. Mary, d. Jan. 5, 1685.

From Wby. Ch. Rec.—ASA, m Violet Case, Feb. 1, 1778, and had Violet, bap. July 19, 1778 ; Frederick, bap. Apl. 2, 1780.

JACOB, m. Huldah Filley, Oct. 29, 1806. Children : Huldah, bap. Dec. 25, 1808; Jacob Mills, bap. Apl. 22, 1810 ; Rachel, bap. Dec. 1, 1811 ; Jason, bap. May 8, 1814; Watson bap. June 23, 1816.

JUSTUS, had Justus Pennoyer, Anson Center, Norman Hubbard, Sylvia Permela, bap. Sept. 3, 1815 ; Edward, bap. Nov. 5, 1820 ; Simeon, bap. Oct. 13, 1822; Flavia Eliza, bap. May 21, 1826.

SYLVESTER, had Sybil Lavinia, bap. June 23, 1816; Susan Merrilla, bap. Nov. 9, 1817.

LEVI, had Joab, bap. Oct. 16, 1786.

Wid. ANNE, prob. wid. Stephen, m. Mr. Isaac Fosbury of Sheffield, Sept. 11, 1750. ELIZABETH, m. Ezra Kent of Suffield, Nov. 8, 1750. HANNAH, m. Wm. Shepard of Hartford, Mch. 28, 1754. EUNICE, m. David Ives of Goshen, Feb., 1761. AGNES, m. Asahel Smith of Suffield, June 28, 1763. LUCY, m. David Lane of Suffield, Dec. 26, 1770. LUCY, m. Seth Talcott, Feb. 14, 1788. MERCY, m. John Wells, Jr., of Johnstown, Jan. 1, 1798. SUSANNAH, m. Harry McClellan, Dec. 21, 1808. SALLY, m. Henry Goodrich of Barkhamstead, Nov. 8, 1810. MARY, m. Diodate Taylor of Hartford, June 5, 1817. BETSY, m. Nathan N. Parsons of New Hartford, May 16, 1827.

AMOS, Senr., m. Miriam Brown, Apl. 29, 1824.

BENJAMIN'S wife, d. Apl. 15, 1751, a. about 23. Capt. JONAH, d. Mch. 14, 1792, in 64 yr. ELIZABETH, wife of Jonah, d. May 28, 1753, a. about 44. JONAH, d. Sept. 18, 1825, a. 69, and his wid. d. Dec. 30, 1825, a. 61. Sgt. JONAH, d. May 21, 1782, a. 79. ELIZABETH, wife of Jonah, Jr., d. July 30, 1786, in 23d yr. Wife of JONAH, d. May 30, 1797, a. about 30. Wid. DEBORAH, d. Sept. 29, 1753, a. about 74. Wid. MARY (mother-in-law to John Burr), d. Jan. 4, 1755, a. about 82. Thomas, son of Thomas, d. Aug. 9, 1779, a. 9 d. DANIEL, drowned Jan. 2, 1761, in a mill-pond, a. about 18. MARY, dau. of Jonathan, d. Oct. 17, 1807, a. 5 yr. CHAUNCEY, d. Jan. 1818. CHESTER, d. Oct. 31, 1821, a. 23. ASHBEL, d. Mch. 16, 1823. Capt. JUSTUS, d. Oct. 17, 1825, a. 42. Miriam, wife of Amos, d. Nov. 15, 1828, a. 74. BETHUEL'S wife, d. Nov. 25, 1829, a. 28. Capt. AMOS, d. Apl. 4, 1830. Wid. Abel, d. July 9, 1830. SAMUEL, d. Oct. 1819. JOEL'S wife, d. Mch. 10, 1795, middle aged. ASHBEL, had a dau., d. Sept. 30, 1803, a. 4 yr., and child, d. Sept. 1795, a. 1. AARON, d. Jan. 25, 1804, a. 45. Wid. ESTHER, d. Feb. 24, 1804, a. 95. ABEL, d. Nov. 22, 1807, a. 63. BETSY, wife of Jonathan, d. Oct. 25, 1804, a. 22.

Capt. JONATHAN, had Elizabeth, bap. Feb. 26, 1764; Deborah, bap. May 18, 1766; Lucy, bap. July 10, 1768; Wealthyann, bap. Aug. 26, 1770; Mary, bap. May 2, 1773; Jonathan, bap. July 27, 1777; David, bap. Oct. 10, 1779; Jacob, bap. Aug. 28, 1785. (Wby. Ch. Rec.)

JULIA, m. Wm. Perkins, Nov. 8, 1826. (W. C. R.)

BENJAMIN, had children bap. June 10, 1771; May 16, 1773; Oct. 1776; Dec. 20, 1778; Dec. 24, 1780; Sept. 15, 1782; May 23, 1784; June 18, 1786; Jerusha, bap. Oct. 31, 1790; Eli, bap. June 3, 1792. (E. W. C. R.)

BENJAMIN, Jr., had Sarah, June 12, 1814; children bap. July 14, 1816; Seth, May 15, 1825; May 6, 1827; Re——, Oct. 4, 1829. (E. W. C. R.)

LEVI, had Levi, bap. May, 1781. (Wby. Ch. Rec.)

ASA, had Asa, bap. Aug. 25, 1782; Jemmy bap. June 26, 1785. (Wby. Ch. Rec.)

GILMAN, p. 634, l. 11, Benjamin had ——, bap. Apl. 15, 1787; Henry, Feb. 6, 1791. (E. W. C. R.)

GLEASON, p. 634, Phineas, (E. W.) m. Catharine Wolfe, Aug. 29, 1816. (W. C. R.)

GOFF, David, had Ellenor, Sept. 11, 1762; Sarah, bap. July 22, 1764; Betty, bap. Nov. 2, 1766. (Wby. Ch. Rec.)

GOODRICH, Jacob, d. and was buried at Wethersfield, Nov. 1745, a. 52 (perhaps). (Wby. Ch. Rec.)

P. 634, l. 22, Jacob's birth, according to R. MSS., "Feb. 26." His father Stephen, d. July 20, 1758, in 28th yr. (Wby. Ch. Rec.) Seth, d. May 5, 1828, a. 45. Stephen, also had Stephen, bap. Apl. 10, 1757. (Wby. Ch. Rec.)

P. 634, l. 23, Elijah, who m. Margery Gillett, 1752, had (besides those given in the text) Elijah, b. Jan. 2, 1754; John, bap. Dec. 28, 1755; Jeremiah, bap. Aug. 7, 1757; Jesse, bap. Oct. 8, 1759; Solomon, bap. Oct. 11, 1761. (Wby. Ch. Rec.)

Seth, had Hannah, bap. July 30, 1780; Elizabeth, bap. Dec. 9, 1781. (Wby. Ch. Rec.)

From Wby. Ch. Rec.—Isaac, m. Sarah Moses, Jan. 12, 1756. Daniel, m. Zeruiah Moses, Feb. 6, 1759. Simeon, who d. June 5, 1785, had Ruth, bap. Nov. 9, 1777; Luther, bap. Feb. 9, 1781. Benjamin, m. Candace Bidwell, Nov. 27, 1794. Wid. Sarah, d. April 4, 1803, in 72 yr.

GOODWIN, p. 634, James, m. Hannah Mather, Mch. 10, 1783.

GRAHAM, p. 634, l. 33, Elisha, m. Anna Humphrey, June 20, 1754. (R. MSS.)

GRANT, p. 635, Matthew Grant's Family Record (from his MSS. Note Book), furnished by the *Hon. J. Hammond Trumbull* of Hartford, Conn.

"Matthew Graunt was married to his first wife Prissilla, in the year 1625, Nov. 16. She died in the yeare 1644, April 27, being 43 year of age and 2 months. Children—Prissilla Graunt, was borne in the yeare 1626, September 14; Samuel Graunt was borne in the yeare 1631, Nouember 12; Tahan Graunt was borne in the yeare 1633, Februarie 3; John Graunt was borne in the yeare 1642, April 30.

"May the 29, 1645, Matthew Graunt and Susanna [wid. of William Rockwell] ware maried. Matthew Graunt was then three and forty years of age, seven months and eighteen dayes; borne in the yeare 1601, October 27, Tuesdaye. Susanna Graunt was then three and forty years of age, seven weeks and 4 days; borne in the yeare 1602, April the 5, Monday. Children of Susanna by her first husband—Joan Rockwell was borne in the yeare 1625, Aprell the 25; John Rockwell was borne in the yeare 1627, July the 18; Samuel Rockwell was borne in the yeare 1631, March the 28; Sara Rockwell was borne in the yeare 1638, July the 24.

"Nouember 14, 1666, my wife Susanna died, being aged 64 years and ¼, 5 weeks and 4 dayes, and since shee and I maried is 21 year, 24 weeks."

P. 635, l. 18, for 1847 read 1647.

P. 635, l. 20, Samuel, Jr. (E. W.), had Hannah, b. Sept. 2, 1684. (Col. Rec.)

P. 635, l. 28, Tahan, m. Hannah Bissell, prob. in 1690. (Col. Rec.)

P. 635, l. 34, John, son of John,[4] b. Oct. 20, 1671, and Mary b. 1674. The said early John, Jr., d. May 17, 1686. (Col. Rec.)

DAVID (of Wby.), d. June 14, 1748.

P. 636, l. 12, Matthew,[7] m. Oct. 29 ; John, d. July 22, 1684. (Col. Rec.)

P. 636, JOHN,[6] had son, bap. 1690-91. (Col. Rec.)

P. 636, l. 37, Capt., afterwards Col. ROSWELL, had Ebenezer, bap. Feb. 18, 1789 ; Henrietta, bap. Feb. 22, 1789 ; Ann, bap. Mch, 29, 1789 ; and children bap. Mch. 21, 1790 ; May 20, 1792 ; Apl. 6, 1794 ; May 27, 1798.

P. 637, l. 10, ASHBEL,[18] who d. June 29, 1774, m. Elizabeth Chapman, Mch. 29, 1764, who d. May 10, 1772. (Wby. Ch. Rec.) This also corrects item on l. 25.

From E. W. C. R.—AARON, had Reuben, bap. Aug, 28, 1763, and children bap. June 20, 1765 ; June 20, 1767 ; Jan. 1, 1769 ; Sept. 20, 1771 ; Feb. 20, 1774.

AARON, Jr., had children bap. Aug. 16, 1784; July 23, 1786; Aug. 10, 1788 ; Pitkin, Oct. 17, 1790 ; Aaron, Dec. 11, 1791; Hannah, May 18, 1794; Lucy, Dec. 24, 1797 ; Ha——, June 29, 1800, and Samuel, Nov. 28, 1802.

SAMUEL ROCKWELL, had Thomas, bap. May 13, 1764.

AZARIAH, Jr., had a child bap. Sept. 26, 1775.

EUNICE, had a child bap. Dec. 5, 1776 ; LUCRETIA, had children bap. April 24, 1785 ; SAMUEL, had a child bap. July 10, 1774; OLIVER, had Orrin, bap. Feb. 19, 1804 ; DAVID, had Abner, bap. Mch. 2, 1794 ; ALFRED, had ——, bap. Nov. 17, 1805.

P. 637, the whole paragraph, commencing on l. 15, is a tissue of errors. MATTHEW of E. W. is evidently *not* Matthew[7]. Lusina's bap. is given in E. W. C. R as Apl. 3, 1763, which does not agree well with her death in 1762. Daniel and Matthew, on line 19, are evidently out of place in this family. E. W. C. R. also give Matthew of E. W. (the father), children, bap. July 28, 1765, and May 11, 1768.

P. 637, l. 35, Edward Chapman had Ellet, bap. Apl. 28, 1762; Sept. 26, 1771. (E. W. C. R.)

EPAPHRAS, had Frances Maria, bap. May 22, 1825, and ——, bap. July 30, 1826.

GIDEON (prob. the same ment. on l. 24, p. 638), had child. bap. Nov. 22, 1761; Hezekiah, July 17, 1763 ; ——, May 5, 1765.

DAVID, had David Wadsworth, bap. June 24, 1798 ; Rhoda Emma, bap. Sept. 28, 1806. (Wby. Ch. Rec.)

JONATHAN, had Jonathan Baxter, bap. Nov. 25, 1810 ; Mary Fields, bap. July 4, 1818 ; Johnson Keyes, bap. Nov. 13, 1814 ; Susanna, bap. May 4, 1817 ; Sophronia, bap. Aug. 8, 1819. (Wby. Ch. Rec.)

JONAH, m. Sarah Griswold (both of Wintonbury), Oot. 9, 1752, had ——,
b. Jan. 31, 1753; Mrs. Gillet, d. May 28, 1753, he m. 2, Esther Filley, Oct.
10, 1754. (R. MSS.)

RHODA EMMA, m. Asahel C. Washburn of Royalton, Vt., 1828. (Wby. Ch.
Rec.)

BENJAMIN, m. Elizabeth Cadwell, Dec. 20, 1753; had ——, b. Nov. 7, 1754.
(R. MSS.)

ABIGAIL and STEPHEN, of Wby, "drowned, Feb. 25, 1752." The wid. Gillet, d. Sept. 29, 1753. (R. MSS.) Rhoda, d. Nov. 12, 1829, a. 62.

Wid. ELIZABETH, d. Sept. 30, 1807, a. 63. Ens. DAVID (prob. David,[12] p.
636) wife, d. Nov. 2, 1775, in 72 yr. He d. Dec. 27, 1791, in 90 yr. They
lost an inf. son, Feb. 3, 1793, and a still born child, Oct. 26, 1794.

GRAY, WILLIAM, m. Annie Fosbury, Dec. 8, 1777. (Wby. Ch. Rec.)

GREEN, p. 638, third line from bottom, JOEL's gravestone says, he d. Aug.
26, 1813, a. 62, which makes his birth in 1751 or '52; his wid. Sally, d.
Sept. 5, 1833, a. 73. JOEL, had children bap. Mch. 18, 1781 ; Sept. 15, 1782.
(E. W. C. R.)

HARRIET, m. Moses Casey, Nov. 28. (W. C. R.)

GRIFFIN, p. 639, l. 32, ALFRED and Fanny, had a dau. Sally, who d. Dec.
23, 1829, a. 2 yr.

MILTON, d. Jan. 8, 1819, in 25 yr.

GRIMES, p. 639, insert, ELISHA, m. Anne Humphrey, June 20, 1754.
(Wby. Ch. Rec.)

GRISWOLD, p. 640, l. 15, from *Col. Rec.*, for *Ann* read *Anna.*

P. 640, l. 18, Joseph, bap. Mch. 12 or 22, the latter prob. correct.

P. 640, l. 19, John, bap. Aug. 1.

P. 640, l. 34, George,[2] m. Oct. 3, 1655.

P. 641, l. 8, for July 14, read July 10.

P. 641, l. 31, a Daniel s. of Daniel, d. Mch., 1684-5. Can this be Daniel[28] ?
(Col. Rec.)

P. 641, l. 38, among children of Thomas,[7] insert Samuel, b. Dec. 15, 1684.

Corrections furnished by Henry Bright, Esq., of Northampton, Mass.—P. 641,
l. 30, JOHN,[21] year of birth, 1703.

P. 642, l. 35, BATHSEBA, *b.*, should be *d.*

P. 643, l. 3, the date of SAMUEL's birth *should be* 1720.

P. 643, l. 26, for *Adan* read *a dau.*

P. 643, l. 30, Nathaniel, b. 1742, is prob. same one who had Friend, bap.
June 10, 1764; Agnes, bap. Sept. 29, 1765. He then lived in Poquonnoc.
(Wby. Ch. Rec.)

P. 643, l. 33, DAVID,[26] m. Huldah Brown, Dec. 23, 1731. He died Aug. 1,
1760. (Wby. Ch. Rec.)

P. 643, l. second from bottom, Capt. THOMAS,[27] was m. in 1728, instead of
1725.

P. 643, l. 36, date of Asinah's birth should be 1751. (Wby Ch. Rec.)

P. 644, 2d line from bottom, Capt. BENJAMIN,[31] was m. 22d July; and she d. in 1776.

P. 645, l. 7, Moses,[38] and wife buried in old Poq. burying ground, had Elizabeth, bap. Feb. 26, 1759. (Wby. Ch. Rec.)

P. 645, l. 12, Shubal,[34] also had dau. Phebe, b. Sept. 14, 1719.

P. 645, l. 16, for 1837, read 1737.

P. 647, l. 1, for *Jedidah*, read *Jedidiah.*

P. 647, l. 5, date of Mary's birth *should be* Aug. 28.

P. 647, line 20, for *Simon*, read *Simeon.*

P. 648, Abiel,[59] strike out all said about his second and third wives, as they belonged to Abiel, son of George, Jr.[61] *Dridania* should be *Diadema.* I believe Abiel,[59] had a second wife, Rebecca, who d. April 12, 1819, a. 48. My original memoranda says Abiel[59] committed suicide.

P. 648, l. 18, SENECA, positively the son of Abiel Buckland, was b. July 21, 1801. Abiel Buckland's other children were Mary, m. a Cook; Jane, m. Bushrod Clark; Julia, m. the same Bushrod Clark; More, m. near Hartford.

P. 648, l. 38, for 2d and 3d wives of GEORGE, Jr.,[61] see note above.

P. 649, l. 29, the date of marriage should be 1789.

P. 649, l. 30, the date of her death should be 1847.

P. 650, l. 22, for *Frederica* Elvira, read *Fredonia* Elvira.

P. 650, l. 26, for *Casmer*, read *Casimir.*

P. 650, l. 24, Leonora Fredonia, was b. Nov. 1st.

P. 650, l. 44, ELIAS of Poquonnoc, had also ——, d. Dec. 12, 1803, a. 3 yr.; his son Erastus Fitch, b. 1779, d. Oct. 12, 1807; also a child, who d. Nov. 11, 1793, while on a visit at Wby.

P. 650, last line, for *None* read *Nona.*

RHODA, m. Joshua Abby of Enfield, May 3, 1827. (W. C. R.) OLIVE H., m. Roland S. Fox of E. H'tf'd, Sept. 9, 1840. (W. C. R.) DANIEL E., m. Eliz F. Baker, Nov. 16, 1842. (W. C. R.) ISAAC P., m. Cynthia M. Hillyer, Apl. 7, 1841. (W. C. R.) John E., m. Caroline Griswold, Nov. 5, 1832. (W. C. R.) LUCIA ANN, m. Cadwell Strickland, of Simsbury, July 29, 1834. (W. C. R.) MARCUS, m. Martha Holcomb of Granby, Feb. 15, 1827. (W. C. R.) MEHITABLE, m. Henry W. Miner of Vernon, Apl. 11, 1827. (W. C. R.) ELIZABETH, m. Chas. Hollister, May 1, 1828. (W. C. R.) GAYLORD, m. Mary Hooker, Aug. 3, 1796. ERASTUS, m. Charlotte Pinney, Jan. 10, 1809. WILLIAM, m. —— Case of Simsbury, Sept. 8, 1814. (W. C. R.) OWEN, m. —— Soper, Dec. 26, 1814. (W. C. R.) GUY, m. Elizabeth Marshall, July 2, 1818. (W. C. R.) JOEL, m. Mary Evans, May 11, 1758.

ELIJAH, m. Sarah Thrall, Oct. 1806.

From Poquonnoc New Burying Ground.—ELIJAH, above named, d. Apl. 26, 1835, a. 56; his wife Sarah, d. Nov. 14, 1834, a. 53. Eunice, their dau., d. Oct. 22, 1845, a. 25. Elijah, Jr. (prob. their son), d. Nov. 26, 1840, a. 34; an inf. dau., d. Jan. 10, 1813, a. 13 days.

Lt. ELIJAH, d. Apl. 12, 1826, a. 76, and his wife Eleanor, d. Aug. 18, 1830, a. 85.

ELISHA, d. June 22, 1842, a. 30 ; EDWIN T., d. Nov. 30, 1840, a. 26.

ORIGEN, d. Sept. 28, 1855, a. 70 ; by his wife Selma, he had James Ethelbert ; d. Apl. 20, 1854, a. 14 yr.; HECTOR ABIEL, d. Apl. 15, 1844, a. 18 ; JAMES W., d. Mch. 20, 1836, a. 3 yr.; Everett, d. Mch. 27, 1836, a. 2 mo ; NATHAN S.. d. Mch. 30, 1853, a. 31; his dau. (by wife Clarinda H.) Emma F., d. Dec. 30, 1848, a. 6 mo., 13 d.; JONN, d. May 18, 1815, a. 38 ; his wife Mary, d. Dec. 8, 1834, a. 56, and son, Abiel Wolcott, d. Jan. 9, 1817, a. 3 yr.; EDWARD W., d. Feb. 27, 1845, a. 62; his wife Harriet, d. Aug. 26, 1832, a. 49 ; their dau. Elizabeth (wife of Wm. S. Loomis), d. Feb. 27, 1847, a. 27; SAMUEL B., d. Aug. 29, 1853, a. 24; BRADFORD, d. Sept. 3, 1855, a. 59 ; his wife Sophia, d. Aug. 25, 1854, a. 58 ; FRIEND, d. Feb. 4, 1831, a. 67, his dau. (by wife Dolly), ALLISSA, d. Feb. 4, 1833, a. 44 ; BRIDGMAN, d. Oct. 9, 1836, a. 45; his wife Hannah, d. Aug. 4, 1829, a. 39 ; MARSHALL B., son of Bridgman and Maria, d. Jan. 1, 1842, a. 4 yr. 9 mo.; ABIGAIL, wife of Nathaniel, d. Apl. 26, 1820, a. 73 ; GILES (see Giles, 1. 7, p. 647), d. Dec. 13, 1850, a. 53 ; LEVI, d. Mch. 19, 1844, a. 75 ; his wife Azubah, d. June 18, 1841, a. 66; BENJAMIN, d. May 25, 1823, a. 57; his wife Sally, d. July, 1811, a. 43 ; MARTHA, of Marcus, d. Aug. 30, 1846, a. 42; RICHARD P., d. Jan. 19, 1842, a. 4 yr. 10 mo.; SYLVIA, of Warham and Sylvia, d. Dec. 12, 1840, a. 2; LOTHROP and Jennette's dau. Ada Eliza, d. Apl. 8, 1857, a. 2 ; GEORGE M. GRISWOLD, d. July 18, 1853, a. 31; his son CHARLES A. (by wife Emily), d. July 4, 1853, a. 2 yr., 6 mo.; PHINEAS, d. Sept. 18, 1829, a. 47; GILES, d. Dec. 13, 1850, a. 53 ; his son GAYLORD B. (by Charlotte), d. July 10, 1846, a. 11 ; ALFRED, d. Sept 28, 1826, a. 26.

Poquonnoc Old Burying Ground.—GROVE and TIRZAH, children of Nathaniel and Abigail, d. June 11, 1771, a. 3 days. FRANCIS, d. Nov. 9, 1796, in 78th yr.; his wife Keziah, d. Dec. 28, 1798, in 75 yr. ANNE, wife of Joab, d. May 28, 1799, in 28th yr.

Bloomfield Burying Ground.—Capt. William, d. May 10, 1830, a. 55 ; wf. Anna, d. Feb. 7, 1813, a. 36. Children : Erastus Wolcot, d. Apl. 1, 1807, a. 5 ; William Pomeroy, d. Apl. 10, 1807, a. 10; Anna Maria, d. Mch. 10, 1811. a. 14; Mary Anna, d. Apl. 14, 1812, a. 2 ; Capt. EDWARD, d. Feb. 22, 1785, a. 56 ; EDWARD, d. Mch. 27, 1788, in 80.

From Wby. Ch. Rec.—JONAH, m. Oct. 9, 1746, to Ruth Barnett ; had Ruth, bap. Mch. 11, 1750; Ann, bap. May 9, 1757.

JOEL, who d. Feb. 3, 1814, a. 80, m. Mary Evans, May 11, 1758; had Joel, bap. Nov. 5, 1758 ; Elijah, bap. July 22, d. 23, 1761 ; Elijah, bap. Aug. 22, 1762; Mary, bap. Dec. 2, 1764 ; Luther, bap. Sept. 28, 1766 ; Rufus and Eleanor (twins), bap. Sept. 1769 ; Eleanor, d. Nov. 28, 1776; Rebecca, bap. May 3, 1772 ; Ralph, bap. Apl. 30, 1775.

NOAH of Poq., had Elisha, bap. Dec. 23, 1757. NOAH, Jr. of Poq., had Aurelia, bap. June 23, 1765 ; Frederick, bap. Apl. 26, 1766 ; Noah, bap.

10

Sept. 15, 1771; Zuba, bap. May 14, 1775. Edward of Poq., had Simeon, bap. Aug. 25, 1765. Deborah, m. William Watson, Oct. 30, 1768. Solomon, m Abiah Allyn, Apl. 27, 1780. Friend, m. Dorothy Weller, Mch. 12, 1787. Abiel of Poq., m. wid. Rebecca Phelps, May 13, 1802. Lydia, m. Asahel Bliss of Canton, June 7, 1810.

Erastus, d. Apl. 1821; wid. Rebecca, d. Apl. 12, 1819.

Wid. Huldah, d. June 4, 1785, a. 73. Frederick, d. Nov. 1829. Pamela, d. Oct. 14, 1825, a. 21. Joel, d. Apl. 11, 1811, a. 84.

From Col. Rec.—Hannah, m. Jonas Westover, Nov. 19, 1663. Daniel, son of Daniel, d. Mch. 1684-5. Joseph, d. Jan. 6, 1673, a. 23 yr.

Miscellaneous.—Esther, b. Mch. 1, 1695-6; Daniel, d. Mch. 1684-5. Ann, b. Mch. 20, 1718.

GUNN, p. 651, l. 9. Col. Rec. appear to give date of Elizabeth's b. as 1649. She d. Jan. 3, 1655. Deborah, was *bap.* on date given.

HAKES, p. 651, l. 13, John, son of John, was b. Aug. 10. (Col. Rec.)

P. 651, l. 19, for Aug. 12, 1659, Col. Rec. give Sept. 29, 1657.

HALL, p. 651, l. 20, Timothy, m. Sarah Barber, Nov. 26, 1663, and had Sarah, b. Aug. 9, 1665. (Col. Rec.)

P. 651, Daniel's wife had a child, bap. Jan. 1, 1775; he had a child, bap. Nov. 16, 1777. (E. W. C. R.)

HALLIDAY, p. 651, insert Jonah, m. Mary Rowel, Nov. 21, 1781.

HALSEY, p. 651, James, m. Keziah Ellsworth, Oct. 10, 1811; Helen T., m. James Buckit, Oct. 12, 1836. (W. C. R.) Philip (l. 27), had Philip, bap. July 6, 1783, and James L., bap. Sept. 2, 1787. (W. C. R.)

HAMLIN, p. 651, Harper, m. Mary Fox, Feb. 25, 1779.

HASKELL, p. 652, l. 27, (Hou.) Eli B.,[1] d. in Toledo, O., Aug. 20, 1861, in 83d yr.; John, m. Polly Allen, Dec. 7, 1808. (Wby. Ch. Rec.)

HAWKES, p. 653, *evidently* same as *Hakes*, p. 651.

HAWKINS, p. 653, l. 4, Isabel, wife of Anthony, d. July 12, 1655. (Col. Rec.)

HAYDEN, p. 653, l. 33, William's (the emigrant) wife, d. July 17, 1655. (Col. Rec.)

P. 654, l. 31, for 1637, read 1737.

P. 654, l. 34, according to N. S. R., Anna, m. *Daniel* Dibble of Farmington, Nov. 17, 1768.

P. 654, last l., for 1837, read 1737.

P. 655, l. 15, the date 1741-2 here, is an obvious error.

P. 655, l. 29, Thomas,[16] was m. Nov. 19, 1767. (N. S. R.)

P. 655, l. 31, Chester, d. Sept. 17, 1777. (N. S. R.)

P. 656, l. 1, for *Altumia*, read *Almira*. (N. S. R.)

P. 656, l. 20, for *Nathan*, read (according to N. S. R.) *Nathaniel*.

P. 657, l. 6, Norman, bap. Aug. 13, 1786; Arabella, bap. Dec. 28, 1793, (W. C. R.); Sidney *Prior*, bap. 1797.

P. 657, 1. 6, N. S. R. says, " *Rosanna*, dau. of Ebenezer, Jr., and Rosanna, bap. July, 1784."

P. 657, line 7, Elvira was bap. May 1, 1791.

P. 657, 1. 10, the following large and valuable addition to the Hayden genealogy is owing to the zealous labor of Mrs. MATTHEW PATTERSON of Dansville, N. Y., and the coöperation of D. WILLIAMS PATTERSON of W. Winsted, Conn. The arrangement is our own.

DAVID,[29] of *Newington*, not Harwinton, m. Jemima (dau. of William, see p. 600. 1. 18,) Ellsworth, and d. near Angelica, N. Y., Feb. 12, 1813 She d. at Painted Post, N. Y., Feb. 13, 1828, a. (85, according to her gravestone, but really) 86.

DAVID[61] (see l. 23, p. 660, *Hist. and Geneal. of Windsor, Ct.*), had children :
I. *William Ellsworth*, b. June 3, 1799, m. Eunice Jacobs, moved to Wisconsin. Mrs. Wm. E. Hayden, d. Aug. 3, 1839, had (1) Eliza, b. at Post Town, N. Y., Nov. 11, 1800, m. Elijah Dickson of Erie, N. Y., 1823 ; issue, Gleason Fillmore, Millard Fillmore, Susannah, Elizabeth, Minerva, Angelica, Barnett Hayden; Edward, George White, Ann Eliza, deceased. This family live in Pulaski, Mich., whither they removed from Williamsville, N. Y. (2) Nancy, b. Aug. 7, 1802, m. Joseph Rice of Angelica, N. Y., removed to Chester, Ohio, where she d. 1839. (3) Sophia. (4) Perry. (5) Walker. (6) Jemima.

II. *Matilda Ann*, b. Feb. 18, 1805, m. Lyman Hitchcock, 1840, in Painesville, Ohio, mechanic, no issue. Mrs. H. was the first white child b. on Church's Purchase, near Angelica, N. Y.

III. *Lyman Munson*, b. Apl. 9, 1807, d. near Dansville village, 1838, of quick consumption ; was a millwright, unmarried.

IV. *Olive*, b. Sept. 28, 1809, m. Dr. Stephen Matthews of Painted Post, now lives at Candor, N. Y. No issue.

V. *David Napoleon*, b. Aug. 15, 1810, m. Miss Rice of Angelica, 1831, had one child, removed to Iowa, on the Desmoines river, 1832.

JEMIMA (incorrectly given in the Hist. as *Jerusha*), b. Feb. 25, 1764, m. at Newington, Ct., Apl. 10, 1785, Ichabod Patterson, b. 1763 [son of Ephraim and Sarah (Chandler) Patterson.] They lived a year or two at Newington ; removed to New Lebanon, Columbia co., N. Y., where they lived till 1790, then removed to Painted Post, N. Y., where he d. Aug. 1796, aged 33 years. She was the third white woman in that new town; she reached there at evening, while her mother-in-law, the second in town, reached there in the morning of the same day. Mrs. Calkins, the pioneer white woman, had then lived there nearly a year. Ichabod Patterson kept the first tavern at Painted Post (several years before Benjamin Patterson opened his, as noticed in French's *N. Y. Gazetteer*, p. 624, foot note 7), which she continued to keep some three years after his death (according to her son Matthew Patterson), when she m. 2d, Nehemiah Hubbell, from New Lebanon, N. Y. (prob. a native of Weston, Ct.), who d. at Knoxville (in the town of Corning), June

21, 1835, a. 70 yrs., 2 mo., 14 days.   She d. at Bath, N. Y. (buried at Knoxville), May 27, 1842, a. 78 yrs., 3 mo., 2 days.   Children:

I. *Matthew* (Patterson), b. New Lebanon, N. Y., Aug. 31, 1788; m. Feb.
12, 1815, Rebecca, dau. of Robert and Sarah (Green) Irwin; he was a
merchant at Northumberland, Pa, from 1812 to 1821, when he settled in
Dansville, N. Y., where he has since resided, engaged in lumbering and
agriculture; had (1) Harriet, b. Northumberland, Pa., Dec. 28, 1815; m. Oct
1, 1850, James Galbraith, of Glenairn, Co. Antrim, Ireland, son of Patrick
and Elizabeth (McIlvane) Galbraith.   He is a physician, removed in 1857 to
West Unity, Fulton co., Ohio; is a member of Co. G, 68th Ohio Volunteers;
issue, James Matthew Patterson, b. Groveland, N. Y., June 23, 1852; Alexander Hunter (twin), b. Sept. 7, 1853, d. a. 9 mo.; George Green (twin), b.
Sept. 7, 1853, d. ——; Rowley Patterson, b. South Dansville, N. Y., Sept.
16, d. Sept. 21, 1855; (2) Robert Irwin, b. Northumberland, Aug. 6, 1817;
m. May 1, 1850, Harriet (dau of Robert and Martha) Land of Corning, N. Y.;
live at Sparta, N. Y.; issue, Chauncey Land, b. Corning, N. Y., Mch. 8,
1851 (made a wonderful Sam Patch leap, down Patterson Falls, near Sparta,
N. Y., in 1855); Helen Adelaide, b Sparta, N. Y, July 17, 1854; Elizabeth
Peat, b. Sparta, N. Y., Sept. 19, 1862; (3) George Green, b. Northumberland, Pa., Dec. 8, 1819, d. Sept. 18, 1822; (4) George Rowley, b. Dansville,
N. Y., Sept. 26, 1822, d. Feb. 8, 1824; (5) Jonathan Rowley, b. Dansville, N.
Y., Jan. 11, 1826; resides with his father 4 miles south of Dansville, N. Y., a
farmer, unmarried.

II. *Harriet* (Patterson), twin, b. Painted Post, Aug. 14, 1796 (after the
death of her father), m. Dr. Robert Hoyt, and d. at Painted Post, Aug. 12,
1830; issue, (1) Jane, d. in Philadelphia, unmarried; (2) Harriet, m. Charles
Campbell, a lawyer of Bath, N. Y., and d. leaving 2 children; (3) Patterson,
resided in Philadelphia, and after the death of his sister Jane, removed to
Virginia; (4) Ichabod, d. before his mother; (5) Robert, d. before his
mother.

III. *Jemima* (Patterson) twin, b. at P. P., Aug. 14, 1796, m. Bath, N. Y.,
Aug. 29, 1817, John McBurney, b. near Bath, Pa., Aug. 29, 1796, son of
Thomas and Mary (Mulhollon) McBurney.   She d. P. P., Feb. 8, 1831.   He
has represented his county in the New York legislature; has, since her
death, been three times m., and has several children by the 2d and 3d wives;
issue, (1) Mary, b. P. P., Sept. 2, 1818, m. 1837, Charles K. (son of Robert)
Miller of Big Flats, N. Y., she d. P. P., Oct. 20, 1838, leaving one child,
Mary Jane, b. Oct., 1838, who now lives in Aurora, Ill; (2) James, b. P. P.,
Sept 4, 1820, m. Lucy Briant, lives at Ottawa, Ill.; issue, John, James,
Thomas, and twins, name, unknown to compiler; (3) Thomas, b. P. P., Aug.
22, d. Oct. 9, 1822; (4) John, b. P. P., Apl. 25, 1824, d. Feb. 19, 1827; (5)
Jemima, b. P. P., Aug. 3, 1826 m. John Dodge, lives at Harbor Creek, Erie
co., Pa.; issue, Edward, John, Thomas, Charles; (6) Sarah, b. P. P., Sept.
3, 1828, d. Feb. 8, 1830.

IV. *Philo P.* (Hubbell) resides at Winona, Minnesota.

V. Hon. *William Spring* (Hubbell), b. 1801, m. Maria McCall of Painted Post, N. Y.;· is a banker at Bath, N. Y., has Mary, m. —— Halleck, and has one child, Edward ; Fanny, m. Mr. Waterbury of Avoca, N. Y.; William.

PELETIAH[62] (see 1. 24, p. 660, *Hist. and Geneal. of Windsor, Ct.*).

LYMAN, when a young man, lived with his sister, Mrs. Jemima Patterson, and tended the Patterson Mill ; d. 8 days after his father ; was a major, and filled offices of trust in his neighborhood ; m. Betsey Fairchild. He lived at Aogelica, N. Y., his farm, on the Genesee river, adjoining that of his father. He left a son *Frank*, b. 8 days after his father's death, and seems to have also left a son *Nathaniel*.

ABIJAH, had *Manly Lord, Miles Lester, Almira*. These all lived in Pompey, N. Y., and with their families moved to Michigan.

OLIVER[63] (l. 28, p. 660, *Hist. and Geneal. Windsor, Ct.*), was an intelligent and well educated man, a school teacher; m. Abigail Cleaveland of Wyalusing, Pa., and had two children, *William* and *Henry H.*; enlisted in war of 1812, was not heard from for two years, and his wife m. again. On returning and finding his " claim jumped," he left the country, changed his name, and m. a second wife. One of his sons by his second m. had his name changed to Hayden, by act of legislature.

OLIVE, m. Robert Bonham of Northumberland, Pa., was then a merchant, but bought a farm on the Coshocton river, 6 miles above P. P. where he lived and d.; his wife d. at P P., July 10, 1821. They had,

I. *Elizabeth*, b. July 13, 1803, m. Enos Smith, Campbelltown, N. Y., Sept. 22, 1830, and had 6 children, all of whom d. young, but one, *Olive B.*, who was b. June 20, 1843, at Big Flats, N. Y., and d. May 3, 1845, at Caton, N. Y.

II. *Jemima Hayden*, b at Painted Post, N. Y., July 14, 1805; unmarried.

III. *William*, b. June 3, 1807, m. Eliza Cook, Feb. 16, 1841 ; issue (1) Joseph Boyd, b. Feb. 26, 1842 ; (2) Gertrude E. b. Oct. 5, 1843; (3) Van Wye, b. Apl. 4, 1852.

IV. *David Hayden*, b. Aug. 17, 1810, m. at Big Flats, N. Y., Sept. 7, 1842, to Sarah G. Reynolds; issue, (1) Frances Matilda, b. July 28, 1844; (2) Eloisia Margaret, b. May 16, 1847.

V. *Charles*, m. Mary B. Goodwin, Sept. 18, 1835 ; he d. Jan. 26, 1859; issue, (1) Martha E , b. Dec. 18, 1839 ; (2) Robert T., b. Oct. 10, 1841, now a volunteer in the Union army ; (3) Delphine, b July 12, 1843, d. May 12, 1859 ; (4) John Charles, b. Aug. 1, 1846.

Sarah, b. at P. P., Dec. 27, 1815, m. George Cook of Campbelltown; have dau. Regina, b. about 1840.

George, m. Lovisa Sharp; she d. leaving 4 children; he lives at Addison, N. Y.

Mary, b. 1820, m. Melwin Fanton of Conn.; are now both dead. They had, (1) Edmund B., b. Oct. 5, 1846 ; (2) Charles ·R., b. May 14, 1849 ; (3) Manfred G., b. July 21, 1851.

P. 657, l. 11, for *Jerusha*, read *Jemima*.

P. 657, l. 40, ANSON B.,[36] m. on 16th Feb. 1815.

P. 657, l. 42, ISAAC,[37] was m. Dec. 6, 1809.   (W. C. R.)

P. 657, l. 43, Juliette was bap. July 9, 1815.   (W. C. R.)

P. 658, l. second from bottom, date of Nathaniel L., m. Oct. 24, 1808. (W. C. R.)

P. 659, l. 11, according to W. C. R., HEZEKIAH,[48] m. Hannah Hayden, Dec. 7, 1801: on same authority his dau. *Fanny* was bap., as *Frances Henry ; Alanson*, was bap. Dec. 15, 1805, and *Hezekiah*, bap. Oct. 6, 1804.

P. 661, l. 40, GEORGE P.,[50] m. Frances *A.* Loomis, Dec. 30, 1840.   (W. C. R.)

Capt. NATHANIEL'S wife Ann, d. Jan. 16, 1761.   (N. S. R.)

MELINDA, m. Levi Joy of Amherst, Mass., Dec. 29, 1829 : MINDWELL, m Joseph Kent of Suffield, Jan. 8, 1799 ; ALETHINA, m. Norman Griswold of Norwich, Oct. 16, 1822 (W. C. R.) ; SUSAN ANN, m. James H. Wells of·H., Feb. 26, 1840.   (W. C. R.)

DANIEL'S wife Elizabeth, d. Feb. 17, 1761.   (N. S. R.)   ELIZABETH, had Pascal, bap. Jan. 1805.   (E. W. C. R.)

HEART, Elisha, d. Aug. 15, 1683.   (Col. Rec.)

HIGLEY, p. 664, l. 3, HANNAH, b. in 1677, is recorded as dead in 1680. (Col. Rec.)

P. 664, l. 7, NATHAN, had also children, bap. Sept. 13, 1767; Feb. 11, 1770; Dec. 18, 1774; Nov. 23, 1777.   (E. W. C. R.)

P. 664, l. 9, ELIJAH, m. Anne ——; his son Elijah, d. Oct. 17, 1776. (N. S. R.)   Anna, d. Oct. 30, 1776.   (N. S. R.)   Chloe, bap. Jan. 22, 1775, d. Oct. 19, 1776.   (N. S. R.)   Elijah 2d, bap. May 11, 1777.   Oliver, bap. Sept. 19, 1779.

NATHAN, Jr., had Nathan Allyn and Sally, bap. Mch. 30, 1794, ——, Feb. 23, 1797 ; ——, July, 8, 1798 ; Wil——, Nov. 1, 1801.   (E. W. C. R.)

HORACE, had Horace, bap. Jan. 4, 1795 ; ——, May 14, 1797; Peter, May 30, 1802.   (E. W. C. R.)

ARODA, had Job Loomis, bap. Mch. 28, 1802; Hiram, bap. Sept. 30, 1804. (E. W. C. R.)

OLIVE, d. Nov. 1819.   (Wby. Ch. Rec.)

MATTHEW (E. W.), m. Hannah Allyn, Nov. 11, 1790.   (N. S. R.)

JOB, m. Dorcas Eggleston, May 9, 1792.   (Wby. Ch. Rec.)

HILLIER, p. 664, l. 34, *John's* wife was *Ann*, who afterwards m., Dec. 9, 1656, John Fitch of Hartford.   John Hillier, d. July 16, 1655.   In inventory of John's estate, July 24, the ages of the other children are thus stated : John, a. 18 yrs. ; Mary, a. 15 yrs. and 9 m. ; Timothy, a. 13 yrs., 17 wks. ; Andrew, 9 yrs. 4th of next month; Simon, 7 yrs. 25th of next month.   (Col. Rec.) Add to this family the name of Abigail, b. Aug. 21, 1654.

P. 664, l. 38, JAMES, son of James, b. 1678, d. Apl. 27, 1679.

P. 664, l. 39, John had a dau., d. July 25, 1680, also Elinor Elizabeth, b. ——, and d. Dec. 23, 1682. (Col. Rec.)

HILLS, p. 664, LUCRETIA, m. Sam. Jabez Vernon, Sept. 11, 1816. (W. C. R.)

STEPHEN, son of wid. of Stephen, d. Sept. 29, 1741, a. about 4. (Wby. Ch. Rec.)

All the following from E. W. C. R.—JOHN (prob. same as on l. 27, p. 664), had Norman, bap. May 22, 1763; and children, bap. Dec. 1, 1765; Apl. 3, 1768; June 6, 1773. Wid. HILLS, had a child bap. June 22, 1777.

OLIVER, had Anna, bap. Mch. 10, 1765; ——, Feb. 23, 1766.

HINSDALE, p. 664-5, insert, Rev. THEODORE, m. Ann Bissell, July 14, 1768. (Wby. Ch. Rec.) Had Ann, bap. Apl. 23, 1769; Lucy, bap. Jan. 6, 1771; Theodore, bap. Nov. 17, 1772; Josiah Bissell, bap. Nov. 20, 1774; James, bap. Oct. 27, 1776, d. Sept. 17, 1777; Levi, bap. Jan. 14, 1781; Almira, bap. Dec. 13, 1782; Daniel, bap. May 1, 1785; Horatio, bap. Dec. 16, 1787; William, bap. Apl. 24, 1790. (*All the foregoing from N. S. R.*)

HITCHCOCK, p. 665, CALEB, Jr., m. Electa Foot, Jan. 15, 1797, had Samuel Foot and Electa Amelia, bap. May 18, 1800, d. Mch. 2, 1805, a. 5; Abigail, m. Levi Dudley of Berlin, Dec. 23, 1802; Eliza Abby, bap. Aug. 30, 1801, d. 1802; Eliza, bap. Aug. 28, 1803; Mary, bap. Sept. 9, 1810, d. Aug. 1, 1829; Electa, bap. May 8, 1814; Julia Ann, bap. Apl. 12, 1818, d. Apl. 17, 1818; Gaylord, bap. June 4, 1820. (Wby. Ch. Rec.)

P. 665, l. 7, Stephen, b. 1767, d. July 3, 1775, in 8th yr.; Eleanor, b. 1770, d. Jan. 20, 1819; wid. Deborah, d. Jan. 24, 1809, a. 98; Eleanor, d. Dec. 31, 1827, a. 86; Dea. Caleb (prob. same as Doctor), d. July 11, 1818, a. 81.

HODGE, JOHN, p. 665, l. 5, also had Thomas, b. Feb. 13, 1668; Mary, b. Feb. 15, 1670; Henry, b. Aug. 19, 1676; William, b. April 10, 1678. (Col. Rec.)

P. 665, insert, SUSANNAH, a member of church in Windsor, had Susannah, Abigail and Samuel, bap. in Middletown, Sept. 18, 1692. (Stearn's Mem.)

HOLCOMB, p. 666, ELIJAH, m. Mary Smith, Feb. 13, 1785; MARY, m. Henry Moshier, Sept. 4, 1834. (W. C. R.)

Miscellanea and Addenda, p. 840, l. 19, the statement here made relative to the death of Hezekiah's wife, is pronounced incorrect by our friend, *Henry Bright, Esq. of Northampton, Mass.*, who furnishes the following from his own original memoranda, copied from her gravestone in Scotland burying ground, Simsbury, viz: "Mrs. Chloe Holcomb, wife of Hezekiah Holcomb, and dau. of Capt. Abraham and Elizabeth Pinney, d. January 20, 1787, a. 37 yrs."

Also the following inscriptions: "Hezekiah Holcomb, Esq., d. Nov. 8, 1820, a. 70," and "Capt. Hezekiah Holcomb, d. July 17, 1794, a. 69."

He also adds his opinion "that the name should be spelled with a final *e*.

Digitized by Microsoft®

Burke, in his *Armory*, and in his *Landed Gentry of England*, etc., etc., spells the name *almost uniformly* with a final *e ;* in one place he spells the name *Holcombe* or *Holtcombe*, and remarks in a note, " Holtcombe is compounded of *Holt*, a Saxon word signifying woody, and *cum*, or, *as written in Devonshire, combe*, a valley between two hills." The W. Holcombes, coming from the west of England, would naturally have retained the final *e*, and there are some families of the name in the Southern States which so spell it.

P. 665, l. 18, Abigail, was bap. in Jan. (Col. Rec.)

P. 665, l. 22, for Sept. 15, read Sept. 13. (Col. Rec.)

P. 665, l. 27, for 1687, read 1681. (Col. Rec.)

P. 665, l. 30, NATHANIEL[3] and Mary Bliss, m. Feb. 27. (Col. Rec.)

JOSEPH, m. Olive Marshall, Jan. 15, 1787. JABEZ of Poq., m. Anne Hosmer of Hartland, Nov. 27, 1805.

HOLLIBUT, p. 666, insert, Dr. JOSIAH, had Abigail, bap. Mch. 26, 1748. (Wby. Ch. Rec.)

HOLMAN, p. 667, add JOHN, had Henry, bap. Aug. 20, 1815. (E. W. C. R.)

HOOKER, p. 667, l. 13, DOLLY G., m. Charles Beebe Strong, June 22, 1814, and MARY CHAFFEE, m. James C. Maguffin of N. Y., Feb. 4, 1818.

HORACE, m. Elizabeth Filer, Aug. 2, 1769, and had Mary Elizabeth and Hannah, bap. Nov. 20, 1774 ; also Nathaniel, bap. June 18, 1775 ; Ann, bap. Apl. 5, 1778 ; Samuel Fowler, bap. Feb. 13, 1780 ; Eunice, bap. Dec. 13, 1782 ; Harry, bap. Oct. 15, 1785.

HOSFORD, p. 667, l. 21, JOHN, d. Aug. 7, 1683. (Col. Rec.)

P. 667, l. 27, strike out " or Marcy." (Col. Rec.)

P. 667, l. 29, for Sept. 28, read 23. (Col. Rec.)

P. 668, l. 2, SAMUEL,[2] had Mary, b. Feb. 15, 1690–1. (Col. Rec.)

P. 668, DANIEL, m. Abigail Welch, Oct. 4, 1769. (N. S. R.)

HOSKINS, p. 668, l. 18, Col. Rec. supply the date of John's burial, May 5, 1648. Anthony,[3] b. 1664, d. July 9, 1747. (Wby. Ch. Rec.)

P. 668, l. 26, for 1772, read 1672. A Thomas, son of Anthony, d. Apl. 13, 1666.

P. 668, l. 27, for Jan. 27, read 29.

The wid. Hoskins, d. Mch. 6, 1662 ; Thomas, m. Elizabeth Birge, widow, Apl. 20, 1653. The wid. Elizabeth (prob. this one), d. Dec. 22, 1675 ; John, son of (this prob.) Thomas, was b. May 29, 1654. *All above from Col. Rec.*

P. 669, l. 1, Zebulon,[6] d. Apl. 21, 1813 ; his son Zebulon, b. 1728, d. Aug. 27, 1768.

P. 669, l. 4, Alexander, m. Mindwell ——, who d. Oct. 17, 1751, a. per. 40 ; the same Alexander, also lost a child about 10 d. old, on Jan. 29, 1742. His son, Alexander, b. 1739, d. Mch. 15, 1773.

P. 669, l. 11, Pure, d. Nov. 13, 1781.

P. 669, l. 13, for *June*, read *May*.

EzEKIEL (prob. the son of John, l. 28), and wife Elizabeth had Esther, bap.
Oct. 19, 1776 ; Elizabeth, bap. Oct. 25, 1778 ; Sarah, bap. Mch. 28, 1781 ;
Eli, bap. May 1, 1785 ; Silas, bap. 1787. (N. S. R.)
AUGUSTUS, m. Electa Palmer, Dec. 4, 1814. (W. C. R.)
THANKFUL of Wby., d. April 23, 1753. (R. MSS.)
LYDIA, d. Mch. 22, 1761. (N. S. R.) JONATHAN, d. Jan. 20, 1761. (N.
S. R.) Wid. ELIZABETH, d. Jan. 1777, " worn out with age." (N. S. R.)
CATHARINE, d. Nov. 8, 1776. (N. S. R.)
P. 669, l. 31, DANIEL, m. Abigail Welch, Oct. 4, 1769. (N. S. R.)
The following from Wby. Ch. Rec.—ALEXANDER, m. Martha Parsons, Feb.
13, 1752.
ALEXANDER, Jr., m. wid. Mary Drake, Feb. 14, 1765.
TIMOTHY, m. Rhoda Gillett, Apl. 30, 1772, had Timothy, bap. Dec. 25,
1774; Alexander, bap. Nov. 2, 1777 ; Joab, bap. Jan. 2, 1780 ; ——, bap.
Aug. 25, 1782 ; Rhoda, bap. Aug. 29, 1784.

JOSEPH,[8] p. 669, l. 8, had also Joseph, bap. Feb. 25, 1738 ; Benjamin, bap.
June 15, 1740, and Elisha, bap. Dec. 22, 1745.

P. 669, l. 9, for Alfred, read Alson.

P. 669, l. 10 ABEL,[10] had also Abiah, bap. Nov. 23, 1777.

ELI, p. 669, l. 27 and l. 37, whose wife d. June 22, 1818, had Eli, bap.
Jan. 31, 1773 ; Matty, bap. Aug. 14, 1774 ; Kezia, bap. Nov. 10, 1776, d.
Sept. 6, 1777 ; Kezia, bap. Jan. 31, 1779 ; David, bap. June 3, 1781 ; Alethea,
bap. Aug. 29, 1784 ; George, bap. July 1, 1787 ; Chloe and Clara, bap. Sept.
21, 1788 ; Augustus, bap. Oct. 17, 1790 ; ——, bap. Nov. 2, 1793.

THOMAS, p. 669, l. 32, m. April 23, 1760 ; had also Mary, bap. June 29, 1766 ;
Ruth, bap. Mch. 13, 1768; Lucy, bap. Apl. 18, 1773, d. Oct. 18, 1775 ; Moses,
bap. Oct. 15, d. Oct. 20, 1775; John, bap. Feb. 11, 1770; JoHN, had Faircina, bap.
Feb. 16, 1755 ; JoHN, Jr., had Jerusha, bap. Dec. 7, 1755 ; George, bap. Feb. 13,
1758; INCREASE, m. Martha Persons, Mch. 20, 1779 ; he d. Apl. 1824; had Mol-
ly, bap. and d. Oct. 7, 1777 ; Molly, bap. July 11, 1779 ; Nabbe, bap. 1786 ;
Gordon, bap. 1783 ; " ye wid. Hoskins," had Mary and Jemima, bap. Apl. 8,
1759 ; HANNAH, had Abigail, bap. July 28, 1771; wid. MARY, m. Capt. Reuben
Loomis, Nov. 23, 1777 ; CHLOE, m. Thomas Dyer, Sept. 27, 1807; HITTY, m.
Roderic Adams of Onondaga, Oct. 11, 1807 ; OLIVE, m. Joseph Allen of
Hartford, Nov. 7, 1820; GEORGE, m. Lovicia Parsons, June 3, 1811 ; John 3d
(p. 669, l. 37), for June, read July ; ZEBULON, d. Mch. 10, 1776, in 80 yr.;
ZEBULON, d. Feb. 21, 1826, a. 38 ; JoHN, d. May 5, 1777, in 64 yr.; THANKFUL,
d. Apl. 23, 1753, a. about 42; HENRY, d. at Philadelphia, Aug. 22, 1796, a.
about 20 ; BETTY, d. Mch. 7, 1813, a. 87 ; wid. MARTHA, d. May 31, 1803,
a. nearly 99 ; wid. HANNAH, d. Dec. 2, 1751, a. about 84.

The following curious advertisement appeared in 1767, in the columns of the
Conn. Courant :

" ZEBULON HOSKINS of Windsor, hereby informs the publick, that for the
space of four years, he was grieviously afflicted with the Gravel, to such a

11

degree as to cause him to make water a hundred times in 24 hours, but could void but very little at a time, sometimes but a few drops, attended with the most distressing pain, and, after the use of many things to no benefit, he was accidently informed by a travelling gentleman, that a tea made of rushes, viz: such as the women scowr their pails with, had been found by experience to be a sovereign remedy for that disease ; he, therefore, immediately applied the medicine, and it had the desired effect—he drank plentifully of it, made it his constant drink, and in about eight or ten days his pain abated, and he voided abundance of gravel. He kept on in the use of it for about two months, when he found he was perfectly cured, and has remained well now for about two years, except when once he wet himself and took a great cold, which brought on the disease again, but the same medicine removed it immediately."

HOSMER, p. 670, l. 1, Joseph, had children, bap. Dec., 1781 ; Dec. 20, 1789 ; Mch. 19, 1797.

P. 670, l. 2, Prosper, had Marcus, bap. Nov. 8, 1801.

P. 670, l. 4, Thaddeus, was bap. Apl. 1, 1792.

P. 670, l. 5, Horace, bap. Sept. 21, 1794; Miriam, bap. Oct. 6, 1799. (E. W. C. R.)

HOWARD, p. 670, l. 21, Nathaniel, had Nathaniel, bap. June 30, 1776. (N. S. R.)

P. 671. (Col. Rec.) Lydia, d. May 4, 1676. (Col. Rec.) Samuel, was bap. Aug. 9, 1778. (E. W. C. R.)

HOYT, p. 671, l. 23, for "he d., read "she d.;" Nicholas, d. July 7, 1655.

P. 671, l. 26, for May 1, read May 7.

P. 671, l. 28, Daniel d. in yr. 1655. (Col. Rec.)

HUBBARD, p. 671, l. 2d from bottom of page, John, Jr.,[1] had also Timothy, bap. Dec. 16, 1750, and is the rightful father of all the children accredited (on p. 672) to Nathaniel,[2] from Agnes to Oliver, inclusive ; he (John[1]) d. Nov. 24, 1760. (Wby. Ch. Rec.)

P. 672, l. 1, Nathaniel,[2] being thus despoiled of half his family, deserves the credit of Sarah, bap. Aug. 22, 1762, and Dothesius, bap. Sept. 30, 1764. He (Nathaniel[2]) is prob. the one who d. Nov. 16, 1773, in 50 yr. (W. C. R.)

P. 672, l. 6, Asa[3], whose wife d. Nov. 2, 1823, a. 67, had Mitty (prob. the "short" of Submit, her mother's name), bap. Feb. 16, 1777 ; Asa, bap. Jan. 3, 1779, d. Mch. 15, 1786; Benoni, bap. Oct. 17, 1784 ; Augustus, bap. Jan. 29, 1785 ; Asa, bap. Apl. 30, 1787 ; Hannah, bap. Aug. 22, 1788 ; Julianna and Alethea, bap. May 4, 1800 ; Susannah Hosmer, bap. June 29, 1800.

Nathaniel, Jr. (prob. son of Nathaniel[2]), m. Dolly Cole of Hartford, Nov. 28, 1770; "Dorothy, wife of Nathaniel," d. Jan. 19, 1820, a. 66 ; Nathaniel, b. Jan. 31, 1773; he d. Mch. 14, 1774; Nathaniel, bap. Apl. 30, 1775 ; Thede, bap. Aug. 24, 1777; Dolly, bap. Sept. 24, 1780; Frederick, bap. Aug. 17, 1783; Chloe, bap. June 24, 1792. (Wby. Ch. Rec.)

Dothesius (prob. son of Nathaniel[2]), had Dose (Dothesius?), bap. Sept. 21,

1788; Nathan, bap. Oct. 10, 1790; Alvin, bap. Feb. 19, 1792; Orrin, bap. Oct. 13, 1793. (Wby. Ch. Rec.)

TIMOTHY (prob. son of John), m. Sarah Gillett, June 18, 1772, who d. May 31, 1811, a. 58; he d. Oct. 15, 1824, a. 74, and had Sarah, bap. Oct. 18, 1772, d. Oct. 6, 1795; Timothy, bap. Aug. 21, 1774; Hannah, bap. Dec. 1, 1776; Eleanor, bap. Mch. 21, 1779; Roger, bap. Aug. 17, 1783; Erastus, bap. June, 1787. (Wby. Ch. Rec.)

JOHN (prob. son of John[1]), m. Susannah Mills, June 15, 1775, and had John, bap. Apl. 21, 1776; Joab, bap. Jan. 18, 1778. (Wby. Ch. Rec.)

NATHAN (prob. son of Dothesius), m. Orinda Colton, May 10, 1819. He d. June 22, 1826, a. 38; Orinda Pamelia, Oct. 8, 1820; Emily, Susan Jane, and James, bap. June 16, 1822; Nathan Edwards, bap. Aug. 10, 1823; Samuel, bap. June 18, 1826. (Wby. Ch. Rec.)

ALVIN (son of Dothesius), had Louisa, bap. Nov. 13, 1814; Drusilla, bap. Sept. 21, 1817; Mary Cornelia, bap. Aug. 13, 1820; Louisa, bap. Apl. 24, 1825; Harriet, bap. June 27, 1830. (Wby. Ch. Rec.)

OLIVER (poss. son of John[1]), had Silva, bap. Sept. 28, 1788; Wealthy, bap. Aug. 11, 1793; Flavia, bap. May 4, 1794; Oliver Kellogg, bap. June, 1796; John Flavel, bap. June 24, 1798; Thomas Jefferson, bap. June 10, 1804; Simeon Edwards, bap. Aug. 10, 1806; Anna Sophia, bap. July 3, 1808. (Wby. Ch. Rec.)

LEVI, m. Juliana Smith, Apl. 23, 1818, had Levi Smith, bap. June 27, 1819; John Newton and Samuel Newell, bap. July 1, 1821; Juliana Matilda, bap. July 6, 1823. (Wby. Ch. Rec.)

BISHOP, who d. Aug. 24, 1823, a. 43, had Sarah Maria, bap. July 29, 1821. JOHN, m. Mabel Barnard of Simsbury, Nov. 14, 1803; JOAB, m. Ruth. Brown, Dec. 2, 1804; NATHANIEL, Jr., m. Sarah Hubbard, Aug. 27, 1828; AGNES, m. Ebenr. Center of W. Hartford, Mch. 17, 1768; RACHEL, m. Dan. Olmstead of Simsbury, Nov. 24, 1774. (Wby. Ch. Rec.)

DOLLY, m. John F. Waters, Nov. 26, 1800; Rachel, m. Wm. Crosby of W. Hartford, Apl. 4, 1802; Maria, m. Edward Francis, Nov. 18, 1823; ANNA SOPHIA, m. Edward Medcalf of E. Hartford, Mch. 25, 1824; EMILY, m. Levi Hough of Glastenbury, Oct. 18, 1830. (Wby. Ch. Rec.)

AGNES, dau. of Lt. John, d. Apl. 11, 1773, a. 88; ORRIN, d. June 29, 1811, a. 18; THEODORE, son of Nathaniel, Jr., d. Aug. 2, 1812, a. 7; THEODORE, d. July 22, 1800, a. 23; ASA, Jr., d. July 16, 1808, a. 19; JOHN's wife, d. Nov. 27, 1806, a. 49; FRANCIS, d. Oct. 15, 1815, a. 2; SUSAN, d. Sept. 20, 1824, a. 15; SALLY (Mrs.) d. Mch. 26, 1828, a. 51; JOHN, d. Sept 11, 1830, a. 9. (Wby. Ch. Rec.)

HUIT, p. 672, line 22, Rev. Ephraim's wife's name was Isabel; so ment. in a record of land purchased by Henry Clarke, Esq., where she is spoken of as wid. of Rev. Ephraim deceased. His dau. Lydia, m. Joseph Smith of Hartford, April 10, 1656. (Col. Rec.)

HULL, p. 672, l. 42, for Sarah, b. *Aug.* 9, read b. *Apl.* 9. (Wby. Ch. Rec.)

HUMPHREY, p. 673, l. 15, SUSANNA, bap. Jan. 12, 1752. (Wby. Ch. Rec.)

P. 673, l. 17, for 1736, read 1756. (Wby. Ch. Rec.)

NOAH, had Sarah, bap. Oct. 2, 1743; JONATHAN, Jr., had Jonathan, bap. Oct. 2, 1743; LYMAN, had Trumbull Lyman, Chloe, bap. May 21, 1815; George, bap. Aug. 25, 1816; Hector F., bap. June 21, 1818; Mary Ann, bap. June 18, 1820; ——, bap. Oct. 6, 1822; Laura Maria, bap. April 25, 1824; Cordelia, bap. Oct. 28, 1827; Henry and Henrietta, bap. July 12, 1829. (Wby. Ch. Rec.)

THOMAS, d. at Sheffield, April 13, 1768, a. about 57; wid. ABIGAIL, d. Sept. 2, 1775, a. about 62; Lot's son TRUMBULL, d. July 30, 1797, a. 2½; ASA's wife, d. March 26, 1826; Mrs. CHLOE, d. May 5, 1829, a. 62. (Wby. Ch. Rec.)

MAHALA, m. Stephen Fosbury of Simsbury, June 28, 1802. (Wby. Ch. Rec.)

P. 674, l. 12, for Luicus, read Lucius.

HUNTINGDON, p. 674, THOMAS went to Branford from W. It is supposed that three sons accompanied Margaret Huntingdon, then Mrs. Thomas Stoughton, from Roxbury or Dorchester to W.

P. 674, l. 19, Geo. W. Sward, read Seward.

HURLBUT, Dr. JOSIAH, had Elizabeth, bap. April 4, 1748; Josiah, bap. Jan. 28, 1750; Ruth, bap. Feb. 23, 1752; SAMUEL, had Bildad, bap. June 17, 1750, d. Oct. 21, 1754. (Wby. Ch. Rec.)

HUTCHERSON, p. 675, d. June 11, 1743, a. about 11 yrs. (Wby. Ch. Rec.)

JARNIELS, (Gerrils, Jurrels, Garls) p. 675, insert HARDEN or ARDEN had children, bap. July 18, 1773; Dec. 21, 1777; April 22, 1781; Sept. 15, 1781. (E. W. C. R.)

JOHNSON, p. 675, HANNAH, was bap. Dec. 17, 1797. (E. W. C. R.)

JONES, p. 675, MARY, d. Nov. 13, 1666. (Col. Rec.)

KELLY, p. 675, JOSEPH, had Aaron, bap. Aug. 30, 1741.

JOHN (from Ireland), m. —— Loomis of Simsbury, June 8, 1766, had John, bap. June 21, 1767; Roger, bap. Nov. 19, 1775. (Wby. Ch. Rec.)

KELSEY, WILLIAM, Jr., m. Tryphena Allyn, Jan. 27, 1774; Oliver, m. Lydia Fish, both of W., Sept. 4, 1807; Zaccheus, d. May 26, 1818. (Wby. Ch. Rec.)

KERR, p. 676, insert, WILLIAM, had Moses, bap. Sept. 4, 1748. (Wby. Ch. Rec.)

KING (all from E. W. C. R.), p. 676, l. 21, ALEXANDER, had children; bap. Feb. 24, 1782; June 25, 1786; May 11, 1788; April 25, 1790; Anne, bap. April 28, 1793; Havi—, March 1, 1796; Cla—, July 2, 1799; B—, Sept. 8, 1799; Theron, Dec. 6, 1801.

P. 676, l. 28, AUGUSTUS, had children, bap. Nov. 9, 1788; Feb. 24, 1790; July 7, 1793; Laura, March 22, 1796.

TIMOTHY's wife (perhaps mother of above), d. May 20, 1785, in 50 yr.; TIMOTHY, son of Timothy, d. Sept. 8, 1760, a. about 32 mos.

P. 676, l. 25, TIMOTHY, who d. 1765, was bap. Jan. 9, 1763; his parents were m. in 1753.

JOEL, had Eliza Verstille, bap. July 21, 1816 ; Charlotte, bap. Nov. 23, 1817; Mary, bap. June 5, 1824, and two children, bap. July 30, 1826. *Wby. Ch. Rec.* supply the following members of this family : Miriam, bap. Aug. 30, 1767 ; Nabby, bap. Jan. 31, 1773 ; Timothy, bap. Dec. 12, 1775 ; Reuben, bap. March 7, 1779.

GEORGE, m. Triphena Latimer, Aug. 13, 1776, and had George, bap. Jan. 12, 1777 ; Triphena, bap. July 11, 1779; ―― Sept. 16, 1781; Chesterfield, bap. Sept. 1787.

ERASTUS, had Moses, bap. Aug. 1, 1802; Sarah, m. Aaron Bates of Hartland, Sept. 8, 1779 ; Abigail, m. Isaac Hunt of Sharon, March 31, 1793.

KINGSLEY, p. 676, NATHAN, had Nathan, bap. May 20, 1764. (E. W. C. R.)

KIRTLAND, p. 676, insert, wid. SARAH (mother-in-law to Samuel Webster), d. Dec. 12, 1762, a. about 85.

LADD, p. 677, l. 15, ELISHA, m. Chloe Barber, Nov. 8, 1785.

LAMBERTON, p. 677, l. 18, OBED, had also Mabel, bap. March 21, 1761 ; Moses, bap. Feb. 10, 1765 ; Elizabeth, who d. Sept. 21, 1777 ; Keziah, who d. Sept. 20, 1777 ; Nathaniel (l. 19), also d. same day as Keziah. (All foregoing from N. S. R.) From same we get the d. of Mehitable, wife of Obed Lamberton, May 27, 1790, a. 69 ; OBED, Jr., m. Ruth ―――, and had Nathaniel, bap. March 23, 1777; Samuel Taylor, bap. Aug. 1781. ELIZUR, m. Mary Winslow, April 29, 1811.

LAMFIRE, p. 677, RACHEL, was bap. Dec. 17, 1797 (E. W. C. R.); prob. the same who d. Nov. 17, 1828, a. 36.

LANE, p. 677, DAVID, had Lucy, bap. Feb. 15, 1773. (Wby. Ch. Rec.)

LATTEMORE, p. 677, CHAUNCEY, m. Polly Newring, Feb. 16, 1815; GEORGE, m. Hannah Loomis, April 3, 1783; JOHN, m. Dorcas Skinner, Dec. 1780 ; JACOB, m. Mary Mather, Dec. 17, 1795 ; HANNAH, m. Jeremiah Woodford, April 2, 1807; LEVI, m. Rebecca Filley, June 1, 1791.

LAWRENCE, p. 677, AMOS, whose wife Sarah, d. June 8, 1794, had first child Amos, bap. March 12, 1752. (Wby. Ch. Rec.)

ELIHU ―, bap. Jan. 14, 1759, and dau. Eunice, d. April 27, 1760, a. about 15 mo.; his wife Eunice, d. Nov. 20, 1760, a. about 30 yrs. (Wby. Ch. Rec.)

SARAH, d. Oct. 10, 1778, a. about 18 yrs. (Wby. Ch. Rec.)

P. 677, BEZALEEL, had also Mary, bap. March 31, 1765; Ebenezer Whetmore, bap. Oct. 25, 1766 ; Nabbe, bap. Nov. 19, 1769 ; Bille, bap. Oct. 1771; Jacob, bap. Dec. 29, 1772; Aholiab, had Elihu, bap. Aug. 29, 1789. (Wby. Ch. Rec.)

ELIHU (prob. son of Aholiab above), had Lucretia, Elihu, Hector, d. Jan. 21, 1817, a. 23; Abiram, bap. June 16, 1822 ; Mary Maria, bap. April 24, 1825; Clarissa, bap. July 16, 1826. (Wby. Ch. Rec.)

LEVI, d. April 13, 1810, a. 41, had Nancy, Maria, Eliza, bap. Nov. 17, 1799; Leicester Filley, bap. Oct. 12, 1800; Emily Susan, July 2, 1809; he lost a dau., d. May 28, 1806, a 4. (Wby. Ch. Rec.)

EBENEZER, m. Eunice Hoskins, Jan. 9, 1766 ; had Eunice, bap. Feb. 16, 1767; Ebenezer, bap. Jan. 22, 1769; Alexander, bap. Jan. 27, 1771 ; Eunice and Ebenezer, bap. July 27, 1800; Orrin, bap. Aug. 23, d. Nov. 6, 1801; Eliezer Curtis, bap. July 15, 1810; Herman, bap. July 4, 1813, d. Aug. 11, 1814, a. 1¼ yrs.; Anson Herman, bap. April 28, 1816; Ebenezer's " youngest child," d. April 14, 1812. (Wby. Ch. Rec.)

HEZEKIAH, m. Tryphena Gillett, Jan. 26, 1758, had Tryphena, bap. Jan. 28, 1759; Hezekiah, bap. June 28, 1761; Wealthyann, bap. May 27, 1764 ; Ruth, bap. Feb. 1, 1767; Levi, bap. July 23, 1769 ; Rockee, bap. Aug. 16, 1772; Elihu, bap. May 7, 1775, d. Sept. 17, 1776. (Wby. Ch. Rec.)

HEZEKIAH, Jr., had Rebecca, Clara, Hezekiah, Elihu, bap. Sept. 28, 1788; Laura, bap. Oct. 1790 ; John Thrall, Mahala, Mary Ann, bap. Sept. 21, 1800; Parmela, bap. Oct. 21, 1804. (Wby. Ch. Rec.)

ELIHU, had Edward M., bap. Aug. 31, 1783; ELISHA, had John and Submit, Prudence, Comfort and Lucina, grown children, bap. June 15, 1766. (W. C. R.)

HEZEKIAH 3d, m. Bede Butler, Dec. 25, 1808 ; CLARISSA, m. Henry Shepard, Dec. 4, 1806; LAURA, m. Augustus Shepard, Nov. 23, 1809 ; Eunice, m. Silas Corel of Glastenbury, June 18, 1807; MAHALA, m. Roger Rowley of Bennington, N. Y., Feb. 8, 1829; ELIZA, m. Luther Pratt of Granby, Aug. 30, 1820 ; JOHN J., m. Abigail M. Shepard of Farmington, Nov. 25, 1819.

STEPHEN, Jr.'s child Molle, d. May 21, 1773 ; ELISHA, d. Jan. 24, 1779, in 65 ; SARAH, dau. of Bezaleel, d. Oct. 16, 1783, in 30 ; LUCINA, d. March, 1784, in 19; BEZALEEL, d. May 29, 1786; wid. Abigail, d. 1810, a. 90; ABIGAIL (dau. of John), d. Feb. 18, 1828, a. 67 ; JOHN, d. Oct. 8, 1828, a. 32; MINDWELL, wife of Hezekiah, d. June 20, 1820 ; HEZEKIAH, d. April 29, 1818, a. 82. (Why. Ch. Rec.)

LEE, p. 677, l. 31, OLIVER, m. Abigail Roe, Oct. 4, 1769 ; Oliver's death must have occurred before May 14, 1778, at which time his son Oliver is bap., as son of Abigail Lee, " widdow." (N. S. R.)

LEWIS, p. 677, JOHN, m. Hannah Drake, March 11, 1779.

P. 677, l. 34, JOHN, who d. 1713, m. Mary (dau. of Michael Humphrey) at Hartford, June 16, 1675, and his son John, b. 1675, d. May 10, 1676 ; JOSEPH, m. Elizabeth Case, April 30, 1674. (Col. Rec.)

LOOMIS, p. 678, l. 22, DAVID, b. 1665, d. June 24, same year. (Col Rec.)

P. 678, l. 26, MARY CHAUNCEY, 2d wife of Joseph, Jr.,[2] d. April 22, 1631.

P. 678, l. 33, MARY JUDD, was of Farmington. (Col. Rec.)

P. 678, l. 34, for 1655, read 1655–56. (Col. Rec.)

P. 678, l 35, HANNAH, was b. Feb. 23, not 20. (Col. Rec.)

P. 678, l. 36, ELIZABETH, b. Jan. 21. (Col. Rec.)

P. 678, l. 42, NATHANIEL,[4] m. 1st, Nov. 24, 1653; his second wife was dau. of Josias Ellsworth. (Col. Rec.)

P. 679, l. 39, for March 19, 1684, read 1685.

P. 679, l. 39, JOSEPH,[13] m. 1, Lydia (dau. of John) Drake, April 10, 1681.

(Col. Rec.) The same authority gives his son Caleb, "of Joseph, of Joseph," d. March 5, 1686-7.

P. 680, l. 39, ABRAHAM,[26] settled in Torrington, where his wife Isabel, and their daus. Jerusha and Isabel, joined the church July 17, 1754. Their son Abraham, Jr., and wife, owned cov. in T. church, Dec. 25, 1757. Their son, Epaphras and wife, did the same, June 6, 1756 ; Epaphras, d. at Winchester, Sept. 10, 1812, a. 80 ; his wife Mary, d. at W., Feb. 12, 1813, a. 78.

P. 680, l. 14, for 1682, read 1683. (Col. Rec.)

P. 681, l. 4, ICHABOD,[29] and his wife Esther, joined the church in Torrington, July 17, 1754, but did not long remain there. Ichabod, Jr., settled there, and many descendants now live in W. Winsted, Ct.

P. 681, l. 5, Lucy, Elijah and Abigail, given as children of ICHABOD,[29] prob. belong, rightfully, to some other Ichabod (see note in this Supplement on l. 1, p. 685) ; and Elijah's death, mentioned in same line, belongs to some other Elijah.

P. 681, l. 7, ELIJAH, was bap. Nov. 18, 1753, in Torrington church. ICHABOD (same line), m. Jan. 29, 1766, in Winchester, Mindwell Lewis, both owned cov. in T. church, March 1, 1767, and descendants lived in Winchester.

P. 681, l. 17, AARON,[32] and wife joined Torr. church, May 6, 1744, and also at same time, Aaron, Mindwell and Esther, their children. AARON, Jr. m. Hannah ——, who joined T. church, March 30, 1746 ; MOSES, m, Sarah ——, and both owned cov. in Torrington, June 6, 1756 ; ABNER, m. Sarah ——, and both owned cov. in T. church, Oct. 23, 1757 ; EPHRAIM, owned cov. in T. church, Aug. 6, 1758. Above, from l. 3, furnished by *D. W. Patterson of W. Winsted.*

P. 682, l. 10, *Justin*, according to W. C. R., should be *Justus.*

P. 682, l. 11, OLIVER,[42] had children, bap. March 20, 1768 ; March 5, 1769; July 28, 1771; May 4, 1777 ; April 16, 1780 ; March, 1782. (E. W. C. R.)

P. 682, l. 14, OZIAS,[43] had Odiah, bap. Dec. 7, 1783. (W. C. R.) OZIAS,[43] m. Sarah Roberts (b. 1747, and d. Aug. 10, 1820), and had children, Sarah, b. and d. March 5, 1773; Sarah, b. Dec. 20, 1775, d. May 10, 1790; James,[1] b. Oct. 24, 1779; Odiah,[2] b. Sept. 24, 1783 ; Ozias, b. Oct. 31, 1788, d. Sept. 10, 1793.

JAMES,[1] m. March 7, 1805, Abigail Sherwood (dau. of Dr. Hezekiah Chaffee of Windsor, Ct., by his wife Charlotte Bradley of Greenfield Hill, Ct.), b. April 24, 1787, and had children, Abigail Sherwood, b. Nov. 28, d. Dec. 30, 1805 ; James Chaffee,[3] b. April 29, 1807 ; Hezekiah Bradley,[4] b. Feb. 27, 1809 ; Samuel Odiah, b. April 19, 1811, m. June 2, 1847, Charlotte (dau. of Alfred) Bliss of Windsor, Ct., and d. July 18, 1855; Osbert Burr, b. July 30, 1813, m. Dec. 19, 1843, Jeannette Hart (dau. of Rev. Dr.) Jarvis of Middletown, Ct., lives in New York city ; Abigail Sarah, b. Sept. 23, 1815, m. Hezekiah Sydney (son of Levi) Hayden of Windsor, Ct., Aug. 9, 1848 ; John Mason,[5] b. Jan. 5, 1825; Col. James, the father of this family, d. May 11, 1862.

ODIAH,[2] m. Harriet Allyn, Sept. 16, 1807, and d. Oct. 14, 1831. Children : Dr. William Ozias, b. July 21, 1808, d. Feb. 1, 1836; Eli Odiah, b. Dec. 14,

1809, d. May 9, 1842; Edgar,[6] b. Feb. 14, 1812; Sarah Jerusha, b. March 12, 1814, d. April 22, 1832; Harriet Emily, b. June 14, 1818, m. Dr. J. P. Jewett of Lowell, Mass., has four children: Charles Henry, b. Jan. 17, 1820. d. Nov. 10, 1848; Thomas Warham,[7] b. March 1, 1827.

JAMES CHAFFEE,[3] m. 1, May 1, 1833, Eliza Cesarine (dau. of J. S.) Mitchell of New Haven, Ct., who d. March 24, 1840; he m. 2, April 24, 1844, Mary Beach (dau. of Ira) Sherman of Bridgeport, Ct., where he now lives. Children by 1st wife: James Mitchell, b. March 24, 1836, d. Dec. 16, 1841; by 2d wife, James Sherman, b. May 8, 1846; Mary Sherman, b. March 17, 1848, d. March 5, 1855.

HEZEKIAH BRADLEY,[4] now of New York city, m., Aug. 13, 1835, Caroline Elizabeth (dau. of Luther) Loomis, of Suffield, Ct., who d. April 23, 1844. He m. 2, Sept. 9, 1849, Euphemia (dau. of Dr. James) Anderson of New York city. Children: Luther, Jr., b. Sept. 18, 1836, d. July 7, 1843; Elizabeth Leavitt, b. Sept. 20, 1843, d. Feb. 2, 1844.

JOHN MASON,[5] now of Chicago, Ill., m., Aug. 20, 1849, Mary Jane Hunt of Sherburn, N. Y. Child: Mary Hunt, b. June 16, 1855, d. Jan. 5, 1861.

EDGAR,[6] m. Harriet (dau. of Nathaniel) Smith, Torringford, Ct., and had William Edgar, and Charles.

THOMAS WARHAM,[7] m. Mary Jane (dau. of Allen) Cook of Poq. in Windsor, Nov. 17, 1858, had Allen Cook, b. Nov. 21, 1860. The foregoing records furnished by Osbert B. Loomis, Esq., of New York city.

P. 682, l. 19, WARHAM, son of John, Jr.,[44] had John, bap. Dec. 9, 1792; Mary, bap. July 10, 1796.

All the following from E. W. C. R.—LUKE[45] (E. W.), p. 682, l. 21, had a 2d dau. Anne, bap. July 14, 1765. His son Simeon, had Luke, bap. March 2, 1794; Charles, bap. Jan. 29, 1797; Robert C., bap. March 30, 1806; William, bap. July 30, 1809; Eliza Ann, bap. Oct. 9, 1811; Julia, bap. May 7, 1815. His son Russell, had Eli, bap. April 22, 1792; ——, Sept. 8, 1793; Anne, Nov. 16, 1794; Russell, July 17, 1796; ——, Sept. 23, 1798; Eliza, June 8, 1800; Lorena, June 21, 1801; Us—, Jan. 9, 1803; ——, June 10, 1804; Mary, Jan. 1806; Francis, March 27, 1808; Jo—, Aug. 16, 1809.

P. 682, l. 26, Dea. AMASA,[47] has been badly treated, and I am surprised to find how many people are interested in him, and anxious for the preservation of his fair fame. I've received letters from Wisconsin to Connecticut relative to Dea. Amasa, and will now endeavor to straighten out some of the kinks.

1st. All the children from Amasa, b. 1785, to Betsyvilla, b. 1805, inclusive, belong not to the Deacon, but to his son Amasa (l. 25), b. in 1763. Having taken so much of the load off the Deacon's back, we proceed to remark

2d. That a principal cause of the confusion is probably in the fact that the wife of the second Amasa was also a *Priscilla Birge.* This fact may clear away the seeming defamation which rests upon Dea. Amasa[47] of having a child b. while he was a widower. Amasa, b. 1785, grad. Y. C., 1807. For *Betsyvilla,* read *Betsyrilla.*

P. 682, l. 29, ELIAKIM (prob. Eliakim,[33] l. 22), Wby. d. March 29, 1753. (R. MSS.)

P. 682, l. 32, CHAUNCEY, son of Amasa,[47] had Juliet, bap. March 27, 1808; Harriet, bap. June 25, 1809 ; Olive Elmer, bap. Nov. 10, 1811.

Mr A. S. KELLOGG says there was a *third* Amasa, who with his wife (name unknown) joined the church in No. Bolton, Jan. 26, 1783. The church record shows two children, bap. there—Nancy, bap. Feb. 9, 1783 (named on page 682, line 33, as b. July 10, 1782), and Samuel, bap. Sept. 26, 1784.

GERSHOM (prob. son of Amasa[47]), had children, bap. Aug. 3, 1806 ; Jan. 14, 1810. (E. W. C. R.)

P. 683, l. 32, ELIJAH, had Sylvester, bap. April 15, 1787, d. Jan. 14, 1797. (Wby. Ch. Rec.)

P. 683, l. 35, ELIPHALET, m. Theodosia Clark, March 28, 1749, and had also Israel, bap. Oct. 8, 1758, d. Nov. 3, 1759 ; Lizzie, bap. March 8, 1761. (Wby. Ch. Rec.) For *Theisdamia*, read *Thedean*, prob. *Theodosia*.

P. 683, l. 37, GIDEON, d. May 7, 1802, a. 67.

GILES (prob. the one ment. on l. 15, p. 684), had children, bap. Dec. 23, 1781; May 23, 1784, and June 20, 1794; Feb. 25, 1786; Horace, bap. Feb. 15, 1789 ; Harry, bap. June 26, 1791; Sally, bap. April 7, 1793. (E. W. C. R.)

P. 684, l. 24, JOSEPH, Jr., d. Sept. 5, 1739. His wid. Mary, d. Sept. 12, 1740.

P. 685, l. 1, Mr. *D. W. Patterson* of W. Winsted, Ct., informs me that he has been informed by one of this Reuben's descendants, that he (Reuben) was son of Ichabod, who was son of Timothy, and his being m. in 1742, would indicate his birth as early as 1720. Mr. P.'s theory, therefore, is that Ichabod, b. 1692, m., and had Ichabod, who m. 1738, and had this Reuben and possibly one or two more before Lucy, b. 1727. See l. 5, p. 681, and note of correction on same, on page 87 of this Supplement. This (Capt.) REUBEN's 2d wife Rebecca, d. Jan. 11, 1775, a. about 55; he d. Oct. 12, 1801, a. 82. (Wby. Ch. Rec.)

P. 685, l. 38, ROMAN W., had Lucretia Barber, bap. Nov. 6, 1836. (W. C. R.)

ODIAH, m. Harriet Allyn, Sept. 16, 1807, and had William Ozias, bap. Dec. 11, 1809 (W. C. R.); and Eli Odiah, bap. June 17, 1810; Edgar, bap. July 20, 1812 ; Sarah Jerusha, bap. Oct. 9, 1814. (W. C. R.)

ARTHUR, had Laura, bap. Nov. 21, 1813. (W. C. R.)

JOB (prob. Job, b. 1743, l. 13, p. 684), had Simeon, bap. April 22, 1798 ; James, bap. 22 June, 1800 ; Willard, bap. Oct. 21, 1805 ; Simeon, bap. Dec. 20, 1807; Harris Allyn, bap. Oct. 20, 1811 ; Lester, bap. Sept. 14, 1815. (All above from W. C. R.)

GILBERT and wife Abigail N., had Mary Jane, bap. May 6, 1853.

ELIHU, m. Rhoda Phelps, May 6, 1813 ; HARRIET E., m. J. R. Jewett of Lowell, Mass., May 26, 1841 (W. C. R.); MELINDA, m. Abial King of Suffield, May 12, 1841. (W. C. R.)

12

Justus (prob. the same as on l. 2, p. 682), had children, bap. July 29, 1770; Sept. 13, 1772; June 4, 1775. (E. W. C. R.)

Gideon (prob. the same as on l. 37 and 39, p. 683), had children, bap. Aug. 2, 1772. This Gideon was prob. the same as one on line 43, same page.

Simon (poss. Simeon), had Simon Lorenzi, bap. March 11, 1792. (E. W. C. R.)

Lucy, had Lucy, bap. Nov. 4, 1764; Hannah, had child, bap. Oct. 29, 1775 ; Naomi, had child, bap. Aug. 15, 1775. (E. W. C. R.)

The following from Wby. Ch. Rec.—Samuel, m. Jerusha Filley, Dec. 13, 1759, and had Jerusha, bap. May 25, 1760, Samuel, bap. Aug. 23, 1761.

Samuel (of Windsor), had Zedekiah, bap. Nov. 10, 1766 ; David, bap. Feb. 26, 1771.

Stephen, Jr., m. Mary Mumford, June 13, 1765 ; had Andrew, bap. July 13, 1766 ; Kesiah, bap. Nov. 15, 1767 ; Molly, bap. March 22, 1772; Molle, bap. March 27, 1774 ; Ralph, bap. April 7, 1776; Elven, bap. Oct. 25, 1778 ; Heman, bap. April 24, 1780; Russell, bap. May, 1780 ; ——, bap. Aug. 31, 1783.

Jacob, m. Diademia Hubbard, Aug. 15, 1771, and had Diademia, bap. Jan. 12, 1772 ; Jacob, bap. Oct. 31, 1773 ; Becky, bap. Jan. 12, 1777.

Elijah (p. 683), m. Abigail Gillet, May 10, 1778, had Clarissa and Erastus, bap. Nov. 3, 1799 ; Abigail and Eunice, bap. Aug. 31, 1783 ; Aurelia, bap. July 10, 1785.

Abijah, had Timothy, bap. June 22, 1787.

Eliphalet (poss. one ment. l. 35, p. 683), had Ann, bap. Oct. 22, d. 27, 1750.

Eliakim[33] (see p. 681, l. 22), who d. March 28, 1753, a. 52 yrs., 9 mos., had Mary, bap. May 3, 1747 ; Sarah, bap. Dec. 31, 1749.

Abel (l. 25, p. 685), whose wife Eunice, d. Feb. 13, 1757, a. about 38, had Eunice, bap. July 25, 1742 ; Abel, bap. May 6, 1744; Ezon, bap. March 23, 1746; Daniel, bap. Aug. 21, 1748 ; Elizabeth, bap. Jan. 27, 1751; Hezekiah, bap. Oct. 7, 1753.

Joab, had Susannah, Reuben, Harrison and Sarah Ann, bap. Nov. 18, 1821.

George, had Eunice Aurelia, bap. July 4, 1813.

Jacob, had Julianna, bap. May 5, 1799.

Samuel, 1st Society Windsor, had David, bap. Aug. 5, 1764.

Samuel, had Russell, Jesse, George, bap. April 19, 1789.

Joab, bap. Feb. 19, 1781, d. Aug. 9, 1783; Anna, bap. Aug. 29, 1784 ; Jacob, bap. June, 1787.

Timothy, m. Wealthy Ann Hubbard, May 2, 1811, and had Timothy Dwight, bap. May 31, 1812.

Jedidiah, m. Sibel Case, Nov. 25, 1748; and had Sybil, bap. Dec. 3, 1749.

Lucy, m. Robert Joyner of Sheffield, March 3, 1757; wid. Theodosia, m. Simeon Judd of Hartford, June 20, 1771.

Rebecca, m. Hez. Goodwin, Aug. 29, 1798 ; Nabby, m. Jonathan Hutchinson of Granby, May 11, 1802; CLARISSA, m. Romanta Woodford of Winchester, Jan. 26, 1809 ; CHARLOTTE M., m. Horace Daniels, Feb. 18, 1830. WILLIAM, m. Densy Burr, Sept. 27, 1807. ABIJAH, had Huldah, bap. Aug. 25, 1782 ; Wealthy Ann, who d. April 17, 1796, a. 8.

Wid. SARAH, d. Aug. 3, 1794, a. 88 ; Eds. JOHN, d. Sept. 6, 1765, in 77 ; wid. LOOMIS (sister to Jno. and Isaac Brown), d. Jan. 6, 1766, a. about 60 ; wid. ABIGAIL, d. April 13, 1793 ; inf. of STEPHEN, Jr., d. Feb. 10, 1785 ; STEPHEN, d. Oct. 30, 1794, in 78 ; DAVID, d. Aug. 20, 1797, a. 78. ELIAKIM, d. April 15, 1802, in 66; wid. GRACE, d. April 2, 1803, in 82 ; wid. MARY, d. April 25, 1804, a. 73 ; ABIJAH, d. June 27, 1805, a. 49 ; wid. MARY, d. Nov. 13, 1806, a. 59 ; PAMELIA, dau. of Hez., Jr., d. May 23, 1807, a. 3 ; JACOB, d. Jan. 13, 1826, a. 75 ; HANNAH, d. June 25, 1823, a. 87 ; JERUSHA, d. July 26, 1823 ; Dea. ELIJAH, d. May 10, 1820, a. 66 ; LYDIA, d. Nov. 9, 1818, a. 91.

MOSES, m. Nancy Loomis, May 5, 1834. (W. C. R.) " Left. Richard Burnham of Hartford, and ye widow Hannah Loomis of W., m. Oct. 15, 1742."—*Tim. Loomis's MSS.* BENJAMIN, m. Chloe Brown of E. W., May 18, 1778, is prob. the father of George, b. Sept. 24, 1783 ; JEDEDIAH, m. Martha Drake, May 18, 1783; ELEANOR, m. Henry Wilson, Nov. 5, 1809 ; HORACE, m. Lula Clark, April 22, 1800, and had Triphena, bap. (W. C. R.) May 21, 1809 ; LOVEL, m. Zuba Phelps, Feb. 20, 1793; AMELIA, m. John Hills (E. W.), Feb. 8, 1815 : BENJAMIN, Jr., m. Mary Gaylord, Feb. 21, 1805.

WILLIAM, had Fanny, bap. May 20, 1798 (W. C. R.); Sally, bap. April 20, 1800 (W. C. R.); SAMUEL, had Harriet, bap. Sept. 11, 1796 (W. C. R.) ; Sarah, b. Dec. 11, 1733; SAMUEL, Jr., had Eleazer, Keziah and Sally, bap. Aug. 10, 1794 (W. C. R.); HANNAH, wife of Gideon, d. May 3, 1817, a 77; see page 683; JONN, d. Nov. 30, 1732, his wife 1734; wid. RUTH, d. July 11, 1767; MARY, d. Dec. 18, 1819, in 33d yr. (E. W. O.); ERCLE (?), of Moses and Eunice, d. Dec. 21, 1794, in 35 yr.

P. 685, l. 30, HENRY, m. Ruth Bidwell, 1727; see p. 683 foot.

" JOSEPH, son of Joseph," had Joseph, who d. March 19, 1682-3 ; Joseph, b. Oct. 8, 1684; Caleb, who d. March 5, 1686-7; Martha, b. Oct. 31, 1690. (Col. Rec.)

JOSIAH, had Josiah, b. Feb. 17, 1684. (Col. Rec.)

P. 841, l. 29, *Addenda and Miscellanea*, JOHN, b. Jan. 30, 1782, d. July 16, 1854.

In Bennington, N. Y., Nov. 19th, 1862, Capt. GEO. LOOMIS, in his 75th year. Capt. Loomis was the last of the eight original settlers of the town of Bennington, who came from Windsor, Ct., in 1806. During the last war, he with his company of militia, was called out to assist in protecting our Canadian frontier. For more than thirty years, almost from its first commencement, he has been a subscriber to *The Evangelist.* He had been considered a consistent christian by all who knew him, for many years, but never made a public profession of religion till the autumn of 1857, when he, with nearly his whole family, united with the Baptist church. This had long been the church of his choice, yet he was no sectarian, but loved all christians wherever he met them. The unanimous testimony of neighbors and acquaintances is, " No one can say aught against him." And in view of his long and useful life, and peaceful death, all feel to say, " Mark the perfect man, and behold the upright, for the end of that man is peace."—*N. Y. Evangelist.*

EZEKIEL, Sen., d. May 24, 1857, a. 42. (Wp. N.)

LORD, ELISHA, had Bidwell, bap. July 4, 1795. (Wby. Ch. Rec.) P. 686, JAMES, m. Rhoda Loomis, April, 1813; ELISHA, m. Susannah Alcott, Dec. 13, 1794, he d. Feb. 29, 1808, a. 59. (Wby. Ch. Rec.) THEONOSIA (perhaps first wife), of Elisha, d. Sept. 19, 1793.

LOTHROP, p. 687, insert THARSHER (Thatcher ?), had children, bap. Jan. 30, 1763; Jan. 20, 1765; Oct. 12, 1766; May 11, 1768 ; May 30, 1770. (E. W. C. R.)

LUCAS, p. 687, insert ICHABOD, m. Abigail Smith, Dec. 29, 1783.

LYMAN, p. 691, insert NATHANIEL, was bap. and had children bap. April 1, 1792; Oct. 27, 1793; July 31, 1796 ; Backus, Oct. 6, 1799; William, Nov. 8, 1801. (E. W. C. R.)

McCLURE, p. 691, insert Rev. DAVID, had children bap. Sept. 10, 1786; Nov. 16, 1788 ; Hannah Pomeroy, Aug. 28, 1791. (E. W. C. R.)

MACK, p. 691, l. 5, ANDREW's wife's name was *Sarah* ——.

McLEAN, HECTOR, m. Esther Chaffee, June 1, 1789 ; had Esther Chaffee, bap. Sept. 3, 1797; Henry Augustus, bap. Oct. 6, 1799. (W. C. R.)

BETSY GOODWIN, d. Nov. 15, 1810, a. 23 ; Sarah, d. May 5, 1817, a. 70; John, d. Sept. 1822.

THOMAS, had Sally, bap. May 29, 1785.

LAUCHLAN, m. Lucy Humphrey, April 11, 1762, and had Hector, bap. Dec. 1762; Charles, bap. Oct. 20, 1765 ; Mariann, bap. March 27, 1768; Archibald, bap. April 28, 1771 ; James, bap. July 11, 1779 ; Lucy, bap. Aug. 31, 1783. (Wby. Ch. Rec.)

NEAL, had child, d. July 6, 1772, a. about 14 days. (Wby. Ch. Rec.)

JOHN, had John, bap. June 16, 1776 ; William, bap. July 11, 1779 ; Betsy Goodwin, bap. Aug., 1787. (Wby. Ch. Rec.)

ALLYN, had inf., d. Oct. 27, 1795 ; Roderick, bap. Dec. 6, 1777. (Wby. Ch. Rec.)

MANLEY, p. 691, l. 22, EBENEZER, d. in 1776. He m. Mary Gillet, Dec. 24, 1762. His son Allyn was b. in 1766, and he also had dau. Permena, bap. March 6, 1774. (Wby. Ch. Rec.)

GEORGE, had George, bap. April 8, 1753. This corrects line 32, page 691.

Dea. WILLIAM's first child, b. 1753, was named William; also had Mary, bap. Nov. 2, 1755; his wife Molly (prob. 2d wife), d. June, 1786. The month of Dea. William's marriage is given as *Nov.* by Wby. Ch. Rec.

MARY, m. Jacob Merrils of W. Hartford, Feb. 17, 1755.

WILLIAM's wife d. Dec. 1, 1802 ; WILLIAM, d. July 22, 1805, a. about 30 ; William (prob. Dea.), and wife were adm. to Wby. Ch., March 3, 1744-5, from Wethersfield. (Wby. Ch. Rec.)

P. 691, ERASTUS, m. Abigail Brown, Jan. 15, 1835. (W. C. R.)

TIMOTHY, had child, bap. June 18, 1786. (E. W. C. R.)

PAMELA, m. Chester Rice of Sandisfield, Feb. 27, 1797. (Wby. Ch. Rec.)

MANNING, p. 691, JOHN, m. Lydia Holcomb, Dec. 29, 1777. (Wby. Ch. Rec.)

MANSFIELD, p. 691, l. 33, JOHN, m. 1683. (Col. Rec.)

MARSH, p. 692, JOHN, m. Sarah Strong, April, 1779. NATHANIEL of Htfd., m. Naomi Barber, Feb. 20, 1795.

MARSHALL, p. 692, 1676 (under autograph), read 1672.

P. 692, l. 47, for *their* generations, read *three* generations.

P. 696, l. 13, SAMUEL's wife Joanna, d. March 13, 1783; he d. Nov. 7, 1797. (Wby. Ch. Rec)

Wid. MARY, had Reuben, bap. Aug. 2, 1778 ; ALEXANDER, had Zeruiah, bap. Aug. 2, 1778; ALEXANDER, d. April 25, 1801, a. 54; OLIVER, d. April 18, 1804, a. 34 ; Wid. LYDIA, d. Nov. 7, 1804, a. 53; SAMUEL, d. June 4, 1813, a. 39. *Col. Rec.* say that MARY (wid. of Capt. Samuel ?) d. Aug. 25, 1683.

P. 697, l. 1, ELIAKIM,[14] m. Anne *Palmer*, Dec. 27, 1785 ; his son Warren, m. Elizabeth Wolcott, Sept. 26, 1811.

P. 697, l. 21, Capt. ELIHU,[16] m. March 7, 1793.

P. 697, l. 27, SAMUEL,[17] d. Aug. 14, 1800. He m. Sabra Mills, Jan. 12, 1769. (Wby. Ch. Rec.)

P. 697, l. 34, CALISTA, who m. Mr. *Herron*, has two children, Fred. M., Calista S.

P. 697, l. 38, ELISHA G., now Captain 6th Infantry, U. S. A., and Colonel of the 13th N. Y. V., Army of the Potomac. Same line, for Josepha *Toule*, read Josepha *Youle*.

CANDACE, m. Odiah L. Sheldon, Aug. 1, 1826. (W. C. R)

SAMUEL, s. of Samuel, m. Rebecca Newberry, June 22, 1675. (Col. Rec.)

EDWARD W. m. Julia A. Haydon, Nov. 10, 1836. (W. C. R.) ALEXANDER, had Lydia, bap. March 31, 1771. (Wby. Ch. Rec.) Geo. Loomis, Sarah and Noah, children of JOSIAH, bap. June 22, 1794. (W. C. R.) Wid. LYDIA, had Ruth, bap. Nov. 1, 1801. (Wby. Ch. Rec.) MARION, m. Hiram Wells of West Hartford, July 22, 1824. (Wby. Ch. Rec.)

MATHER, p. 699, l. 21, for 1634, read 1635.

P. 700, l. 23, Rev. Samuel,[2] had also dau. Hannah, b. Sept. 1682, d. prob. in 1683. (Col. Rec.)

P. 702, l. 2, WILLIAM (with his brother Samuel), was bap. Nov. 15, 1761. (N. S. R.) He d. Jan. 1, 1800. (Wby. Ch. Rec.)

P. 702, l. 13, ALLEN, bap. April 4, 1773. (N. S. R.)

P. 702, l. 14, add WILLIAM, bap. Aug. 4, 1776.   (N. S. R.)

P. 702, l. 15, Rev. ALLYN,[9] grad. Y. C., 1771; ord. Feb. 3, 1773, at *Fair* Haven, Ct.

P. 702, l. 17, ALLYN (prob. Allyn, Jr.), and Parthenia, had Edward, Mary, Samuel, d. June 10, 1830, a. 19.   (Wby. Ch. Rec.)   Julia, Harriet and Sarah, bap. Nov. 21, 1819.   (W. C. R.)

P. 702, l. 30, EPAPHRAS, had Henry, William, Charles, Caroline, bap. Aug. 30, 1827; Lydia, bap. Sept. 12, 1831; Mary Ballantine, bap. Oct. 31, 1834; Sarah Jane, bap. Nov. 2, 1839.   (W. C. R.)

P. 702, l. 20, ELLSWORTH, bap. May 10, 1783; (W. C. R.)   ROBERT TREAT, bap. June 25, 1786.   (W. C. R.)

P. 702, l. 22, JEMIMA, bap. July 8, 1781.   (W. C. R.)   She m. *Allyn* Hyde, May 30, 1805.

P. 702, l. 23, TIMOTHY MATHER, M. D., m. Roxana Phelps, about 1784 or 85.   Children : Roxana, b. Oct. 14, 1786, d. Sept. 3, 1787 ; Timothy, b. June 6, 1788, d. in 1792 or 93.   After the Doctor's death, his wid., in 1802, m. Stephen Clarke, and removed to Litchfield, Ct., and had children, Roxana, William, Sarah.   Mrs. Roxana (Mather) Clarke, d. 1857,   *Letter of Sarah Whiting of Litchfield, Ct., a descendant of Dr. Mather's wid.*

P. 702, line 29, ELIJAH, Jr., m. Jerusha Roberts, Nov. 7, 1790; had Talcott, bap. Dec. 18, 1791 ; Timothy, bap. Oct. 28, 1793; Epraphras, bap. Nov. 1, 1795 ; Jerusha, bap. April 15, 1798, all from W. C. R.

P. 702, l. 30, THADDEUS, d. at Binghamton, N. Y., Dec. 8, 1854, a. 75.

P. 702, l. 33, WILLIAM, bap. June 21, 1801.   (W. C. R.)   Elijah, bap. July 3, 1803.   (W. C. R.)

P. 702, l. 34, Lydia *Clark*, bap. Sept. 22, 1805.   (W. C. R.)

P. 702, l. 35, ALLEN, M.,[16] m. Parthagenia Huntingdon, Feb. 27, 1806.

P. 702, l. 37, ELLSWORTH,[16] m. Laura Wolcott, July 30, 1807.

P. 702, l. 42, TIMOTHY, bap. Feb. 15, 1769.   (N. S. R.)

AZARIAH, Jr., m. Charity Gibbs, and had Charity, bap. Aug. 13, 1788; Eunice, bap. May 1, 1791; Samuel Nathaniel, bap. May 19, 1793.

RUHAMA, m. Joel Stevens of Pittsfield, Jan. 8, 1799 ; TIMOTHY, m. Roxanna Phelps, Aug. 16, 1785.

ELIJAH, m. Ruhama Roberts, Nov. 6, 1791.

TIMOTHY, s. of Timothy, bap. Nov. 25, 1788.   (W. C. R.)   A child of Cotton, d. April 15, 1761.   (N. S. R.)

EDWARD, s. of (Return ?) Strong, bap. Oct. 22, 1799.   (W. C. R.)

ELIHU, had Meducy (Medusa ?), bap. Aug. 26, 1787.   (Wby. Ch. Rec.)

MATSON, JOHN, p. 703, had Sarah, who d. July 19, 1756, a. about 21; Elizabeth, bap. Sept. 23, 1744, d. Feb. 14, 1771; David, bap. July 5, 1747; John, bap. June 18, 1769, d. Jan. 30, 1770 ; Moses, bap. Aug. 15, 1771, d. May 1, 1772.

JOHN, Jr.'s, wife, d. July 5, 1765, a. about 22.

ASA, had Lucretia, bap. April 10, 1763.   (Wby. Ch. Rec.)

MAUDSLEY, p. 703, l. 6, Capt. John, m. Dec. 14, 1664; his dau. Mary, b. 1673, m. Isaac Phelps of Westfield, Dec. 17, 1690. (Col. Rec.)

MAY, p. 703, Charles, b. Feb. 17, 1764, s. of Samuel and Mary (Pierce) May, m. Chloe Reed, Aug. 20, 1788; she d. suddenly, Jan. 26, 1795, a. 30 yrs. 29 days; child, Chloe Reed, b. Nov. 15, 1789, m. William Phelps, had Erasmus, dec.; (Rev.) Winthrop, now of Hitchcockville, Ct.; Charlotte, Marietta; Elizabeth Pierce, b. Jan. 1, 1792, m. Charles Loomis, now of South Windsor, Ct.; May Huntingdon, b. Nov. 29, 1794, m. Simeon P. Haskell. E. W. C. R. give two others, viz., Elmira W. and Charles Williams (prob. by 2d wife), bap. July 26, 1801.

MAYBEE, p. 703, l. 15, for *buried*, read *died*. (Col. Rec.)

MEARS, p. 703, l. 22, Seth, was bap. March 12, 1763 ; a child of John was bap. Sept. 20, 1767. (E. C. W. R.)

Cyprian, had Anne, d. May, 1, 1777, in 15 mo.; Moses had Sarah, bap. Sept. 6, 1747 ; Rhoda, bap. Sept. 2, 1750.

MERREL, p. 703, insert Jacob, m. Mary Manly, Feb. 17, 1755. (Wby Ch. Rec.)

MESSENGER, p. 703, Edward had Dorcas, b. Sept. 23, 1650, and Deliverance, bap. April 7, 1655.

P. 703, l. 28, Nathan, b. April 7; Rebecca, b. 1684-5. (Col. Rec.)

MICHEL, p. 703, Mariann (prob. Mary Ann), bap. May 7, 1774. (E. W. C. R.)

Silas of Hartland, m. Roxana Barber, Feb. 9, 1795.

Rev. Wm. F., d. Feb. 5, 1818, a. 50. (Wby. Ch. Rec.)

MILLINGTON, p. 704, l. 1, John, m. 1663. (Col. Rec.)

MILLS, p. 704, l. 14, *Hist. of Windsor* (in common with the Mills family sketch in the *Memoirs of Rev. Wm. Robinson*, and that in the *Genealogical Sketches of West Simsbury* by Abiel Brown) is in error in relation to Peter Mills, the emigrant, called in an early record "Peter Miles the taylor." He could not conveniently have been born in 1666, as there stated, for he had a lot in Haddam before Nov. 30, 1669. It is not known that he ever lived in Haddam, but March 13, 1670, the town of Haddam voted to Thomas Shailler "the lote that was Peter Milesis the donchemanes." (*Had. Rec. 1st Book.*) D. W. Patterson of West Winsted, Ct., who contributes the foregoing item, also suggests that Dorcas was the first wife of his son Peter, Jr., and Ebenezer and Return, were sons of said Peter, Jr. Wby. Ch. Rec. mention a Peter who d. May 14, 1756, a. about 87, prob. this same Peter, Jr.

From W. C. R.—Elijah, m. Huldah Drake, Nov. 6, 1783; had Oliver, bap. Jan. 20, 1788; Huldah, bap. Nov. 21, 1790; Samuel Webster, bap. April 20, 1794.

Elijah, prob. same as above, had Timothy, bap. July 10, 1803; Julia Ann, bap. Nov. 17, 1805 ; Oliver Williams, bap. Aug. 29, 1796. (W. C. R.)

Augustus, had children bap. Nov. 8, 1789 ; Nov. 10, 1792 ; April 3, 1796 ; Timothy, Feb. 24, 1799. (E. W. C. R.)

Augustus, of E. W., m. Anne Barber, Oct. 15, 1783; had Samuel, bap. April 25, 1784.

Drusilla, m. Henry A. Marvin of Bloomfield, N. Y., Aug. 27, 1817; Oliver W., m. Ann T. Phelps, Feb. 23, 1825; Samuel, m. Candace Allyn, May 8, 1823; Huldah, m. Horace Turner of Hartford, Nov. 12, 1812; Alethea, m. Frederick Mills of New York, Dec. 4, 1806.

Capt. Roswell, had Augustus, bap. Feb. 20, 1763 ; and children bap. April 14, 1765; March 22, 1767; Aug. 6, 1769; Sept. 6, 1771; Feb. 19, 1775; March 23, 1777; Aug. 20, 1779. (E. W. C. R.)

From W by. Ch. Rec.—P. 704, 1. 36, Daniel,[3] had also Anne, bap. Feb. 24, 1740 ; Susanna, bap. Jan. 3, 1742.

P. 705, l. 3, Peletiah,[4] his son Roger, bap. June 4, 1749; d. Oct. 14, 1751; Martha, was bap. July 5, 1752; Eli, was bap. Nov. 4, 1753; Frederick, bap. Feb. 28, 1756 ; Susanna, bap. Oct. 2, 1757.

Peletiah, Jr. (prob. the same), m. Lois Gillet, June 29, 1763 ; Lois, bap. July 1, 1764; Jesse, bap. March 2, 1766; Bildad, bap. July 10, 1768; Sarah, bap. Sept. 6, 1772.

Elijah, m. Hannah, who d. Feb. 13, 1782, in 71 yr.; he d. Jan. 1, 1811, a. 86. Children: Hannah, bap. Nov. 10, 1745; Lucina, bap. Oct. 7,'1750; Diadema, bap. July 1, 1753 ; Judith, bap. May 2, 1756 ; Nabbe, bap. Jan. 7, 1759 ; Elijah, bap. Sept. 20, 1761 ; Oliver, bap. June 19, 1765 ; d. a few days old ; Sarah, d. March 30, 1768; a. 7 mos.; Sarah, bap. Sept. 18, 1768.

Capt. Roger, m. 1, Mary Webster, March 23, 1768 ; who d. Oct. 23, 1768, in 24th yr.; and had Roger, bap. Oct. 16, 1768. He m. 2, Abigail Griswold of Poquonnoc, April 17, 1771. Children : Nabbe Griswold, bap. Nov. 10, 1771; Molle, bap. Dec. 5, 1773; Peletiah, bap. March 17, 1776 ; Elisha, bap. Nov. 1778 ; George, bap. June 17, 1781 ; Rufus, bap. Aug. 31, 1783 ; Betsy, bap. Dec. 9, 1787; Drusilla, bap. June 10, 1790.

Eli, m. Sarah Filley, Jan. 23, 1775; and had Eli, bap. July 9, 1775 ; Abial, bap. Jan 4, 1778 ; Sally, bap. June 3, 1781; Betsy, bap. Aug. 31, 1783.

Samuel, m. Kezia Filley, March 13, 1766; had Kezia, bap. Feb. 16, 1767; Linda, bap. April 8, 1770.

Mrs. Susanna, m. Mr. Joseph De Forest of Stratford, Aug. 18, 1757.

Martha, m. James Barnett of Nine Partners, March 31, 1774.

Peter, Esq., d. April 9, 1762. Wid. Martha, d. July 21, 1779, in 82d yr. Nabby, had Nabby, d. Feb. 21, 1781, a. 1½ yr. Peletiah, Esq., d. July 1, 1786, in 63d yr. Wid. Hannah, d. Jan. 26, 1806, a. 89. Elihu's wife d. July 3, 1807, a. 44. Elihu's wife Huldah, d. June 18, 1808, a. 41. Elijar, d. Jan. 1, 1811, a. 86. Miriam, wife of Elihu, d. April 12, 1816, a. 43.

MOORE, p. 705, Concerning the ancestor, Mr. W. B. Trask of Dorchester, Mass., makes the following queries, somewhat unanswerable, but worthy of consideration : " You infer that Dea Moore went to Windsor, with Mr. Warham in the first immigration. Do you find his name on the records of Windsor, previous to Jan. 2, 1637 ? You state that Dea. John was deputy in 1643, and in Matthew Grant's old church record is a list of those church members who " were so in Dorchester and came up here with Mr. [Warham] and still are of us." You have the name of "[Dea. M]oore," and " Dea. Moore's wife," in that list. Now can the John Moore of Dorchester, in '37, be the Dea. John of Windsor? May it not have been that he either returned to Dorchester (if it was the same individual), and tarried a while, and, in 1643, or before settled permanently in Windsor? Or, that he went to Windsor a few years after the immigration of the church and pastor, and that Mr. Grant in his summary, years after that, put him down among the early comers, as he might have been, if he had gone thither subsequent to the first immigration. Or, this John Moore of Dorchester, 1637, may have been another individual, if so, I should like to know what became of him. I have not had time to make an investigation as to whether he is mentioned on the records subsequent to '37."

P 706, l. 39, *Taintoe*, read *Taintor*, and for *Bradford*, read *Branford*.

P. 707, l. 12, E. W. C. R. gives following dates for WARHAM's [13] family, Jan. 17, 1779 ; Nov. 5, 1780 ; Sept. 1, 1782; June 20, 1784; June 25, 1786; April, 1788; Feb. 21, 1790; Elizabeth, bap. Oct. 16, 1791 ; Jan. 5, 1794.

P. 707, l. 16, Capt. afterward Major Eli,[14] has his family record filled out by the E. W. C. R., as follows : Peter was bap. Feb. 1, 1795 ; Anne, bap. Nov. 13, 1796; Sally, ditto; John, bap. March 9, 1800; Eli, bap. (after his father's death) July 19, 1801.

P. 707, l. 18, EDWARD, 3d,[15] m. Wid. Ruth Parsons, Jan. 31, 1771. (Wby. Ch. Rec.)

P. 707, l. 20, EDWARD, was bap. Sept. 1, 1782 ; Roger, bap. Dec. 12, 1784. (W. C. R.)

P. 708, l. 21, Ann *Maria*, bap. Oct. 25, 1807. (W. C. R.) Minerva C., bap. June 4, 1809. (W. C. R.)

P. 708, l. 41, HANNAH, was bap. Nov. 20, 1798. (W. C. R.)

P. 709, l. 3, WILLIAM's three first children were bap. Oct. 25, 1807, the eldest dau. by name of *Esther* Jane. (W. C. R.)

NATHANIEL, had child, bap. Sept. 2, 1776 ; Aug. 29, 1779 ; (his wife had child bap.) April 24, 1785; Oct. 14, 1787. (E. W. C. R.)

P. 709, l. 21, ANDREW, m. Sarah, "yᵗ was dau. of Samuel Phelps," Feb. 15, 1671. (Col. Rec.)

P. 709, l. 28, HARLOW, was m. May 4. (W. C. R.)

MARIA A., m. Wm. E. St. John, Oct. 30, 1833. (W. C. R.) HARRIET, m. Henry Holman of E. W., Dec. 18, 1842. (W. C. R.). ELIZABETH, m. Wm. G. Morgan, Nov. 27, 1828. (W. C. R.) PHILANDER, m. Sarah R. Holcomb, Dec. 28, 1791. ELIZABETH, m. John May, July 6, 1797. THEOPHILUS, m. —— Griswold, July 10, 1777. JULIA (p. 709, l. 4), m. Ferdinand M. Calkins of Harwinton, Oct. 20, 1836. (W. C. R.)

13

JOHN, son of John, Jr., was b. June 26, 1665. (Col. Rec.) ˙

ANSON, had Harriet, bap. Nov. 17, 1799. (W. C. R.) Olive, dau. of ABI-
JAH, bap. April 15, 1781.

From Wby. Ch. Rec.—WILLIAM of W., m. Lydia Case of Simsbury, Jan.
25, 1803. FANNY, m. Henry Spencer of Hartford, Nov. 23, 1815. THOMAS,
had Elisha, bap. Sept. 28, 1806.

All from E. W. C. R.—MORTON, p. 710, WILLIAM, had a child bap. Jan. 9,
1774; JOHN, had a child bap. June 28, 1778; ALEXANDER (see line 18), had
child bap. May 30, 1778 ; HORACE, had a child bap. Oct. 5, 1828; DEODAT[us]
and child bap. May 10, 1778; another child bap. Jan. 11, 1789.

"ABNER M., got himself bap." Jan 16, 1780; his wife Eliza was bap. Dec.
16, 1798, and children bap. March 25, 1781; March, 30, 1783 ; April 24, 1785 ;
Aug. 20, 1786; Feb. 4, 1816. ZEBULON, was bap. Oct. 14, 1798, also a child;
HORACE bap. Oct. 6, 1799.

ANDREW, d. May 28, 1752, a. about 79 yr.; "had resided in Wby. at Zebulon Hoskins' a few months." JOEL'S child, Olive, d. Oct. 11, 1792. (Wby.
Ch. Rec.)

MOSES, p. 710, MARTIN, had Martin, Jabez, Herschel and Roxana, báp.
July 6, 1800. (W. C. R.)

P. 710, l. 30, JOHN, d. Oct. 14, 1683 ; his son John, was b. July 15. (Col.
Rec.)

TIMOTHY, m. 1, Sarah *PHELPS*, who d. Sept. 12, 1751, a. about 38; m. 2,
Sarah ——, who d. Nov. 19, 1759, in 51 yr.; m. 3, Elizabeth *HUMPHREY* of W.
Simsbury, who d. Oct. 6, 1763, a. about 50 ; ~~possibly~~ a 4th wife, *ANNE* as ˙ a wife
of Timothy (Lieut.), d. March 19, 1786," her name as we learn from the
list of admissions to the Wby. Church, was Anne, and her previous residence
New Milford ; had Zeruiah, bap. Nov. 9, 1740; Martin, bap. July 17, 1743;
Kezia, bap. June 15, 1746; Dorcas, bap. Nov. 6, 1748; Lydia, bap. Aug. 11,
1751. (Wby. Ch. Rec.) *⁊ son. by 1st wf.*

MARTIN, m. Lydia, and had Martin, bap. April 30, 1766; b. after his father's
death. (Wby. Ch. Rec.)

MARTHA, aunt of Timothy above, d. July 9, 1764, a. about 56 ; MARTIN, d.
Jan. 27, 1766, in 23 yr. (Wby. Ch. Rec.)

MOSS, p. 710, insert CHESTER, had dau. Leverich, bap. Nov. 1782. (N.
S. R.)

MUNSELL, p. 711, JACOB,[1] was the son of Thomas Monsell of New Lon-
don, Ct., mentioned in 1681; on a highway committee in 1683; had wife
Lydia, and children *Jacob*, Elisha, Mary and Deliverance; d. 1712. In 1723,
Jacob was of Windsor, and Elisha of Norwich. See Caulkins' *Hist. of New
London*, page 358.

P. 712, l. 10, JOEL, b. *Aug.* 3, according to *Pres. Stiles.*

EDWARD B. m. Lucy Stevens, Oct. 19, 1834. (W. C. R.)

ZACHEUS, m. Hannah Drake, May 4, 1768. (Wby. Ch. Rec.)

P. 712, l. 26, GURDON[11] and family should be differently located in the record. For interesting biography of this Gurdon, see *Vermont Quarterly Gazetteer*, i, 21.

NASH, p. 719, l. 5, for 1659, read 1659-60.

P. 719, l. 7, for 1663, read 1663-64.

P. 719, l. 11, Moses, b. 1696; d. Jan. 26, 1760, in 64 yr. (Wby. Ch. Rec.)

P. 719, l. 16, TIMOTHY, m. March 1, 1722.

P. 719, l. 23, for *Tolland*, read *Windsor*.

P. 719, l. 25, for *Poalk*, read *Paulk*.

P. 719, l. 28, insert the name of Stephen, b. April 13, 1762; d. Oct. 21, 1776, and Timothy, b. March 19, 1764. (See *Nash Genealogy*.)

JOSEPH, who d. March 22, 1771, a. about 35, m. Ann Skinner, March 16, 1758; had Joseph, bap. Feb. 18, 1759; d. March 19, 1759; Anna, bap. June 13, 1762; Joseph, bap. March 16, 1760; Rebecca, bap. Jan. 28, 1765; Rivera, bap. April 12, 1767; Jemme, bap. July 22, 1770. (Wby. Ch. Rec.)

JOHN, had Mary, bap. Dec. 15, 1754; Moses, bap. March 20, 1757; John, bap. Aug. 27, 1758; John, d. Oct. 19, 1758, a. about 28. (Wby. Ch. Rec.)

NEARING, ASAHEL, m. Molly Loomis, Oct. 21, 1792, and had Polly, Ashbel, Henry, Maria, bap. Sept. 15, 1799; Heman Loomis, bap. May 11, 1801.

ASAHEL H., m. Mary Ann Latimer, Oct. 19, 1820.

NEWBERRY, p. 720, l. 33, Capt. BENJAMIN was *Major* at time of his death.

BENJAMIN (can this be B.,[10] p. 722?), m. Sarah Drake, Oct. 13, 1763.

P. 721, l. 2, Hannah, b. 1652, d. Sept. 21, 1663. (Col. Rec.)

P. 721, l. 7, for *May*, read *March*

P. 721, l. 8, Thomas, b. 1677, d. Feb. 10, 1680; another son Thomas seems to have been b. March 28, 1681.

P. 721, l. 32, for June 19, read June 29.

P. 722, l. 3, the family of Gen. ROGER,[9] receives the following *addenda et corrigenda*, from family papers kindly loaned us by Mrs. Rhoda Simmons of Windsor, Ct. His first wife was the dau. of Alexander and Hannah Allyn of W. His second wife was the dau. of John and Eunice Ely of Springfield, Mass., b. Sept. 11, 1741. His first son ROGER, d. Oct. 14th, in the same year he was b. His dau. ELIZABETH, d. Sept. 27, 1766. His son PERICLES, d. Nov. 7, 1791, a. 21 yrs., 9 mos. 20 days. His dau. FANNY, was b. March 7, 1775; m. John Sargeant, June 26, 1799; he d. 23 Jan, 1829; she d. Dec. 12, 1851. His second dau. ELIZABETH, was b. March 2, 1773. His second son, ROGER, and dau. EUNICE (twins) were b. Oct 7, 1779; Roger grad. at Y. C., and studied law, and Eunice d. at age of 19 yrs. His son HENRY, was b. Jan. 27, 1783, m. *Elizabeth* Strong, Oct. 7, 1803, and in 1824 moved to Ohio, and d. Dec. 2, 1854, a. 72; had the following children: Elizabeth, b. Oct. 28, 1804, m. Elisha N. Sill of W., removed to Cuyahoga Falls, O., has Alfred and Ethelbert. Mary Strong, b. Sept. 13, 1808, d. Dec. 30, 1855; Fanny, b. April 4, 1810, m. Elisha N. Sill (husband of her deceased sister), and has

Elizabeth and Mary; Julia, b. April 1, 1812, m. Ogden Wetmore, who d.
young, and she afterward m. Henry Holbrook, and lives at Cuyahoga Falls,
O.; Almira, b March 18, 1814, m. —— Fagle, has one son, lived at C. F.,
he d. young; Eunice, b. Sept. 18, 1815, m. Charles Sill, lives at Cuyahoga
Falls, O., has Henry, John and Sarah. His dau. RHODA, was b. April 11,
1786, m. Dr. Abel Simmons of Ashford, Ct. (who was b. Aug. 13, 1787),
Sept. 8, 1812; he d. Nov. 23, 1818 Children: Eunice N., b. June 13, 1813,
m. Anson Loomis, Oct. 26, 1836, and had Mary Elizabeth, b. April 11, 1842;
Abel, b. Nov. 18, 1814, d. at Athens, Ga., Nov. 15, 1838.

Following from Wby. Ch. Rec.—THOMAS, had Aurelia, bap. Sept. 9, 1764;
Sally, bap. June 7, 1767; Mariann, bap. Nov. 6, 1768; Anne, bap. Nov. 10,
1771; James, bap. March 22, 1773; Dolly, bap. March 2, 1777; James, bap.
Sept. 27, 1778.

FREDERICK, m. Mary Gillet, July 21, 1800, had Susan, bap. June 23, 1811;
Eliza Ann, bap. Sept. 19, 1813; Chauncey, bap. June 2, 1816; Huldah, bap.
May 4, 1817.

JAMES, m. Sally Butler, April 19, 1804.

P. 723, l. 8, for Nov. 13, read Nov. 17.

AMASA (E. W.), m. Ruth Warner, March 3, 1784.

BENJAMIN (perhaps Benjamin,[10] p. 722), had child, bap. Oct. 3, 1762; had
Abigail, d. March 2, 1773, a. about 18 mos.; Josiah, d. Oct. 8, 1776, a. about
2 yrs.

All the following from E. W. C. R.—JOSEPH (prob. the one ment. on l. 38,
p. 721), had children, bap. Nov. 29, 1796; Charles, Jan. 21, 1798.

JOHN (perhaps brother of above), had children, bap. May 19, 1785 Sept.
3, 1786; early in 1788; Oct. 25, 1789; Sophia, May 8, 1791; Sally, Aug. 4,
1793; Edward, Oct. 18, 1795; Emily on same day: ——, April 20, 1800;
Solomon, Jan. 3, 1802; Joseph Mosely, April 14, 1805.

AMASA (prob the one on l. 40, p. 721), had children bap. Feb. 6, 1785;
April 30, 1786; early part of 1788; Nov. 22, 1789; Ruth, Oct. 23, 1791;
Jan. 17, 1796; Sept. 1, 1799.

CHAUNCEY (bro. of above), had children, bap. Oct. 13, 1782; May 23,
1784; April 30, 1786; Dec. 16, 1787; Sept. 6, 1789; Sept. 11, 1791; April
31, 1793; Anna, Aug. 16, 1795; July 8, 1798. WILLIAM, had child, bap.
Oct. 29, 1809.

DYER (ment. on p. 721, l. 37), had Dyer, bap. March 16, 1794; Mary, May
21, 1797; ——, June 1, 1800; Seneca, April 3, 1803.

Mrs. MARY, d. July 29, 1689. (Col. Rec.)

We take pleasure in presenting our readers with the following letters of
Gen. ROGER NEWBERRY, addressed to Mrs. Eunice Ely of Springfield, who
afterwards became his second wife. The first, written to her upon her husband's death, and the second written years after, in the sweet confidence of
married life, give us a better view of his character, than pages of description
could do. They are copied *literatim et verbatim*, from the originals:

1.

To Mrs. Eunice Ely, Springfield :

Madam—I know not how to Content myself not to appear in the Ranks of yᵉ many hearty Mourners, whose Sympathy would fain Contribute some Releafe to yᵉ Uncommon weight of affliction that a Holy God has seen meet to bring upon you. I fear my trembling pen will too much Renew yᵉ Grief, which I know is very pressing. I am loath to Stir up the wound which so tenderly affects you—But would fain be Instrumental to administer some Consolation in this hour of yᵉ tryal.

I know when yᵉ tender Branch of yᵉ house was Crop't by Death (as a sweet flower in summer) it touched you in a very tender part—But it seems yᵉ God saw best to lay still a weightier stroak upon you—& the Desire of yᵉ Eyes Must fall a Victim to Relentless Death, tell me, Mad. Did not these lovely Injoyments take up too much room in yᵉ heart. Was n't you Ready to think yᵉ Mountain stood strong, and yᵗ you yᵉ self should Dye in yᵉ Rest, i. e, have a tranquil life or not meet with those providences that would Imbiter Life to you. I am persaded you Did n't think yᵉ portion lay on this side yᵉ grave. But it May be you expected an Easyer passage to it— Well, Remember this is ye Dissepline, that God saw bess to use with you for some holy Ends—Who will be with & support you in yᵉ furnice of yᵉ tryal, if you still make him yᵉ all—I know Nature Unassisted Cant subsist under such heavy stroaks—but Remember yᵉ promise, all things shall work for good to yᵐ yᵗ love God—this Carries yᵉ prospect Beyond time & all its flatering prospects & all its thretning aspects—You know a little time will sit you Beyond yᵉ Care of this transitory life, & it will Be no Grief to you when view'd in yᵉ peacefull harbour of Bliss & glory, to take a survey (from yᵉ hill of Sion) of yᵉ Stormy Ocean on which you have sailed to yᵉ Peacfull Reagon of Immortal Rest! this, Md. I Confidentially hope has terminated yᵉ ut- most Wishes, even in yᵉ Days off yᵉ Earthly tranquillity, & if this be yᵉ case, why yᵉ tresure is still secure. Tho' providence has Deprived you of some Desirable Injoyments in yᵉ passage there, I hope you will find yᵉ tender Consort and loveing ofspring in yᵉ Relms of paradise Consorting with angeli· Beings in hyms of Praise to him yᵗ sits upon the throne & to yᵉ lamb for ever & ever. Well, Md. if yᵉ God sees meet to Disapline you with yᵉ Rᴏ & by that means, together with other Dispinsations, to prepare you for . participation of heavenly Injoyments, let me intreat you to kiss yᵉ Court·· hand that Designs yᵉ Best good, & by these methods is preparing you for Joys Immortal, tho' Earthly Streams fail.—this is yᵉ Earnest Desire of yᵗ uɪ kuown Friend, who hath a tender Sympathy with you under yᵉ Burthen, & prays that all yᵉ Passages of Providence before you may more and more prepare you for   of yᵉ full Completion of yᵉ utmost Wishes in yᵉ Beatific Vision of yᵉ Great Redeemer, in yᵉ Inefable felicities of the heavenly Canaan—Adeau.

May 25, 1754.

II.

New Haven, Oct. 19, 1770.

My Dear—I rec'd yours and the things you sent by Doct'r Wolcott, and Sincerely rejoice to hear you and our little son are well. I hope shortly to Return home, not exceeding the time proposed, and Possibly sooner—I ever thought the man happy that Could be freed from every bodys Buisness but his own; to live with and enjoy his family, and every day experience shews me I have not been mistaken. Certainly a continual hurry of business must be Disagreeable to the Philosopher Mind—and such is my case—but such is the state of human affairs, especially in this part of the world, that but few if any can live without being Imployed in some sort of Buisness to gain a Subsistance—the manner of Life I have chosen Calls too much abroad but at this time of Life a Retreat is Dangerous. I am sure home is agreable. I sincerely wish to be there more than I am, partly on my own & partly on your account. You say you are alone: I am Sensible of it, and that your being alone must Cause you much trouble, but tho' I am absent, you have my best wishes, and I am not without hopes sometimes or another to be more at home and afford you more of my help than I have hitherto done but how that will be, God knows—Perry you say sends his Duty to his Daddy. I thank the Dear Boy that he does not forget me. He is the object of our Care and of our wishes, but poor boy he is born in a Dark Day when Vice Trumps Government Dealing, the Laws against Immorality lie unexecuted. Wickedness has many advocates, & Religiou but few, the Pure Doctrines of the Gospel are Perverted, every one (in this Dark State) attempting to assimilate us to God is call'd a Crime, and Vice the Road to Happiness—hence many fall a sacrifice, and everything dear to us in this Life is threatned, but my Dear there is one that Rules above in whom none ever trusted in Vain, let us make him our Confidence and Teach our Child the same—we have then Done our Duty, and will leave him in the hand of Providence—but our Task is arduous and Difficult—let us then begin early and bend his tender mind to Virtue, that the Road thereof may become habitual—This Task, my Dear, is Principally Devolved on you and may God give success—here may you see the greatest   for Honour although empty as a Bubble, it is courted as a Real substance—and everything sacrificed at its Shrine—but the more I am acquainted with its Votaries and Greatest favorites, the Less it appears and almost Shrivels into Nothing—it is, I confess, agreeable to Receive evidences of the friendship of our fellow men, but mere Titles are empty sounds, and does not alway Discover the Real worth of the wearer and what the Poet says is True

Titles are marke of Honour—and wise
The Fool or Knave that weare a Title lies.

But my Dear there is an end of Scribling and therefore shall end abruptly, and Subscribe myself,

Most affectionately Yours,

Roger Newberry.

P. S. I have no news to write except that America is acting a most Shameful Part & Giving all that is Dear. a General Importation has taken place in this Town and Buy and Sell Publickly with general approbation—Remember my Duty to my mother and Love to Perry and all Friends—I am in usual Health. R. N.

NEWELL, p. 724, add ABEL, d. April 29, 1759, a. about 25. (Wby. Ch. Rec.)

NILES, p. 725, l. 20, PAMELIA, m. Rev. Andrew Yates of East Hartford, June 11, 1810.

OLD, p. 728, l. 3, ROBERT and SUSANNAH, m. Dec. 31, 1669. (Col. Rec.)

OSBORN, p. 728, l. 14, for *May*, read *Jan.* (Col. Rec.)

P. 728, l. 15, for April 6, read April 16. (Col. Rec.)

P. 728, l. 17, ISAAC, d. Nov. 24. JOHN (the emigrant) also had a son John, b. April 23, 1654. (Col. Rec.)

P. 728, l. 19, strike out the words "or Aug." (Col. Rec.)

P. 728, l. 20, for *March* 2 and *Jan.* 2, read "*ye 2d week*," also in next line, for *Jan.*, read "*ye 1st week;*" Mary, was b. Jan. 26. (Col. Rec.)

P. 729, l. 1, MARY, wife of Samuel, d. Aug. 30. (Col. Rec.)

P. 729, l. 23, this MARTHA STILES, was dau. of John, son of John Stiles the 1st. Her dau. Martha, b. Jan. 8, 1738. Her son Abel, d. 1751, and Abel 2d, was b. in 1752. The foregoing corrections are on authority of Pres. Stiles' MSS., who says he had the record of the family from Mrs. Martha (Stiles) Osborn's own lips.

P. 730, l. 14, JACOB,[17] m. Sarah ——, and had Sophia, bap. Jan. 14, 1791 (N. S. R.); Emma, bap. Jan. 1, 1792 (N. S. R.); Celia, bap. 1794 (N. S. R.); Harriet, bap. Feb. 5, 1797 (W. C. R.); Ruth Bissell, bap. Oct. 27, 1799 (W. C. R.)

P. 730, l. 15, NEHEMIAH (E. W.) m. Amelia Phelps, Nov. 17, 1805 (Col. Rec.) ; SAMUEL, m. Rebecca Denslow (prob.), 1683. (Col. Rec.)

P. 730, l. 26, HENRY, m. Keziah Hayden, Nov. 14, 1814. (W. C. R.)

P. 735, for articles 31, 61, read articles 32, 61, etc.; JOHN R., m. Laura Bissell, Sept. 16, 1805.

Pp. 729, 730, the following from a letter by *D. W. Patterson, Esq.* of W. Winsted, Ct., explains itself :

"A bit of tradition often helps one to arrange records. I heard the following the other day : There were two *Samuel* Osborns in Windsor, father and son, who married daughters of Israel Phelps of Enfield. The father was 41 years old, when the son married the eldest sister, and twelve years after that the father married the younger Please see if that would not authorize a reconstruction of some part of your Osborn Record. I think you give Benjamin Osborn (page 729, l. 16) as marrying in 1725, a Mary Phelps, but his children were, several of them, born before that, while Samuel, in the next paragraph above, has no wife, but is evidently the man who *ought* to have had the Phelps wife."

OWEN, p. 731, l. 9, for April 9, read Aug. 29; the John on this line is prob. the same one who d. Jan. 13, 1670. (Col. Rec.)

P. 731, l. 11, BENJAMIN, d. May 26, 1665. Note to l. 14 is also confirmed by Col. Rec. This JOSIAS,[1] had also Isaac, b. June 4, 1678. The DANIEL on line 9, m. Mary Bissell, Jan. 24, 1681, and had Daniel, b. Nov. 25, 1862. Foregoing all from Col. Rec.

P. 732, NATHANIEL, Jr.,[10] is also credited in Wby. Ch. Rec. with "a twin child, bap. July 16, 1764."

PALMER, p. 733, l. 30, for April 16, read April 26.

P. 733, l. 33, TIMOTHY,[1] also had Timothy, b. Jan. 20, 1686. His son Benjamin, was b. 1681. (Col. Rec.)

P. 734, l. 20, "Ensign" JEHIEL, d. Sept. 13, 1777, in 54th yr. (N. S. R.) MARTIN, m. Nancy Chandler. May 17, 1801; MIRIAM, m. —— Osborn, Sept. 29, 1806; JOHN, m. Mindwell Griswold, Aug. 9, 1814. (W. C. R.)

P. 734, l. 14, SAMUEL[4] of Poq., had also Ozias, bap. Oct. 14, 1759; Dr. NEHEMIAH, m. wid. Elizabeth Latimer of Wethersfield, May 26, 1766; JONATHAN, m. A—— Griswold, Oct. 19, 1786. (Wby. Ch. Rec.) BENJAMIN, had Electa, bap. Aug. 5, 1787. JEHIEL, d. Jan. 25, 1806, a. 38; BETSY, d. Feb. 5, 1808, in 19. (Why. Ch. Rec) JONATHAN, d. Dec. 2, 1815, a. 43.

PARSONS, p. 735, l. 24, for Bethnia, read Bethia. (Col. Rec.)

P. 735, l. 26, for 1644, read 1653. (Col. Rec.)

P. 735, l. 31, for 1648, read 1668. Mary of W., m. Nicholas Evenes (?), Nov. 7, 1670. (Col. Rec.)

From Wby. Ch. Rec.—HEZEKIAH (l. 21, p. 736), had also Hannah, bap. May 27, 1739.

JOHN (prob. same ment on l. 20), m. Elizabeth ——, who d. March 6, 1758, a. about 40; had James, bap. Oct. 16, 1748 ; Elizabeth, bap. Aug. 19, 1750; Sile, bap. April 10, 1752 ; John, bap. Feb. 10, 1754, d. Oct. 20, 1758; Olive, bap. Oct. 12, d. Dec. 11, 1755 ; Oliver, bap. Nov. 28, 1756, d. Oct. 24, 1758 ; John, bap. April 13, 1760, d. May 14, 1764 ; Lucy, bap. Aug. 8, 1762; JAMES (prob. son of John above), m. Hannah Phelps, Jan. 25, 1770, and had Hannah, bap. Feb. 10, 1771, d. July 28, 1775 ; Mercy, bap. Oct. 25, 1772 ; James, bap. April 30, 1775; John, bap. Oct. 5, 1777; Gurdon, bap. Sept. 24, 1780; Oliver, bap. Aug. 7, 1783 ; CHATWELL, m Mabel Bidwell, April 4, 1771 ; HEZEKIAH, had Hezekiah (1st child), bap. June 19, 1757; Peletiah, bap. Sept. 20, 1758, d. Jan. 30, 1759; Martha, bap. Nov. 4, 1759 ; Peletiah, bap. Sept. 20, 1761 ; Anna, bap. May 13, 1764; Abigail, bap. Dec. 15, 1765; Hannah, bap. Feb. 6, 1769 ; Biah, bap. Sept. 18, 1774.

P. 736, l. 22, HEZEKIAH, Jr., m. Anna Webster, June 25, 1778, had infant d. March 11, 1779, a. 2 d.; Lizzie, bap. Feb. 27, 1780 ; Anna, bap. Aug. 25, 1782 ; Hezekiah, bap. March 20, 1784; William Webster, bap. Aug. 1787 ; Wealthy, bap. March 14, 1790 ; Daniel Latimer, bap. Aug. 12, 1792 ; Bishop Case, bap. July 5, 1795; Lamira, bap. Jan. 5, 1800.

Roxy and Triphena, bap. Jan. 4, 1789 ; Anne, bap. March 14, 1790.

PELETIAH (son. of Hezekiah), had Lovisa, bap. Sept. 16, 1792; Peletiah, bap. Nov. 2, 1793; Henry Wolcott, bap. Sept. 25, 1808 ; also Electa, Chandler, William Kelsey, Peletiah Lorenzo, bap. Sept. 24, 1815; Edward Rutherin, bap. Oct. 11, 1818.

THOMAS, had Thomas, bap. Sept. 16, 1759 ; Solomon, bap. Nov. 22, 1761.

DANIEL LATIMER (son of Hezekiah), had Susan Camilla, bap. May 28, 1815; Hezekiah Wheeler, bap. Aug. 21, 1816 ; Eunice Philena, bap. May 10, 1818; Wealthy Ann Amelia, bap. Oct. 1820; Anna Webster, bap. May 25, 1823 ; John Keep, bap. Oct. 23, 1825.

WILLIAM WEBSTER (son of Hezekiah), m. Eunice Phelps, Dec. 22, 1808 ; BISHOP C. (son of Hezekiah) of W., m. Sophia Griswold of Simsbury, April 30, 1817; he d. Sept. 26, 1829, a. 34; JONATBAN J., m. Mary C. Griswold of Simsbury, Dec. 1, 1825 ; Claudius Dwight, bap. June 3, 1827; THANKFUL, m. Dea. Isaac Buller of Harwinton, July 1, 1762 ; MARTHA, m. Caleb Talcott of Bolton, March 22, 1759; HANNAH, dau. of Ens. Hez., m. Zebulon Curtis of Torringford, Jan. 5, 1792 ; ABRAH, m. John Thorp, Feb. 16, 1796 ; ELIZA, m. Ralph Wells of Farmington, Oct. 23, 1800; WEALTHY ANN, m. Truman Curtis of New Hartford, May 1, 1807; LAMIRA, m. Dennis Smith of Sandisfield, Oct. 8, 1807.

HEZEKIAH, d. March 18, 1756, a. about 83 ; wid ABIGAIL, d. Oct. 25, 1764, a. about 80 ; JOHN, d. March 14, 1768, a. about 45; Ens. HEZEKIAH, d. March 4, 1802, a. 66 ; HEZEKIAH, Jr., d. Feb. 16, 1809, a. 24 ; Roxy, wife of Peletiah, d. May 7, 1811, a. 46; Capt. HEZEKIAH, d. May 22, 1825, a. 68.

PEASE, p. 737, ELIZABETH, m. Joseph Ritter of Hartford, Nov. 30, 1845. (W. C. R.)

PERRY, p. 737, Rev. JOSEPH, had also Frances, bap. March 18, 1764 ; ——, Oct. 5, 1766 ; ——, Sept. 18, 1768 ; ——, March 10, 1771 ; ——, Aug. 13, 1775 ; ——, May 25, 1777 ; ——, Aug. 21, 1778. (E. W. C. R.)

PETTIBONE, DANIEL, m. Margaret McClean of Berlin, Nov. 25, 1804. ROSANNA, m. Obadiah Gillet of Farmington, Nov. 24, 1800. (Wby. Ch. Rec.)

DANIEL, l. 5, p. 738, m. Sarah Brown, Feb. 15, 1770. JOSEPH's wife Lucy, d. Aug. 25, 1807, a. 44. SARAH, d. Feb. 12, 1808, a. about 57. ABEL, d. May, 1815. Mrs. ELIZABETH, d. Feb. 15, 1816, a. 86. Miss HANNAH, d. 1828, a. 78. ABIJAH, had Abijah, bap. April 28, 1771. (Wby. Ch. Rec)

PHELPS, p. 738, l. 8, GEORGE, had John, bap. Feb. 15, 1652 ; Nathaniel, b. Dec. 9, 1654. (Col. Rec.)

P. 738, l. 28, WILLIAM Phelps, Jr., *ought* to have been credited with the two barren wives (see lines 28-30) for which his brother *Nathaniel* could have had no possible use, inasmuch as he m. (see page 739, line 3) Elizabeth Copley, who was undoubtedly the mother of his children.

P. 739, l. 1, to " d. without issue " add April 30, 1679. (Col. Rec.)

P. 739, l. 14, *omit* the " and " before " removed." He moved to Hebron about 1690, and had Martha, Timothy, Cornelius, Charles[1] and Hannah.

14

CHARLES[1], b. at Hebron, July 4, 1701, m. Hepzibah Stiles, a cousin of Pres. Stiles, and had children, Amy, b. Nov. 11, 1726 ; Charles, b. Sept. 22, 1732; Zeruiah, b. April 3, 1729 ; Ashbel, b. April 28, 1743 ; James, b. May 29, 1745 ; Bethuel[2], b. April 25, 1744 ; d. at Warehouse Point, Conn., a. 85.

BETHUEL,[2] m. Caroline Lord of Marlbórough, Conn. Children : Lydia, m. —— Barber ; Epaphras Lord ; Charles Stiles,[3] b. March 12, 1789 ; m. 1, Flavia Burt of Long Meadow ; 2, Harriet S. Morgan of Westfield ; 3, Catherine Warner of Hartford, Conn.; 4, Elizabeth Sexton of New York, and now resides in Brooklyn, N. Y. Children by second wife : (Rev.) Charles Edward ; Harriet Flavia.

P. 739, l. 20, for 1688 read 1689; Sarah Pratt, same line, was of Hartford. (Col. Rec.)

P. 741, l. 9, JACOB, Jr., had Charity, bap. March 24, 1771; d. Aug. 18, 1771 ; Charity, bap. Sept. 19, 1773; Eveline, bap. Feb. 19, 1775 ; Barshe, bap. Aug. 17, 1777 ; Jacob, bap. Aug. 17, 1783 ; Jacob, bap. Aug. 13, 1786. (Wby. Ch. Rec.)

P. 741, l. 21, for *Livia,* read *Livia Drusilla.* (N. S. R.)

P. 741, l. 24, ELIJAH,[26] had also Caleb, bap. Oct. 6, 1782; Nathan, bap. May 9, 1790.

P. 741, l. 42, CHARLES, m. Hannah Cooke, May 12, 1748 ; who d. May 15, 1786. He d. May 21, 1803, in 95 yr. His son CHARLES, Jr., m. in Feb. 1776, according to Wby. Ch Rec. Same authority gives him following children : Anna, bap. April 13, 1777 ; Patty, bap. May 14, 1779 ; d. May 26, 1779.

P. 743, l. 11, for 1663, read 1665. (Col. Rec.)

P. 743, l. 20, for *Samuel* read *Sarah.* (Col. Rec.)

P. 744, l. 1, THOMAS,[10] had also Margaret, bap. July 29, 1744; Lois, bap. Jan. 11, 1747. (Wby. Ch. Rec.)

ROGER, Jr., m. Rhoda Barber, Oct. 31, 1803 ; ELEANOR, m. Ephraim A. Judson of Sandisfield, Mass., Feb. 1, 1803 ; HENRY, m. Rachel Jacobs, Dec. 12, 1819. (W. C. R.) DANIEL, m. Delia Drake, April 4, 1832. (W. C. R.) JONAH, m. Emily Allyn, Dec. 26, 1820 ; FLUVIA, m. Calvin Brewer of Walbraham, Mass., May 25, 1820. (W. C. R.) RHODA B., m. John W. Dunlap of South Hadley, Jan. 16, 1844. SAMUEL of Poquonnoc, was m. Aug. 28, 1712. (*Tim. Loomis'* MSS.) JAMES, m. Sabry or Sally Phelps, Jan 10, 1797. TIMOTHY, m. Ruth Wilson, Feb. 3, 1785. CANDACE, m. Henry Thompson of Enfield, June 10, 1829. (W. C. R.)

DANIEL (E. W.), p. 742, l. 3, had three children bap. Nov. 3, 1793. (E. W. C. R.) Evidently Daniel, Huldah, and who was the other b. before that date?

JOSEPH, had children bap. June 28, 1795; Nov. 19, 1797; Jan. 12, 1800; Isaac Newton, bap. April 25, 1802; Mary, bap. July 28, 1805; June 25, 1808 ; Oct. 11, 1811.

GEORGE, had Walter, bap. 1789 ; Samuel, bap. Oct. 9, 1791; Rhoda, bap.

Oct. 6, 1793 ; Epaphras, bap. Jan. 20, 1793 ; Anna Theresa, bap. April 6, 1805 (all from W. C. R.).

From Col. Rec.—JOSEPH, m. Mary Porter, June 26, 1673. ISAAC, son of Isaac, b. Sept. 10, 1666. WILLIAM, d. Feb. 17, 1681. SAMUEL (probably son of Samuel,[1] page 738), m. ABIAH (poss. it is meant as Alice), dau. of John Williams, June 21, 1678. Mrs. ANN, d. Aug. 30, 1689. MARY, wife of Jose, d. Jan. 16, 1682. WILLIAM, son of Joseph, d. Oct. 8, 1689. DANIEL, son of Joseph, d. Jan. 4, 1690. ABRAHAM, son of Abraham, b. March 6, 1665-6.

From Wby. Ch. Rec.—NOADIAH, m. Naomi Case, Feb. 24, 1743, had Shubael, bap. Dec. 11, 1743 ; Noadiah, bap. Jan. 26, 1746.

AARON (probably the son of Aaron,[3] page 743), had Aaron, bap. March 14, 1762; Polly, bap. Aug. 12, 1764 ; Daniel, bap. March 2, 1766 ; Nathan, bap. May 8, 1768 ; Israel, bap. July 18, 1773 ; Elihu, bap. Sept. 24, 1775.

CORNELIUS, Jr., had Azuba, bap. Dec. 4, 1768 ; Cornelius, bap. Sept. 9, 1771 ; d. Sept. 20, 1771.

OLIVER, m. Eunice ——, who d. Feb. 5, 1809, a. 47, had Eunice and Oliver, bap. Sept. 21, 1788 ; Chester, bap. Oct. 1790 ; Lucy, bap. Sept. 1, 1793.

BISHOP, m. Amy King, Oct. 12, 1815 ; had Emily, bap. March 9, 1817 ; Eunice Mariette, bap. June 27, 1819 ; George Bishop,'bap. June 10, 1821.

WILLIAM, m. Martha Holcomb of Poquonnoc, Jan. 4, 1740. DAMARIS of Poquonnoc, m. William Moore of Turkey Hills, Jan. 20, 1740. LUCY, m. Aaron Barnard of Simsbury, June 27, 1770. ISAAC, perhaps son of Cornelius,[12] page 740, m. Martha Mills, Sept. 5, 1745.

JOAB, m. Keziah Burr, Oct. 14, 1792, had Kezia, who d. Feb. 12, 1796, a. 27. OLIVER, Jr., m. Nabby Brown, April 27, 1809.

AARON (probably the one who d. 1802, a. 60), had ‚Susannah, bap. Aug. 6, 1780.

CORNELIUS (probably the one who d. Jan. ·5, 1804, a. 59), had ——, bap. August, 1780.

ISAAC, had Theodosia, bap. May 7, 1738 ; Lucy, bap. Dec. 9, 1739.

SAMUEL, had Tryphena, bap. May 7, 1738.

JOSIAH of Poq., had Bildad, bap. Dec. 9, 1739.

ISAAC, 3d of Poq., had Phares, bap. Sept. 29, 1765.

ELIHU, d. April 9, 1804, a. 28. LUCY, d. Feb. 2, 1809, a. 16. ABNER, d. Aug. 9, 1813. TIHZAH, d. Jan. 3, 1814, a. 30. NOADIAH, d. and buried at Hartford, Oct. 15, 1746. NATHAN, d. Nov. 30, 1798, in 31 yr., by fall of a tree.

" April 16, 1762, died SHUBAEL PHELPS, in ye 19th year of his age. (*Eodem die*), Eunice, Daugr. to Nathll. Burr, in ye 13th year of her age. N. B.— These two persons were burnt in Mr. Joshua Case's House, and out of its ruins Part of yr Bodies were taken w[ith]out any Limbs, and buried in one Grave."

JACOB, d. Feb. 5, 1815. CHARLES' wife, d. March 8, 1826. ZELOTAS' child, d. June 30, 1815, a. 1.

PHILLIPS, p. 745, l. 6, add George Phillips (possibly and probably *Phelps*), m. Anna Fitch, May 23, 1784. SARAH, d. May 14, 1662. (Col. Rec.)

PICKET, p. 745, insert, PHINEAS, had Saxton and Henry, bap. Dec. 1786; also Fanny, bap. May 7, 1797; Julia King, bap. Nov. 3, 1799; Eliza, bap. July 5, 1801; Mary Ann, bap. Aug. 8, 1807. (W. C. R.) SAXTON, m. Betsy Roberts, June 6, 1808. CONTENT, m. Barzilla Hudson of Torringford, Jan. 26, 1803. NANCY, m. Roger More, May 26, 1803.

PIERCE, p. 745, NATHANIEL, m. Zeruiah Holcomb, July 24, 1804. (W. C. R.), SAMUEL'S sons, Samuel and Ebenezer, d. Nov. 3, 1754; Lois, bap. Sept. 22, 1755; Susannah, bap. Aug. 28, 1757; Rhoda, bap. Nov. 4, 1759; Samuel, d. Sept. 16, 1768; and Ruth, twins, bap. May 23, 1762; Samuel and Ebenezer (twins), bap. July 30, 1769; d. Jan. 8, 1772; Lieut. Samuel, d. Oct. 1, 1776, a. about 48. (Wby. Ch. Rec.) OLIVE, m. Simeon Judd of Hartford, June 3, 1776.

PINNEY, p. 745, HUMPHREY, the emigrant. In the possession of Miss Lucretia Stiles of Windsor, Conn., are several ancient papers, consisting of letters addressed to Humphrey Pinney by his nephew.John House of Montague, in England; also letters from George Betty of Combe St. Nicholas, Somersetshire, England, relative to certain business which he had entrusted to Mr. Pinne; also concerning Pinne's property in England; and his will, which is dated June 3, 1682. In one of these letters from John House, dated March 1, 1668, is the following postscript: "My uncle William Pinny [see *Windsor Hist.* p. 74, line 13] hath buried his wife, she d. about a quarter of a year since."

The lease, which was executed Feb. 20, 1658, "between Humphrey Pinney now dwelling in Montague, of the one part, and Roger Dunster of Broadway, in the county of Somerset, of the other pte," &c., relates to "four acres of pasture & meadows" lying and being "in the manor of Iilton."

P. 747, l. 21, for 1728, read 1723.

P. 747, l. 39, Capt. ABRAHAM,[12] his son Jonathan bap. March 19, 1738. (Wby. Ch. Rec.)

P. 748, l. 36, Lieut. ABRAHAM,[18] b. Dec. 23, 1735, o. s.; m. his first wife June 9, 1761; d. Dec. 12, 1813. In reference to his children, we give the following extract from a letter of Mr. D. W. Patterson of W. Winsted. "They say up in Colebrook that Stiles' *Windsor*, p. 748, transposes the names of Israel,[34] and Asaph Pinney,[35] they are *sure* that Asaph was the eldest, and give the date of birth (as see below) which they say is recorded in his Bible, in his *own fist-i-graph*. Israel,[34] d. Aug. 30, 1821, a. 52, which you see harmonizes with the above supposition."

P. 749, l. 8, the date of 2d m. of JONATHAN,[19] should be Dec. 29.

P. 748, l. 40, and p. 750, l. 28, GROVE[32] (b. according to family records Oct. 15, 1762), m. Mercy Case of Simsbury, April 25, 1785, settled in Colebrook, and removed about 1838 to Crawford county, Pa., where he d. in fall of 1850; she d. April, 1854. Children: Clarissa, b. Feb. 18, 1786, m. 1,

Joel Miller of Winsted, Conn.; 2, Ethan Pendleton of South Norfolk; Mercy, b. Dec. 9, 1789 ; m. Earl Bancroft, settled in Penn.; Grove, b. June 30, 1792, moved to Ohio, has family ; Friend,[1] b. March 16, 1796 ; Henry,[2] b. Deo. 1799 ; Flora, b. Aug. 20, 1804; m. Fred. Pendleton of Norfolk, and went to Penn., and d. Sept., 1843 ; Damon,[3] b. Feb. 11, 1807; Adeline, b. Feb. 20, 1810 ; m. Albert Beach of Goshen, and d. November, 1853.

FRIEND,[1] m. Clarissa Miner, and d. in Ohio. Children: Allen, Henry, Orville, Minerva.

HENRY,[2] m. Delina Riggs of Norfolk, went to Penn., and then to Texas. Children: Elbirt (M. D.), b. 1825 ; Adeline b. 1828; m. Isaac Cummings.

DAMON,[3] m. 1, Sally Pendleton of Norfolk, Jan. 12, 1830 , went to Penn., m. 2d, Mary Griswold, April, 1851. Children by 1st wife : Michael S.,[4] b. Nov. 14, 1831 ; Hobart Buell, b. Oct. 20, 1833 ; m. Elizabeth Turner ; Nary Esther, b. Oct. 8, 1836 ; m. James Swift; Sarah ·Adell, b. Aug. 28, 1839 ; Orville F., b. Nov. 12, 1841; Elbert Grove, b. Sept. 7, 1846. Children by 2d wife : Chester, b. July 17, 1853 ; Hattie, b. Dec. 19, 1857.

MICHAEL S.,[4] m. Esther Swift. Children : Ida, Sarah, Isaiah.

P. 748, l. 41, and p. 750, l. 30, ABRAHAM,[33] m. Mehitable Case of Simsbury, settled in Colebrook, removed to New Canaan, Columbia county, N. Y. Children : Mehitable, b. March, 1790; m. Anson Hunt of New Canaan, N. Y.; Ovid, b. Jan. 1792; m. Jane Taylor; Hilpa, b. Jan. 1794; m. Edward Rowlandson of Barry, Orleans county, N. Y.; Lucretia, b. March, 1796 ; m. Oliver D. Buel of Canaan ; Polly, b. Nov. 1797, unm.; Abraham, b. Jan. 18, 1804 ; d. 1825.

P. 748, l. 1, and p. 750, l. 32, ISRAEL,[34] m. Belinda Loomis of Simsbury, settled, lived and d. in Colebrook. Children : Israel,[1] b. Oct. 13, 1788 ; Linda, b. Oct. 10, 1790 ; m. Chester Treat of Hartland, settled in Ohio ; Menda, b. March 4, 1793; m. Luman Cowles of Colebrook, went to Lee, Mass., d.; Nathaniel,[2] b. July 30, 1795 ; Reuben,[3] b. April 18, 1798 ; Jasper,[4] b. Sept. 2, 1801 ; Elihu,[5] b. Sept. 21, 1804 ; Carlos,[6] b. Sept. 16, 1808.

ISRAEL[1] m. Eleanor May of N. Carolina, had Alexander, Philander, Belinda, Ellen, Martha, Winford.

NATHANIEL,[2] m. Rebecca Underwood, who was b. Feb. 21, 1796; he d. March 29, 1854 ; she d Aug. 27, 1861. Children : (1,) Rebecca Jane, b. Sept. 28, 1819 ; m. Abiram E. Cook and has one child, Ella Jane, b. Feb. 21, 1861. (2,) Orator, b. Sept. 5, 1823 ; m. —— Brown and has a dau. Mary Louisa, b. March, 1860. (3,) Warren Alonzo, b. Sept. 15, 1825 ; m. May 21, 1849, Abigail Belinda Deming, b. Oct. 25, 1827, dau. of George Gilbert and Belinda (Moore) Deming, has one dau. Georgia Etta, b. Nov. 14, 1856. (4,) Burral "Van Wike " (? Van Wyck), b. Jan 16, 1829 ; m. Augusta Cobb, has a son William Clifford, b. Sept. 30, 1858. (5,) Susan Eliza, b. May 15, 1831 ; d. Jan. 30, 1835.

REUBEN,[3] m. Nancy Moore (b. March 3, 1798) of Barkhamsted. Children : (1,) Jeanette, b. Feb. 15, 1822 ; m. Charles M. Coe, b. Feb. 7, 1821, and has 3

children, viz : Charles P., b. June 2, 1849 ; Adelaide F., b. Oct. 23, 1855 ; Leon
A., b. April 29, 1858. (2,) Martha, b. Dec. 20, 1830 ; m. William H. Ward, b.
Dec. 29, 1831, has one child, Abbie, b. Aug. 12, 1853.

JASPER,[4] m. Maria Fellows of Canaan, has one child, Laura.

ELIHU,[5] m. Eliza Preston, settled in Clarenden, O., has children : Edwin,
Phebe, another son.

CARLOS,[6] m. Elizabeth Sturges of Hitchcockville, settled in Lee, has children : Caroline, Mary, Charles, Alice.

P. 748, l. 41, and p. 750, l. 34, ASAPH,[35] m. Betty Wilcox (b. Sept. 9,
1777); he d. in Colebrook, April 4, 1835 ; she d. June 3, 1847.   Child :
ELIZA, b. Oct. 1, 1798; m. Dorrance Barber of Colebrook, and after his d.
m. Harvey Wakefield.   Child by 1st husband : Eugene Luman, b. Dec. 26,
1820 ; d. Oct. 17, 1843, leaving one son Eugene Luman ; Cero Fayette, b.
April 19, 1822, lives in Spencer, Tioga county, N. Y., which county he represented in New York Legislature in 1861.   EMMA, b. Feb. 17, 1800; m.
Ralzemon (son of John) Phelps of Winchester.   Children : Emeret E. (dau.),
b. Aug. 19, 1830 ; d. Jan. 6, 1842 ; John Pinney, b. Dec. 24, 1834 ; m. Nancy
Gorman of Hamden and has dau. Cora, b. Dec. 21, 1857.   ASAPH ORVILLE,
b. March 9, 1805; m. May 17, 1840, to Elizabeth (dau. of Luther and Maria
Hoskins) Phelps, b. in Colebrook, March. 6, 1817.   ☞ To this gentleman
we are largely indebted for the full accounts of the families of the sons and
descendants of Lieut. Abraham[18]. ⚫ HARVEY WILCOX, b. Dec. 16, 1811;
m. Harriet Wakefield.   Children : Victor Hugo, b. July 27, 1851 ; d. Feb.
12, 1854 ; Lucien Vernet, b. May 9, 1853.

P. 748, last l. The descendants of ELISHA and ELIJAH (twin sons of Lieut.
Abraham[18]), who were b. Oct. 12, 1775, are, as given in the following records,
furnished by A. O. Pinney.

ELIJAH, m. Mahala Grant, Oct. 9, 1806; he d. Aug. 24, 1855.   Children :
Ann, b. Sept. 25, 1807 ; m. Ralzemon Phelps, April 22, 1829 ; Roswell Grant,[1]
b. March 30, 1809 ; Elijah Orson,[2] b. March 2, 1813 ; Horace L.,[3] b. April
14, 1815 ; Milo E.,[4] b. April 12, 1821.

ROSWELL G.,[1] m. Abby L. Strong, Sept. 3, 1835.   Children : George R., bap ·
July 13, 1836 ; m. Sarah Davidson, April 29, 1858 ; Emily J., b. Oct. 17,
1839 ; Lafayette, b. March 14, 1842 ; d. March 23, 1844 ; Louisa Jane, b. Aug.
26, 1844 ; Elijah E. and Elizur E., twins, b. July 7, 1847 ; Elijah E., d. Sept.
11, 1852; Harriet R., b. Oct. 4, 1856.

ELIJAH O.,[2] b. March 2, 1813 ; m. Mary Pendleton, Jan. 10, 1837.   Children : Ethan, b. Dec. 28, 1837 ; Finett, b. May 15, 1839; Sarah, b. Nov. 7,
1840; Uranah, b. Aug. 31, 1842 ; d. Sept. 19, 1853 ; Laroy, b. April 6, 1844;
d. April 16, 1859 ; Charles, b. Sept. 13, 1846; Dothy, b. Dec. 9, 1849 ; Emeline, b. Oct. 7, 1851 ; Ralzemon P., b. June 10, 1854 ; Ward, b. Aug. 19,
1857.

HORACE L.,[3] m. Wid. Sarah Shannon, Dec. 5, 1842.   Children : Ellen, b.
Sept. 3, 1843 ; d. Oct. 4, 1851 ; Anthony and Elijah (twins), b. March 23,

1845 ; Alexander, b. May 21, 1848 ; Rosanna, b. Aug. 17, 1851 ; Catharine, b. May 1, 1853.

MILO E.,[4] m. Harriet Skinner, Dec. 1849, moved to Memphis, Scotland county, Mo. Children: Emma, b. Dec. 1851; William B., b. March 20, 1857 ; Edward Milo, b. July, 1859.

ELISHA (twin brother of Elijah, and son of Lieut. Abraham[18]), m. Rachel Belden, Jan. 1803; d. Dec. 1, 1847. Children: Orpha, b. Oct. 4, 1804 ; m. Luman Andrus, Jan. 1821; Harriet, b. Sept. 22, 1806; d. Oct. 25, 1828; Alta, b. Sept. 1808 ; d. April, 1812; Elvira, b. Aug. 4, 1810; m. Thos. Dunn, Sept. 19, 1837 ; Melissa, b. April 10, 1813; m. Reuben Standcliff, Jan. 13, 1852 ; Martin,[1] b. Aug. 12, 1815 ; Elizabeth, b. Aug. 31, 1820; m. William Torrey, Oct. 6, 1846; Mary, b. Jan. 17, 1823; m. Cyrus Crouch, Feb. 12, 1848 ; Elisha,[2] b. Feb. 14, 1827, and lives in Penn.

MARTIN,[1] m. 1, Louisa Mix, April 6, 1847; she d. July 18, 1848 ; he m. 2, Adeline Standcliff, Dec. 24, 1843. Children by 2d wife: Ovid, b. Nov. 18, 1849 ; Louise, b. July, 1851; Eugene, b. April, 1854 : Amelia, b. August, 1857.

ELISHA,[2] m. Mary Thompson, Sept. 4, 1854. Children : Alice, b. Aug. 14, 1855 ; Lamberteen, b. June 20, 1857; Frank, b. June 26, 1859.

P. 749, l. 2, ELIHU (son of Lieut. Abraham[18]), m. Margaret Langford of Maryland, and had one son, *John Book*,[1] b. in Baltimore, Dec. 25, 1806.

JOHN BOOK,[1]* m. Ellen Agnes Seward of Guilford, Conn. (b. in Savannah, Ga., March 13, 1816), on Sept. 13, 1836. Children : Sarah Agnes, b. in Pittsburg, Pa., Oct. 23, 1838 ; John Patterson, b. Philadelphia, Jan. 15, 1841 ; d. June, 1843 ; Alice Langford, b. in Philadelphia, May 2, 1843 ; d. Oct., 1843.

---

* REV. JOHN BOOK PINNEY, after the death of his grandfather (Lieut. Abraham,18) lived among his uncles in Colebrook and Canaan, from the spring of 1814 until that of 1817, when being 10 years old, he was placed by his father, at school in the Academy at Windsor, Ct., where, to use his own words, "for nearly nine years I was allowed, under the unwatchful, not to say unfaithful care of my guardian, to waste my time among a constantly changing set of incompetent teachers." When nearly 19 years of age he went to Lexington, Ga., where much against his inclination, he was placed at a private school, and during the next season entered the junior class of the Georgia University at Athens, from which he graduated in 1825. While in college, young Pinney became a subject of an extensive revival of religion which occurred among the students, and became a member of the Presbyterian Church Having studied law considerably while in his senior year at college, under the direction of Jos. H. Lumpkin, Esq., then a leading lawyer, and now Chief Justice of the state of Georgia, he was in that year admitted to the bar under William H. Crawford, Esq., formerly Secretary, then judge of the Supreme Court of Georgia. He however soon quit the law, in order to prepare for the ministry, and by teaching school for a year at Walterboro, S. C., he procured the means necessary for the prosecution of a three years' course of theological study, and in the fall of 1829 entered the Theological Institution at Princeton, N. J., where he graduated in 1825. While there, he decided to become a missionary among the great Negro nations of Borneo and Hausa in the interior of Africa. In the fall of that year he was ordained, together with a companion, the Rev. Joseph W. Barr of Ohio, and started on their intended work. Mr. Barr, however, while they were awaiting the departure of the vessel which was to convey them, was suddenly cut off by an attack of Asiatic cholera, and Mr. Pinney proceeded alone. The hardships and fatigues, however, of a journey from the coast of Africa to the interior

Wm. Seward Pierson, b. at Windsor, Conn., Aug. 4, 1846; Annie Foster, b. at Washington, Pa., April 14, 1848; Robert McKennan, b. in New York city, April 2, 1850, d. Feb. 18, 1852; Ella Reed, b. in New York city, July 10, 1852; Fanny Loomis Prime, b. Dec. 25, 1853; Benj. Coates, b. May 6, 1856; Maud Fay, b. Jan. 29, 1858, d. Sept. 13, 1859.

P. 749, l. 4, HORACE (son of Lieut. Abraham[18]), went to Virginia, about 1810, where he m. Nancy Snavely, Oct. 31, 1811, and soon after emigrated to Jackson co., Ohio, where he lived until 1837, when he removed to Laporte co., Ind., where he d. April 25, 1839. His wife d. Jan. 4, 1841, a. 52. Children (still living in Indiana): (1.) David, b. Nov. 9, 1812, lived in Pine Grove, Gallia co., Ohio, and has two children, Aurora and Abraham; (2.) Horace[1], b. Sept. 17, 1817; (3.) William[2], b. July 28, 1819; (4.) Mary, b Nov. 27, 1821, m. Phineas Small (b. Nov. 9, 1805), June 25, 1840, had Lois Cyrena, b. Aug. 23, 1841, m. Sept. 13, 1859, to Elijah Reynolds; Nancy Jane, b. Feb. 6, 1844, m. Emry Jener, Jan. 1, 1862; Eunice Loquincey, b. Aug. 31, 1846; Orlando V., b. May 14, 1849; Riley Francesco, b. March 23, 1852; Harrison, b. Sept. 11, 1854, and a twin with Henderson Thornburgh; Phineas Orange, b. May 25, 1858; (5.) Harvey, b. April 12, 1825, d. Oct. 25, 1834; (6.) Lois, b. June 24, 1827, m. Jacob Thornburgh, Dec. 5, 1848, had Dameris Cyrena, b. Aug. 3, 1850; William Elvin, b. April 10, 1853; (7.) Hester.

HORACE[1], m. May 4, 1843, Angeline C. Haskell (b. Feb. 4, 1827). Children : Jay, b. Jan. 2, 1847; Jane, b. April 20, 1850; Janurah, b. Sept. 4, 1852; Kay, b. Nov. 16, 1854; Elb, b. May 6, 1856; Erastus, b. Feb. 3, 1861.

WILLIAM[2], m. Cynthia Long (b. Sept. 20, 1822), Dec. 23, 1841. Children : Elizabeth Nancy, b. Oct. 6, 1842; Harvey Wright, b. July 15, 1844; James Andrew, b. June 27, 1846, d. July 14, 1846; William Eslis, b. Nov. 10, 1847;

---

so completely broke down his health, as to compel his temporary return to this country in 1833. In the fall of that year, he again set out, with nine missionary companions, and landed at Monrovia on the 1st of January, 1834. Just as Mr. P. was leaving the United States, he had been persuaded to become (temporarily) the agent of the American Colonization Society, which constituted him ex-officio, acting governor of the Colony of Liberia. At the same time the early death of certain missionaries so discouraged the American Board of Foreign Missions, that they consented to the proposition of the American Colonization Society to have him commissioned as governor of the colony, and to suspend their mission awhile. Coincident with the above named commission, Mr. P. received another from the United States government as agent for recaptured Africans. His views, however, were not in accordance with those of the two boards, and though by circumstances obliged to retain the authority conferred upon him until he could be relieved by a successor, Mr. Ploney at once refused to accept the appointment permanently.

Finally, the heavy cares and anxieties incident to such duties, together with repeated attacks of African fever, so undermined his health, as to necessitate his return to the United States in the fall of 1835.

Since that time, with the exception of a little over a year, during which he was the settled pastor of the Presbyterian Church at Washington, Pa., Mr. Pinney has been chiefly engaged as Corresponding Secretary of the Pennsylvania and New York Colonization Societies; meantime, however visiting Liberia in 1840, and again in 1855, on special duties. In 1852, Mr. P. was appointed Consul General for the Republic of Liberia, for the United States, a well merited compliment.

Perry Guilford, b. Feb. 3, 1850; Hermau Franklin, b. March 26, 1852; Lois Charlotte, b. Sept. 1, 1854 ; Elvin Clinton, b. July 17, 1860.

P. 752, l. 6, for *Amelia*, read *Aurelia*.

P. 752, l. 35, for Elizabeth *Melonia*, read Elizabeth *Victoria*.

MARTIN (can this be Martin[51] ?), had Mary, bap. Jan. 13, 1799. (W. C. R.) DAVID, m. Anna Sill of W., Sept. 12, 1822. (W. C. R.) ELIHU, s. of Jonathan, bap. March 5, 1769. (N. S. R.) Elihu and Oliver of Jonathan and Mary, bap. Oct. 6, 1773, (N. S. R.) SARAH, dau. of Noah and Elizabeth, bap. Nov. 15, 1761. (N. S. R.) DANIEL, s. of Noah and Abigail, bap. June 15, 1766. (N. S. R.) NOAH (perhaps the above), d. "of mortification," Aug. 30, 1776. (N. S. R.) FANNY, bap. June 5, 1796. (W. C. R.)

POMEROY, p. 753, l. 5, ELTWED's wife, d. July 5, 1655; Eltwed (prob. the same), m. wid. Lydia Parsons, Nov. 30, 1664 ; his s. Caleb, m. Hep. Baker, March 8, 1664, and had dau. Hepzibah, b. July 27, 1666, *before* he went to Northampton ; Mary, d. April 21. (Col. Rec.)

POND, p. 753, l. 11, SAMUEL, d. March 14, 1654; his wid. Sarah, m. 2, John Linslee of Toket, July 9, 1655; Samuel's son Nathaniel, was b. Dec. 1651, and Sarah, b. Feb. 11, 1662.

P. 753, l. 13, ISAAC,[1] m. May 10. (Col. Rec.)

PORTER, p. 753, l. 33, SAMUEL, was b. in 1664-65 ; and REBECCA, b. 1666-7. (Col. Rec.)

P. 754, l. 4, for *Sept.*, read *Dec.* (Col. Rec.)

P. 754, l. 31, " Cousin MINDWELL PORTER, wid°. went to 'hampton [probably Northampton], with Lt. Joseph King, in order for marriage, Aug. 22, 1733." (Timo. Loomis' MSS.)

HEZEKIAH (Hez.[11] or Hez.[16] ?), had Ruma, b. 1751, m. —— Baker ; also, Israel, b. 1746, m. Happy Sadd. (E. W. Bap. Rec.) If these are children of Hez[.11], the *dates* are evidently incorrect.

P. 756, l. 24, for Capt. *John*, read Capt. *Jonathan.*

P. 756, 2d l. from bottom, strike out *Sally.*

The following from E. W. C. R. HEZEKIAH (is this Hez.[16] p. 755, l. 11?), had children bap. Feb. 12, 1764; Oct. 5, 1766 ; May 2, 1773; March 5, 1775; March 4, 1787; July 18, 1790.

WARHAM[17] (p. 755, l. 12), had child, bap. Jan. 2, 1791 ; Frederick, bap. Sept. 30, 1804; Elijah, bap. Feb. 3, 1793; Elizabeth, bap. Feb. 1797 ; ——, Aug. 25, 1799; ——, May 30, 1802; Warham, Jr., bap. June 7, 1807 ; Mary, bap. July 2, 1809.

NATHANIEL, Jr., had children bap. Oct. 3, 1771; Jan. 16, 1774 ; May 4, 1777; Aug. 22, 1779 ; Aug. 11, 1782; April 3, 1785; Edward, Oct. 7, 1792.

JOHN, had children bap. Nov. 15, 1767; Jan. 7, 1770; Feb. 28, 1773; Feb. 3, 1782; Oct. 12, 1788.

SARAH, had Arethusa, bap. Feb. 22, 1795 ; Huldah, bap. Oct. 29, 1797. LUCINA had child, bap. Sept. 11, 1785.

15

SAMUEL, had children, bap. Feb. 18, 1781; June 1, 1783; JOSEPH, had children, bap. Aug. 31, 1800; July 11, 1802.

From Wby. Ch. Rec.—ANNE, m. Wm. Wallis, Nov. 10, 1738; MARY, m. Thomas Cadwell, Jr., of W. Hartford, Dec. 28, 1752.

Capt. JOSEPH, d. March 24, 1759, a. about 60; his wife d. May 27, 1757.

POWELL, p. 757, last l., Col. Rec. give the name of Thomas' wife as "*Allse* (Alice ?) *Traharne*," (possibly an *Indian* girl). Their son Thomas was b. July 11 —; his son Hannibal, b. Oct. 3, 1682, and d. Jan. 15, 1684; John, d. Jan. 17, 1685. (Col. Rec.)

PRATT, p. 758, insert, Timothy had children, bap. Oct. 11, 1776; Jan. 3, 1779; Aug. 12, 1781; May 23, 1784.

PRIOR, p. 758, l. 5, 4th *Col. Rec.* contain the record of m. (no date given) of Humphrey and Mary Whitcomb. Prob. (from context) in 1686. His first wife Ann, d. Sept. 29, 1682.

P. 758, l. 9, concerning this DANIEL,[2] Mr. Edwin Stearns of Middletown, Conn., sends the following from M. records: "Daniel Prior, formerly of Windsor, m. Sarah (dau. of Samuel) Egglestone, 1697. Children: Thankful, b. Jan. 21, 1698 ; Daniel, b. Nov. 5, 1699, d. June 9, 1710; Daniel,[2] b. April 8, 1701; Susannah, b. March 5, 1702; Mary, b. July 13, 1705 ; Ebenezer, b. Sept. 23, 1707; Mrs. Sarah Prior, d. April 6, 1768; Daniel Prior, m. 2d, Mary, wid. of John Lucas, by whom he had Experience, b. April 16, 1710.

ABNER (see line 20 ?), had Sarah, bap. July 1, 1781.

PURKINS, p. 758, insert JOHN, had child, bap. Feb. 15, 1767.

RANDALL, p. 760, l. 21, ELIZABETH, the 2d wife of Abraham, was the wid. of John Kirby of Middletown, Conn., who had d. 1677. She m. Randall, April 22, 1684. (Ed. Stearns.) He d. Aug. 21, 1690. (Col. Rec.)

Col. Rec. give Phillup, d. May 6, 1662, and "Old Wid." d. Aug. 24, 1665.

REED, p. 759, l. 6, for *Porter of Windsor,* read *Dr. Porter of East Windsor.*

P. 759, l. 11, for 1804, read 1824.

P. 759, l. 12, LUCY WELLS, b. 1804, m. R. Hazlett in 1820.

P. 759, l. 21, CELINA (according to Rev. Julius Reed of Davenport, Iowa), was *living* in 1860-1. If so, the *date* of death belongs to some other Celina, that's sure. E. W. C. R. make her bap. April 14, 1799.

P. 759, l. 22, EMILY, was bap. June 27, 1818. (E. W. C. R.)

P. 759, l. 23, ELIJAH F.[4], M. D., commenced practice in that part of Bolton now Vernon, April 16, 1789. His wife was b. there.

P. 759, l. 27, HARRIET S. REED, who m. John Hall, had also Robert b. 1831, and Harriet, both now dead.

P. 759, l. 29, Rosanna, b. 1810, d. May 20.

ISAAC (prob. same as on p. 760, l. 14), had by his wife Dinah, a son Elijah, bap. May 20, 1764, and Martin, bap. Dec. 7, 1766. The foregoing are from N. S. R.

Isaac of North Windsor, had Elijah, bap. May 1764. (Wby. Ch. Rec.)

RICE, p. 760, insert, Aaron, m. Lucy Burnham, Aug. 7, 1788.

RICHARDS, p. 760, Hezekiar had Hezekiah, bap. Nov. 14, 1756. (Wby. Ch. Rec.)

RILEY, p. 760, Eunice, dau. of Nathaniel, bap. Jan. 30, 1785.

RISING, p. 760, l. 40, James was voted an inhabitant of W., March 11, 1668 (Town Rec.); m. Martha Bartlett, wid., Aug. 13, 1673, prob. the one who d. (see Hist.), April 20 (not 2), 1674. His first wife d. Aug. 11, 1669. (Col. Rec.)

ROBERTS, p. 761, l. 38 [?], Henry, had son Henry, bap. 1786, also Mary, bap. Sept. 4, 1788, and Barzilla, bap. Sept. 19, 1790. (W. C. R.)

James, p. 761, l. 43, m. Lauranna Loomis, June 2, 1783, and had Betsy, bap. Nov. 21, 1784.

Joel, had child, bap. Jan. 31, 1762. (E. W. C. R.)

Elihu, p. 761, l. 44, m.,Deborah Munsell, Feb. 2, 1801. Roxanna, m. —— Taylor, Jan. 2, 1806. Ruhama, m. Timothy J. Dawson of N. Haven, 1814. Lauranna, m. Jabez Gillet of Torrington, Jan. 11, 1798.

Sally, p. 761, l. 43, m. Daniel Talcott, Jr., May 17, 1798.

From Wby. Ch. Rec.—P. 761, l. 2, Samuel, was bap. June 4; Ruth, bap. March 27, 1768; Hannah, bap. May 20, 1770; Samuel,[2] bap. May 3; Eunice and Lois, bap. Oct. 2, 1774; Hezekiah, bap. June 5, 1776; d. same day; Hezekiah, bap. Aug. 26, 1781.

Lemuel, had Lemuel, bap. Oct. 17, 1742; Nathaniel, bap. March 24, 1745; Margaret, bap. May 28, 1749; d. Jan. 8, 1752.

Nathaniel, had Rhoda, bap. Dec. 14, 1766; Nathaniel, bap. Feb. 6, 1769: Lydia, bap. April 28, 1771; Orpha, bap. Aug. 22, 1773; Electa, bap. Feb. 4, 1776; Esther, bap. April 11, 1779; Erastus, bap. Aug. 26, 1781.

Erastus (son of Nathaniel above), m. Lois ——, who d. Oct. 24, 1804, a. 22; had Erastus Seymour (off. by Sam. Colton), bap. June 23, 1805.

Paul had Paul, bap. Nov. 24, 1776; Mindwell, bap. Aug. 2, 1778; John (of Windsor), had Ann, bap. Feb. 4, 1750.

Oliver, m. Anna Bunce, April 15, 1792.

Eunice, m. Jas. Goodwin of Hartford, March 3, 1799.

Esther, m. Joseph Goodwin, Jr., March 23, 1806.

Chester, m. Harriet Wilson, Oct. 12, 1806.

About 1751, Richard, d. a. about 60, and, about 8 yrs. before, his father Richard, d. Lieut. Lemuel, d. September 10, 1772, a. about 70; John, d. March 11, 1773; Abigail, d. Sept. 30, 1773, in 41 yr.; Wid. Deborah, d. March, 1777, about 88; the wid. d. May 8, 1786, in 74th yr.; Nathaniel, d. July 31, 1800, a. 54; Hiram, d. April 27, 1810, a. 16; Nathaniel, d. Nov. 19, 1813, a. 34; Rhoda, d. April 15, 1815, a. 67; Lemuel, d. July 28, 1828; Lemuel, d. July 1, 1829, a. 63.

ROBESON, p. 762, insert, ELIZER (prob. Elizur), had Faith, bap. Sept. 16, 1764. (E. W. C. R.)

ROCKWELL, p. 762. In the 2d Book of Records of Court and Probate of the Connecticut Colony, recently discovered, we find (page 162) the will of JOHN ROCKWELL of Windsor, who must have been the father of Simon Rockwell, who, with his sisters Mary (Watson) and —— Sanford, are mentioned on page 762, lines 19, 21. This will of John Rockwell, dated April 4, 1661, constitutes his son Simon, as his executor, and to have the estate after his mother's death. The house, land, one cow, etc., are devised to his wife. Simon was to have a cow, and himself and sisters Mary, Hannah (wife of Zachary Sanford, mentioned above), were to have one pound each, and their children one pound apiece. The value of the estate was £244.05. He d. May 10, 1662.

Wilmet (Wilmoth, Wilmarth) Rockwell, wid. of the above John, executed a will on the 12th of May, 1662, wherein she gives " to my daughter Mary, one Bed, that which Simon lies on, with two Blankets, two sheets, one pillow " and, "to my daughter Hannah, one little Bed, which my husband died on, with two blankets, two sheets, one pillow," and " all my wearing clothes to my two daughters to be equally divided to them. And all ye rest of my estate I give to my son Simon." She d. May 12, 1662.

Query. Who can inform us of the origin of this family ?

P. 762, l. 19, SIMON, d. June 22, 1665. He and his sisters, as will be seen from the foregoing paragraphs, were children of John and Wilmet.

P. 762, l. 26, DELIVERANCE, wid. of John,[1] afterwards m. Robert Warranar of Middletown, Feb. 2, 1674.

P. 762, l. 30, for Nov. 27, read Nov. 23.

P. 762, l. 35, Abigail, b. 1664, prob. d. May 3, 1665. (Col. Rec.)

P. 762, l. 32, this ELIZABETH m. Lieut. James Ward of Middletown, Conn., Feb. 1, 1694. With her brother Joseph[3], owned the cov. and was admitted to Midd. Ch. Oct. 28, 1694, having both been bap. in Windsor, where their father was in full communion. She d. July 28, 1721; Lieut. James Ward, d. Jan. 4, 1712. Children: Elizabeth, b. Nov. 11, 1694; Mary b. April 9, 1697; James b. March 6, 1700; Samuel, b. March 25, 1703; Sarah, b. Sept. 12, 1705; John b. Sept. 6, 1708. (Communicated by Mr. Edwin Stearns, of Middletown, Conn.)

P. 762, l. 31, strike out the index figure [3] attached to Joseph's name.

P. 762, l. 37, strike out this and next line, being family given to Joseph,[3] but belongs to Joseph,[5] as see below.

P. 762, l. 36, JOSEPH[5], b. in Windsor, May 22, 1670 (this varies as will be seen, from the date in the Windsor Hist., p. 762, l. 31, see also note above), admitted to Middletown 1st Church, Oct. 28, 1694, m. Elizabeth (dau. of Edward) Foster of M., Feb. 1, 1694, was chosen deacon May 31, 1704 ; was captain of a company, and was town clerk from 1708 to 1734, and his son William after him, from 1735 to 1765, and was also deacon after his father's death. Deacon Joseph, d. Oct. 28, 1742, in 75th yr. ; his wife d. Aug. 15, 1753, a. 80 (having been b. May 7, 1673). Children : John, b. Oct. 29, 1694 ; Joseph, b. Oct. 24, 1697 ; Edward and Elizabeth, twins, b. Oct. 10, 1700, both d. March, 1701 ; William, b. July 3, 1702 ; Hannah, b. Dec. 18, 1704 ; Edward, 2d, b. July 23, 1707 ; Ebenezer, b. March, 9, 1711. (Communicated by Edwin Stearns, Middletown, Ct.)

P. 764, l. 19, after *Rockwells*, insert *in Colebrook, Ct.*

P. 764, line 12, Isaac [16] had also a child bap. Nov. 1, 1767.

Furnished by A. O. Pinney.—P. 766, l. 7, Ephraim[23], had, in addition to Sarah, mentioned in the text, Allen[1], b. June 10, 1776 ; Hannah,* b. Sept. 19, 1778, m. David Wadsworth ; Ephraim, Jr. b. Feb. 19, 1781, left home in early life, not since heard from—a silversmith by trade ; Abner C.[2] b. May 4, 1783 ; Eleazer,[3] * b. Nov. 10, 1785 ; Zerah,[4]*, b. March 6, 1787 ; Sally, † b. Jan. 3, 1791, m. Jacob Bowman ; Bernard,[5] *, b. March 30, 1793.

Allen,[1] m. Phebe Davis, and he d. Jan. 25, 1851. He was one of the first settlers of Bradford county, Pa. Children : Allyn, Jr., b. Feb. 22, 1800, m. Cath. Cole, Oct. 23, 1821 ; Polly, b. Aug. 31, 1801, m. David Cole, d. May 23, 1838 ; Nancy, b. March 2, 1804, m. Nathan Bullock, d. Sept. 4, 1846 ; Levi, b. Jan. 11, 1806, m. Lois Davidson ; Oliver, b. Feb. 4, 1807, m. Nancy Smith ; Betsy, b. July 4, 1812, m. Henry Stone, May 20, 1830 ; Hiram, b. Jan. 4, 1814, m. Deborah Greene, Oct. 11, 1837 ; John, b. March 11, 1817, m. Susannah Greene, April 15th, 1841 ; William A., b. Jan. 9, 1820, m. Rachel Craton, Oct. 20, 1844.

Abner C.,[2] m. Betsy Fowler, Dec. 20, 1808, and he d. July 29, 1836. He was one of the first settlers of, and the first sheriff of Bradford county, Pa. Children : Donna M., b. Sept. 29, 1809, m. J. D. Montanye ; Zerab,[6] b. Nov. 17, 1811 ; James L.,[7] Feb. 15, 1814 ; Hannah M., b. Aug. 10, 1816, d. March 21, 1824 ; Mary C., b. Nov. 15, 1818, d. Feb. 12, 1825 ; William A., b. Sept. 10, 1821, d. March 22, 1824 ; William A., 2d, b. July 18, 1824, m. Mary Nichols ; Roland R., b. June 15, 1828, m. Sarah Wilson, July 2, 1851.

Eleazer,[3] m. Kezia Spring, June 11, 1806. Children : Ephraim F.,[8] b. March 4, 1808 ; Lodoiska S., b. April 28, 1810, m. J. W. McFaddan, Oct. 20, 1825 ; Calvin D., b. June 12, 1812, m. Rebecca Blystone, Sept. 6, 1832 ; Clarissa F., b. June 24, 1814, m. Jacob Blystone, Jan. 31, 1833 ; Darius N., b. June 29, 1816, m. Eunice Herrick, Jan. 18, 1838 ; Hannah M., b. Jan. 10, 1818, m. Albert E. Kingsley, Oct. 11, 1842 ; Orville A., b. July 25, 1820, m. Mary Baldwin, Oct. 13, 1842 ; Sally R., b. Nov. 16, 1825, m. George Wilson, May 23, 1844 ; Pamelia M., b. July 5, 1831, m. David Stoke, June 31, 1849.

Zerah,[4] m. Phebe Carter, Feb. 25, 1812, and he d. Feb. 1, 1859. Children : William S.,[8] b. Jan. 6, 1813 ; Louisa M., b. Oct. 17, 1814, m. John O. Hodges ; Laura A., b. Jan. 13, 1817, d. Feb. 11, 1852 ; Abner C., b. May 10, 1819, m. Sarah Grear ; Horace N., b. April 10, 1821, m. Harriet Parker ;

---

* These children were all among the first settlers of Crawford county, Pa.

† A first settler of Bradford county, Pa.

EPHRAIM S.,[10] b. July 13, 1823; Harriet P., b. Dec. 31, 1825, m. Alvah Benjamin ; Phebe L., b. June 19, 1828, m. Henry C. Long.

BERNARD,[5] m. Rebecca Marcy, Feb. 3, 1819. Children: Addison O.,[11] b. Dec. 16, 1819 ; Sally A., b. Dec. 5, 1821, m. Nathan L. Snow, Oct. 9, 1845; Emeline M., b. Nov. 26, 1826; Emily M., b. April 13, 1824, d. July 27, 1825; Eunice L., b. Dec. 10, 1829, m. Justin E. Snow, May 22, 1850, d. Feb. 2, 1855 ; E. Fidelia, b. Oct. 7, 1832, m. S. B. Root, Oct. 10, 1855.

ZERAH,[6] m. Mary A. Hart, and he d. March 19, 1857. Children: Elma S., b. April 28, 1836, d. July 13, 1838; Clarence B., b. Jan. 19, 1840, d. April 7, 1841 ; Maylon L., b. Jan. 29, 1843, d. July 30, 1850; Abner Clayton, b. Nov. 27, 1845 ; Helen E., b. Oct. 24, 1847 ; Mary M., b. Feb. 24, 1849.

JAMES L.,[7] m. Cordelia Lyon, Sept. 15, 1845. Children: Abner L., b. April 21, 1853 ; Mary J., b. April 25, 1855 ; Frank M., b. July 24, 1859 ; John L., b. July 28, 1861.

EPHRAIM,[8] m. Rhoda Washburn, Dec. 23, 1830. Children: Anon B., Sally M., Fanny, Sylvester, Sophia.

WILLIAM S.,[9] m. Elinor A. Snow. Children: Annor A., James William, Jesse Z., Elma A.

EPHRAIM S.,[10] m. Mary E. Dodge. Children: William DeForest, b. July 8, 1850, d. Sept. 12, 1852; Frank DeElmer, b. Sept. 10, 1853.

ADDISON O.,[11] m. Martha L. Root, Oct. 8, 1845. Children: Wilbur Furness, b. April 25, 1848, d. Sept. 19, 1852; La Rue Du Retz, b. Aug. 9, 1849.

The following from E. W. C. R.—ABNER (prob. son of Deacon Daniel,[14] see line 7, page 764), had children bap. Aug. 11, 1771 ; Aug. 8, 1773.

AMASA, had children bap. Dec. 30, 1792; Jan. 17, 1796.

DANIEL (prob. Daniel,[22]), had " a little boy " bap. July 29, 1770 ; Aug. 29, 1773 ; May 28, 1775 ; April, 1777; Feb. 18, 1781 ; Aug. 11, 1782; Dec. 9, 1787; Jan. 11, 1789.

DANIEL, Jr., had children bap. D——, Aug. 4, 1793 ; Jo——, Feb. 4, 1798; B——, June 19, 1803.

ISAAC,[21] had a child, bap. Aug. 23, 1772.

P. 766, l. 9, CHARLES.[24] Emily and Maria, were bap. Oct. 23, 1796; Abigail, bap. July 31, 1799; W. Hayden, bap. April 6, 1800 ; Mary (on records " Mariam " prob. Mary Ann), bap. April 25, 1773 ; Julia, bap. Feb. 24, 1805; Naomi, bap. April 12, 1807 ; Helen, bap. April 7, 1811.

WILLIAM, had William, bap. Feb. 20, 1763; Nov. 3, 1765; child, bap. March 6, 1768; Sept. 15, 1771; June 20, 1774 ; May 25, 1777.

SILVANUS (son of John[6]), had child bap. Dec. 5, 1776.

JOAB, had dau. bap. Jan. 20, 1799 ; ——, Oct. 12, 1800.

RUSSELL (son of Samuel, see line 14, page 766), had children bap. Jan. 30, 1819 ; July 23, 1820 ; Oct. 8, 1826.

EBENEZER [19] (line 1, page 765) had also James Barber, bap. June 26, 1763.

NATHANIEL, Jr., had four children bap. Oct. 31, 1816, and one July 29, 1821.

GEORGE'S wife had children bap. Aug. 31, 1817; June 6, 1819; July 15, 1821.

ISAAC[16] (page 764), had a child bap. Nov. 1, 1767.

DAVID'S wife was bap. Nov. 9, 1788; had two children bap. Nov. 16, 1788; Jan. 3, 1790; David, April 20, 1794.

SAMUEL,[18] had Solomon, bap. Oct. 31, 1762, prob. d. soon, as he had another Solomon, bap. Jan. 22, 1764, the one whose biography is given on page 765.

DANIEL, had Jane Allison, bap. Nov. 14, 1813; Henry, bap. June 2, 1816. (W. C. R.)

Wid. ANNA, d. Jan. 31, 1792. (Wby. Ch. Rec.)

SIMEON, m. Olive Cook, Sept. 28, 1797. Children : Anna, bap. Oct. 14, 1798; Harriet, bap. Feb. 1, 1801. (W. C. R.)

ELIJAH of E. W., m. Nancy Green, Oct. 3, 1832. (W. C. R.)

OWEN, m. Ann Frances, April 28, 1827. (W. C. R.)

ELIZABETH, m. Thomas D. Elliot, Nov. 30, 1843. (W. C. R.)

P. 767, l. 14, for 43, read 53.

P. 767, l. 34, for 1744 read 1744-45.

DAVID (of E. W.), m. Lucy Wilson of Simsbury, Oct. 10, 1808. (Wby. Ch. Rec.)

• *From Wby. Ch. Rec.*—ROWELL, JOHN had Roger, bap. Aug. 26, 1750; JOHN, Jr. had Mary, bap. Nov. 2, 1760; Martin Steele, bap. Aug. 2, 1772; • Simeon, bap. July 16, 1780.

• DANIEL, m. Phebe Spencer of Suffield, Jan. 23, 1775; had Justice, bap. June 30, 1776; Chloe, bap. Oct. 18, 1778; Susannah and Eunice, bap. Oct. 17, 1784.

• ROGER, m. Anne Bunce of New Haven, May 31, 1778.

P. 768, l. 1, SAMUEL, had also Elizabeth, bap. April 3, 1748. (Wby. Ch. Rec.)

P. 768, l. 4, For *Hayes* read *Hayse* (prob. Hays). (Wby. Ch. Rec.)

P. 768, l. 9, Samuel, Jr. m. Catharine Fyler, June 9, 1771; had Sabra, bap. Aug. 25, 1782, and Amelia, bap. Aug. 29, 1784. (Wby. Ch. Rec.)

Wid. MARY, d. June 12, 1739, a. about 90. THOMAS, Jr. (prob. the one ment., line 29 and 30, page 767), d. Oct. 28, 1741, a. about 70; his wid. VIOLET, d. April 1, 1751, a. 70. HANNAH, d. Sept. 23, 1801, a. 78. Wid. MARY, d. Sept. 7, 1806, a. 81. PHILANDER, Jr.'s wife, d. Sept. 16, 1814. Wid. ELIZABETH, d. Sept. 26, 1814, a. 89. Wid. MARY, d. June 12, 1738, a. about 80. GRACE, d. May 18, 1765, a. about 73. WILLIAM, son of Samuel, d. Oct. 28, 1772, a. about 13 mos. DANIEL, son of Daniel, Jr., d. Aug. 23, 1777, a. 6 mos. STEPHEN, d. April 30, 1778, a. about 23. JOB's dau. Naomi, d. Feb. 21, 1794, a. 2¾ yrs. DANIEL, d. March 18, 1798, a. 81.

P. 768, l. 10, THOMAS, had Justin, bap. June 17, 1792; THOMAS (prob. same as foregoing) and Mary, had Thomas, bap. Feb. 11, 1781; Roxanna, bap. May 25, 1783; Horace, bap. Aug. 13, 1786; Allyn, bap. July 10, 1790 ; Polly, bap. Aug. 23, 1795.   (All these from W. C. R.)

P. 778, l. 34, JOHN, b. Feb. 20, 1744-5.   (Wby. Ch. Rec.)

JOHN, Jr.'s wife Roxanna, bap. 1790; Nathaniel Steel, bap. Sept. 7, 1783; Henry Allyn and Timothy were bap. July 25, 1790; Polly, bap. Nov. 18, 1792.   (All from W. C. R.)

JOHN, had Jehiel, bap. July 14, 1799.   (W. C. R.)

JUSTUS, m. Almira Riley, Jan. 6, 1817.   (W. C. R.)

MARTIN, m. Ruth Barber, Nov. 23, 1780.

JAMES, m. Catherine Morgan, March 3, 1836.   (W. C. R.)

ROWLAND, p. 768, l. 20, Rev. HENRY A. m. Elizabeth Newberry, March 25, 1795; ABRAHAM, m. Deborah Gillet, June 1, 1803 ; had Wiliam Frederick, bap. Nov. 3, 1806.   (W. C. R.)   ABIGAIL, m. George Bliss of Springfield, Nov. 15, 1804.

ROWLEY, p. 768, l. 28, THOMAS, m. Mary Denslow, May 5, 1669. His child d. May 22, 1676. He also had Abigail, b. Feb. 10, 1686.   (Col Rec.)

P. 768, l. —, ELIZABETH of Windsor, m. William Lucas, Jr., of Middletown, Conn., July 15, 1695 ; was admitted to Mid. Ch. in 1696, her mother being a member of the Church in Windsor. She had children : Elizabeth, b. August, 1698 ; Martha, b. March, 1699 ; William, b. March 14, 1701; Deborah, b. Nov. 1702; Gideon, b. May 31, 1705 ; Ebenezer, b. May 8, 1707; Samuel, b. Sept. 6, 1709; Anna, bap. May 3, 1712.   (Furnished by Edwin Stearns, Middletown, Conn.)

From Wby. Ch. Rec.—THOMAS, m. Mary Hale of Salmon Brook, Nov. 4, 1779 ; SILAS, had Nabby, bap. Jan. 20, 1814. Job, had Job, Ruth, Bildad, Loomis, bap. July 20, 1800. BILDAN, m. Clarissa Shepard, Sept. 17, 1818. The wife of ROGER, d. May 2, 1821, a. 69; Roger, d. Feb. 11, 1822, a. 73.

ROGER'S wife d. June 24, 1800, a. 52. EUNICE, wid. Daniel, d. Sept. 1, 1800, a. 84. NABBY KING (dau. of Silas), d. Jan. 24, 1804, a. 6. JOB's child, d. Feb. 5, 1809, a. 7. SAMUEL, d. Dec. 6, 1811, a. 101. JOB, d. Feb. 24, 1823, a. 71.

ROGER, Jr. m. Rebecca Lattimer, Nov. 8, 1801.

LEVI, m. Abigail Center of Hartford, Jan. 19, 1804.

MARY and Pamela, bap. Oct. 6, 1808.

THEODORE, m. Hannah Loomis, Nov. 29, 1810.

RUSSELL, p. 769, l. 1, ELLIS, seems to have again been m. to Katharine ——, and their son Walcott was bap. Aug. 17, 1766.   (N. S. R.)

P. 769, l. 4, WILLIAM had, besides William, b. 1767; the following by "his wife Mary :" Theodore, bap. Nov. 19, 1775 ; Mary, bap. Aug. 2, 1777; Joseph Hunt, bap. Aug. 17, 1783.   (All from N. S. R.)

P. 769, l. 6, Rev. WILLIAM, of this gentleman and his family little information remains in Windsor. He d. just as the Revolution commenced, and in the distractions and turmoils of war, almost all traces seems to have disappeared. For the following items concerning him and his descendants, we are indebted to the courtesy of Edwin Stearns of Middletown, Conn., who is engaged upon a history of the Russell family, or the descendants of William Russell of New Haven.

" Rev. WILLIAM, son of Rev. William* and Mary of Middletown, Conn., b. July 23, 1725; grad. at Yale, 1745; member of 1st Church in Middletown June 5, 1749; tutor at Yale, 1749-50; was called to Windsor 1st Church in February, 1751; ord. July 24, 1754; was twice m.: 1, to Abigail Andrew a gr. dau. of Rev. Samuel Andrew of Milford, Conn., about 1754, she d. about 1762; 2, Jan. 18, 1770, to Abigail Newberry of Windsor. Rev. William d. April 19, 1775 (the day on which the battle of Lexington occurred) in 50th yr. and the 24th of his ministry. Children by 1st wife—William Andrew, b. about 1755; grad. Yale, 1774; d. 1786, unm.; Samuel Andrew; Abigail, d. in inf.; Abigail, 2d, m. John N. (son of Nathaniel and Elizabeth) Mather of Windsor (he was b. Oct. 8, 1750; was an officer in Continental army; d. at Kingston, N. Y., during the war). Only child by 2d m—James, d. in inf.

JACOB and Hester (or Esther ?) had Elijah and Hester bap. Nov. 27, 1774; Jerusha, bap. Aug. 4, 1776; Return, bap. May 5, 1778; Elisha, bap. January 1780; Samuel, bap. Dec. 13, 1782; Jerusha, bap. April 13, 1785; Content, bap. Jan. 24, 1787; Hosea, bap. June 3, 1792. All these from N. S. R.

SAMUEL (probably son of Jacob and Hester above), m. Hepzibah Ellsworth, Feb. 28, 1805.

ELISHA (probably son of Jacob and Hester above), m. Lydia Ellsworth, June 2, 1803.

SAMUEL, d. February, 1778; William, d. June 18, 1780.

SADD, p. 769, THOMAS, Jr., also had children bap. June 20, 1774; Oct. 12, 1776; Sept. 11, 1785.

P. 769, l. 20, SIBEL (dau. of Matthew), was bap. Dec. 4, 1763. MATTHEW also had child bap. April 21, 1766.

JOHN, had children bap. Jan. 29, 1764; March 9, 1766; May 8, 1768; June 17, 1770; June 13, 1773.

NOAH, had Lucina, bap. June 27, 1802; Joseph, bap. Feb. 12, 1804; ——, Oct. 12, 1823.

WAITSTILL, had Polly bap. May, 20, 1792. (All foregoing from E. W. C. R.)

SANDERS, p. 770, l. 8, for 1691, read 1690. (Col. Rec.)

SAXTON, p. 770, l. 13, RICHARD and his wife must exchange dates of death. (Col. Rec.)

THOMAS, l. 21, had also Allyn, bap. Oct. 28, 1764. (E. W. C. R.)

SAYER, p. 771, insert, Wid PHEBE, d. May 21, 1753. (R. MSS.)

SEDGWICK, ABRAHAM, had Jonathan who d. being scalded in a milk bowl, with water, May 27, 1748; a. about 27; Thankful, bap. March 29, 1748;

---

* Ancestry of Rev. William of Windsor: 1, William, b. in England, 1612, emigrated to New Haven, 1639; 2, Rev. Noadiah, b. at N. H., 1659, settled in Middletown; 3, Rev. William, b. at Middletown, 1690, successor to his father; 4, Rev. William of Windsor.

16

Ebenezer, bap. April 1, 1750 ; Abi, bap. June 7, 1752 ; Wealthyann, bap. Jan. 17, 1754 ; Linda (d. few hrs.) and Lina (twins), bap. April 7, 1757; Abraham, bap. April 29, 1759.

SEGAR, p. 770, insert, from *Wby. Ch. Rec.*, DARIUS, m. Eunice Drake, Nov. 12, 1772 ; had Darius, bap. Aug. 5, 1773; Elijah, bap. Nov. 8, 1778 ; Hezekiah, bap. May 14, 1780.

JOSEPH, whose wife d. Feb. 19, 1743, a. 73, had Zuba, bap. Nov. 9, 1740 ; d. Feb. 4, 1756; Abigail, bap. July 15, 1744; Elijah, bap. Nov. 8, 1747; d. September, 1750 ; Darius, bap. Sept. 29, 1751.

MICAH, had Micah, bap. June 9, 1765; Mary, bap. Oct. 19, 1766; Amos, bap. Aug. 28, 1768; Anne, bap. July 15, 1770 ; Russell, bap. Dec. 6, 1772 ; Rachel, bap. Oct. 17 (Oct. 23), 1775 ; Daniel, bap. Sept. 7, 1777 ; Levi, bap. Aug. 6, 1780 ; Joseph, d. March 9, 1794, a. 88.

SEWARD, CHARLES, had Charles bap. Feb. 16, 1777 ; Nabbe, bap. March 1, 1778. (Wby. Ch. Rec.)

SHEFFELAND, ELLAS, had dau. Delana, bap. July 22, 1764. (N. S. R.)

SHADDOCK, p. 770, last line, ELIAS, m. Hanna (dau. of John) Osborn, and was buried at W., May 26, 1676. (Col. Rec.)

SHARE (?) p. 770, insert JOHN, d. Sept. 29, 1669. (Col. Rec.)

SHELDING, p. 771, REMEMBRANCE, and Mary (probably this is a second wife of Remembrance, Jr., line 12), had a dau. bap. June 2, 1765 ; Elisha, bap. Nov. 1, 1767. (N. S. R.)

SELAH, m. Amy Drake, Jan. 24, 1782; SARAH, m. Aaron Fish, Feb. 21, 1806.

SHEPPARD, WILLIAM, had William, bap. Oct. 8, 1758.

AMOS, had Jonathan, bap. April 5, 1761; Jesse, bap. March 18, 1764 ; Luther, bap. April 23, 1769.

THOMAS, had Levi, bap. May 2, 1779 ; Aurelia, bap. Oct. 25, 1788.

THOMAS, Jr.'s son d. April 17, 1793, a. 2; his wife d. June 29, 1800, a. 35 ; his youngest child d. October, 1809; Mary, d. July 7, 1810 ; his child, d. Jan. 11, 1809, a. 4; his wife (2d one prob.) d. Jan. 11, 1809, a. 45; all of spotted fever ; another son, d. Feb. 20, 1809.

THOMAS, d. May 26 or 27, 1775, aged about 88. AARON, son of Thomas, d. August, 1775, a. about 18 mos. MARY, wife of Thomas, d. Sept. 20, 1775, a. about 43 ; their child d. June 11, 1786. THOMAS's wife d. Nov. 27, 1822. THOMAS, d. May 22, 1819, a. 90.

SHERMAN, p. 771, insert, NATHANIEL, had child bap. March 18, 1781. (E. W. C. R.)

SIKES, p. 771, insert, WALTER, had child bap. March 25, 1792; Morella, March 13, 1796; ——, May 17, 1795.

SILL, p. 772, RICHARD, had William ; Richard ; Jennet ; Thomas; Hale; Roderic; bap. Oct. 19, 1788. (N. S. R.)

HORACE, son of Elihu, bap. Aug. 13, 1797. (W. C. R.)

P. 772, l. 10, insert " a dau. by wife Mary " before Enoch, bap. Dec. 1779 ; also " Filley " after Joseph. (N. S. R.)

P. 773, l. 3, for 1741 read 1841.

SKINNER, p. 774, l. 1, Isaac, Jr. m. Dorcas Drake, Oct. 8, 1744; their son Hezekiah, d. May 7, 1761. Daniel of E. W. m. Clarinda Barber, June 5, 1799.

The following from E. W. C. R.—Abiram, had children bap. May 25, 1777; Sept. 19, 1778; Aug. 6, 1780; Feb. 24, 1782.

Benjamin (prob. Benj. on line 26, page 774), had Benjamin, bap. March 14, 1762; child bap. Sept. 1, 1765.

Benjamin, had children bap. Feb. 6, 1785; Sept. 3, 1787; Oct. 26, 1788; Norman, Oct. 17, 1790; Seth, Jan. 27, 1793; ——, April 12, 1755; Ti—, April 22, 1798; Wil—, Aug. 1, 1802.

Timothy (line 3, page 774), had also a child bap. June—October, 1777.

Levi (prob. one on line 14, page 774), had children bap. Jan. 3, 1802; Sept. 21, 1800; May 13, 1804; Levi, Sept. 17, 1809; ——, July 14, 1816.

Oliver, Jr.'s wife and child were bap. Nov. 19, 1797.

Daniel, Jr. (line 39, page 774), had children bap. May 20, 1766; Oct. 1, 1769; Oct. 5, 1777.

Giles, and his wife Sarah, had Nathan, bap. Aug. 2, 1795; Si—, July 10, 1796.

Oliver, had child bap. Jan. 4, 1767; Oct. 4, 1772.

Oliver, had child bap. March, 1771; ——, Oct. 4, 1772; William, bap. Feb. 19, 1764; Lizzie, bap. Aug. 21, 1774. (Wby. Ch. Rec.)

From Wby. Ch. Rec.—Isaac, had Anne, bap. Nov. 12; 1738; Isaac, Jr., had Elizabeth, Armin, Skinner and Orson, bap. Nov. 5, 1788; Lucy, d. Feb. 23, 1740, a. about 18 yrs. Ambrose and Kate, bap. Sept. 23, 1792; Isaac, bap. Oct 16, 1796; Ambrose, bap. Oct. 21, 1798; Abby, bap. June 7, 1802; Warren, bap. Oct. 7, 1804.

Deborah (line 39?), Uby, d. Sept. 13, 1750; the wife of Timothy, d. Jan. 31, 1754. (R. MSS.)

Isaac, d. June 13, 1799, a. 82 yrs. Chester, son of Isaac, d. Oct. 2, 1805, a. 12. Orson, d. Nov. 15, 1805, a. about 18. Kezia's child, d. Sept. 23, 1744, a. but a few hours. Deborah, d. Sept. 14, 1750, a. about 18. Sgt. Isaac, d. Oct. 31, 1762, a. about 71. Lizzie, of Lucy, d. Oct. 7, 1776, a. about 2. Wid. Hannah, d. Oct. 17, 1793, in 97. Isaac, d. Oct. 3, 1816, a. 70.

SMITH, p. 775, l. 28, David's dau. Mary, was b. 1756.

"Lt." Samuel, Jr., had children bap. June 10, 1771; Feb. 16, 1772; Anne, April 25, 1773 ——, May 14, 1775.

Samuel (prob. same as line 22, page 775), had Abigail, bap. March 19, 1763; ——, Nov. 23, 1766. (E. W. C. R.)

SNOW, Widow, had four children bap. Sept. 3, 1775. (E. W. C. R.)

SOPER, p. 776, Maria Antoinette, m. S. J. McKinney, Dec. 26, 1836.

From Wby. Ch. Rec.—John, m. Rosanna Blancher of W. Hartford, Jan. 8, 1766.

Levi, m. Hannah Mills, April 14, 1768, had Levi, bap. Jan. 22, 1769;

Hezekiah, bap. Dec. 2, 1770; Allin, bap. Oct. 18, 1772; Roger, bap. Dec. 25, 1774.

PHEBE, m. Roice Beech of Goshen, June 9, 1756.

JOHN (line 11, page 776), d. at Simsbury, Nov. 22, 1749, a. perhaps 41; his wife Phebe, d. May 21, 1753, a. about 42. Wid. SOPER, d. September, 1760, and was buried at Kensington, a. about 84.

STARTWEATHER (Starkweather), p. 776, insert THOMAS, had children bap. Jan. 24, 1773; July 23, 1775; June 22, 1777; Aug. 12, 1781; Aug. 16, 1784. (E. W. C. R.)

STILES, a new and enlarged edition of the *Stiles Family Genealogy* is in preparation.

P. 783, the pastor of Ellington Church is Rev. Thomas K. Fessenden.

STOCKING, p. 807, insert SAMUEL, had Elizabeth, bap. Aug. 11, 1793. (E. W. C. R.)

STOUGHTON, p. 807, l. 12, THOMAS, m. Mary Wadsworth, Nov. 30, 1655. (Col. Rec.)

P. 808, ELISHA (prob. the one whose death is given in line 41), and Anna, had Israel, bap. Jan 22, 1775. ELISHA (prob. the same), had Ruth, bap. Nov. 28, 1784; Harry, bap. June 11, 1786.

SARAH, d. and buried May 3, 1652. (Col. Rec.)

ELIJAH, had Dolly, bap. Dec. 24, 1786; ELIJAH and Mary, had Olive, Patty, Elijah and Clarissa, bap. Sept. 23, 1787. (W. C. R.) ERWIN T. (or J.) of E. W., m. Julia Green, Sept. 5, 1809. (W. C. R.) RUTH, m. James Phelps of Westfield, Nov. 8, 1804.

JOHN, had children bap. March 23, 1766; March 24, 1771; Oct. 23, 1779; July 1, 1781. JOHN, Jr., had child bap. April 23, 1769. EPHRAIM, had children bap. May 7, 1775; March 30, 1777. SILENCE, had child bap. Jan. 11, 1789. ALEXANDER, had children bap. Dec. 3, 1775; May 14, 1780.

SAMUEL, d. April 24, 1806, a. 70. SAMUEL'S inf. child d. April 18, 1792. SAMUEL, d. Jan. 28, 1818, a. 52. SAMUEL A., son of Wolcot, d. Nov. 13, 1827, a. 2.

From Wby. Ch. Rec.—SAMUEL Jr. m. Chloe Gillet, June 6, 1787; she d. Sept. 17, 1805 in 37; their son d. Nov. 29, 1795, a. 6. CHLOE, m. Wm. Case of Say-brook, Dec. 2, 1824. SARAH, m. John A. Hemstead of Hartford, Sept. 7, 1830.

The following from E. W. C. R—OLIVER (prob. son of Nathaniel,[6] p. 808), had children bap. Dec. 20, 1761; April 15, 1764; June 8, 1766; June 19, 1768; Nov. 11, 1770; Aug. 29, 1773.

RUSSELL (prob. son of William, Jr., line 19, page 808), had Russell, bap. July 22, 1793; Elmira, bap. Nov. 13, 1796; ——, Sept. 24, 1796.

WILLIS, had Elizabeth, bap. Feb. 12, 1826.

TIMOTHY, had child bap. Sept. 17, 1797; Lydia, bap. March 10, 1799; Fran—, bap. June 7, 1801.

WILLIAM, had children bap. Feb. 15, 1789; Jan. 30, 1791; March 23, 1794. JOHN, had child bap. Oct. 22, 1786; April 12, 1789.

STRONG, p. 809, l. 18, for *April*, 1643, read *April* 26, 1663. (Col. Rec.)

P. 809, l. 31, for *bap.* read *b.* (Col. Rec.)

P. 809, l. 40, MARY, b. 1658 ; m. Timothy Standly of Farmington, Nov. 22, 1676. (Col. Rec.)

P. 810, l. 6. for 1684 read 1686. (Col. Rec.)

P. 810, l. 34, add to children of ABEL (E. W.), the name of Abel, bap. March 17, 1793. (W. C. R.) ABEL'S son NATHAN, m. Didemia Soper, Oct. 31, 1804.

DANIEL (son of Abel) (E. W ?), m. Wealthy Loomis, July 3, 1799 ; and had Betsy, bap. Feb. 1, 1801. (W. C. R.)

ELISHA and Mary, had Jane, bap. April 8, 1787 ; Elisha Bebee, bap. June, 1789; Samuel, bap. Sept. 25, 1790; Charlotte, bap. June 15, 1794; (the preceding from N. S. R.); Almira, bap. Aug. 20, 1797 ; Oliver, bap. July 28, 1799 ; William Augustus, bap. Nov. 14, 1802. (W. C. R.)

JOHN, m. Elizabeth Bissell, Aug. 24, 1682. (Col. Rec.)

JOHN³ was married in 1686. (Col. Rec.)

RETURN, m. Jennet Sill, Dec. 29, 1799. JULIA, m. Heman Norton of N. Y. Aug. 23, 1807. MARY, m. Ward Woodbridge, March, 1809. SAMUEL, m. Delia Selden, Oct. 14, 1811. ALMIRA, m. Charles Babcock, Oct. 15, 1816. (W. C. R.)

SAMUEL and Delia, had Delia, Charlotte, Mary Jane; Samuel, bap. Nov. 13, 1819 ; Mary Selden, bap. Oct. 4, 1823.

All the following from E. W. C. R.—JOHN, Jr. had child bap. Nov. 24, 1782. JOHN, had children bap. Feb. 19, 1786; July, 1788. NOAH R. had Marilda, bap. March 9, 1800. WARHAM, had children bap. June 12, 1803 ; June 23, 1805 ; Eliza, July 26, 1807.

NATHANIEL, had children bap. Oct. 17, 1778 ; July 23, 1780 ; Sela Jan. 1, 1797.

TIMOTHY, had children bap. June 10, 1764 ; Nov. 25, 1770 ; May 17, 1772; Oct. 17, 1773 ; June—Oct. 1777 ; dau. June 23, 1805.

NATHANIEL (prob. same as on line 6, page 811), had also Harvey, bap. March 27, 1763; Rachel, bap. Dec. 2, 1764. (N. S. R.)

STRICKLAND, p. 811, insert JOSEPH of Hartford, m. Elizabeth Chapman, Dec. 11, 1684.

TAYLOR, p. 812, SAMUEL, m. Mary Bankes of W., Oct. 27, 1670. Wid. T., d. Aug. 5, 1689. (Col. Rec.) Same authority also supplies 1682 as year of Nathaniel's birth, last line.

TERRY, p. 813, GEER, m. Louisa Denslow, Nov. 15, 1798.

Wid. CHLOE had two children bap. Oct. 28, 1821. (E. W. C. R.)

P. 813, l. 2, MARY, b. 1633, m. Richard Goodman of Hartford, Dec. 8, 1659. (Col. Rec.)

P. 813, l. 6, JOHN. b. 1669-70, d. Dec. 30, 1670. (Col. Rec.)

THRALL, p. 814, l. 2, for 1798-9 read 1708-9.

P. 814, l. 9, Mary Roberts, wife of John, Jr.,[1] was probably the wife of John,[5] 23d line same page.

P. 814, 1. 28, CHLOE, b. July 27, 1771, was bap. with Eunice July 23, 1775. (N. S. R.)

P. 814, 1. 29, DAVID's wife was Jane ——.

From Wby. Ch. Rec.—OLIVER J. m. Harriet Moore, Dec. 23, 1817.

ISAAC, m. Rhoda Phelps, Jan. 26, 1775; had Rhoda, bap. June 25, 1775; Linda, bap. Nov. 30, 1777; Isaac, bap. Feb. 19, 1781; Thomas, bap. Aug. 17, 1783; Polly, bap. June, 1787; Patty, bap. Oct. 1790; Friend, bap. June 16, 1793.

JOHN, had Elizabeth, bap. June 14, 1770; Eli, bap. June 26, 1774; d. Jan. 23, 1775.

The Wid. ELIZABETH "the younger" had a dau. Elizabeth, who d. Aug. 29, 1777. (N. S. R.) Wid. ELIZABETH (prob. same as above), had Timothy, Elizabeth (see preceding) and Mary, bap. Aug. 4, 1776. (N. S. R.) The Wid. THRALL, had Mary, who d. Sept. 18, 1776. (N. S. R.) Probably all the same family.

JESSE, had Nathaniel, bap. May 4, 1786; Marilla, bap. June 10, 1787; JESSE and Mehitable had Timothy, bap. Oct. 25, 1789; Anna, bap. Oct. 5, 1793; preceding from N. S. R.; Elizabeth, bap. Oct. 2. 1796. (W. C. R.)

DAVID, m. Zulima, had Henry, Mary, Sarah, Joel, all bap. Oct. 1, 1786; also Huldah, bap. Jan. 30, 1791; William, bap. July 27, 1794. (N. S. R.)

Genealogy of WALTER (son of Jesse, son of Samuel, son of John, Jr.,[1] son of Sgt. John) of Circleville, Ohio, furnished by him.

P. 814, SAMUEL (son of John, Jr.,[1] line 9, son of Sgt. John, line 4), b. July 11, 1737, m. Lucy Winchel of Windsor, and moved thence, before the Revolution, to Granville, Mass., and thence, in 1790, to Rutland, Vt., was an officer in the French war, and a captain in the American army in Revolution. He was one of the insurgents in the Shay's Rebellion, for which it is said he lost his property. In 1788 he was a member of the Massachusetts Legislature, and d. in Vermont in 1821, æ. 84 yrs. He was an honest man, and had considerable influence, for many years was a member of Congregational Church. He had nine children, all of whom had large families, and six of whom moved to Rutland with him. One of his daughters m. Eber Spelman of Stafford, Ct.; one son Worthy, d. in Windsor about 1816, a. 47, and left a good property; he also had sons Jesse, Eliphas, Samuel and Aaron.

Jesse, wife Mabel and family; Eliphas and family, and Aaron's family, he being dead, all moved together from Vermont to Ohio, about 1815-16.

SAMUEL, removed from Granville, Mass., to Granville, Ohio in 1805.

TILTON, p. 816, 1. 1, ELIZABETH, d. July 17, 1655. (Col. Rec.)

TUDOR, p. 816, 1. 17, OWEN's wife, "Wid. Mary Skinner" was the dau. of —— Loomis, she d. Aug. 19, 1680. They had Samuel and Sarah (twins), b. Dec. 5 (and another record says Nov. 26), 1652; Owen, Jr. b. March 12, 1654; Mary, b. March 6, 1660, m. a Judson; Jane, m. a Smith, and d. before 1717.

P. 816, 1. 23, MARY, b. 1690. ELIZABETH, m. Thomas Marshall, and was living in Oct. 1766, but divorced; for interesting documents relative to the case, see *Com. Arch. Lotteries and Divorces,* fol. 1, No. 107, *et alios.* They then lived at Torrington, Conn.

P. 816, l. 34, for *Oliver* read *James.*

P. 817, OLIVER,[6] had Mary Ann, bap. May 15, 1803; David McC. bap. April 7, 1805; Abigail, bap. July 5, 1807; Sophia, bap. April 19, 1818; Pauline, bap. Nov. 5, 1819.

ELIZABETH, had Eliza, bap. May 29, 1803. HENRY, had Mary Sophia, bap. March 29, 1801.

SAMUEL,[4] the dates of his children's baptisms as follows: Naomi, April 8, 1764; June 9, 1765; Sept. 10, 1769; Sept. 6, 1772.

The daus. of JOHN, Jr.[1] (line 9, page 814), LUCY, m. John Hathaway; MARY, m. Elisha Winchell; MINDWELL, m. John Morand.

P. 817, l. 17. for *Elknah* read *Elkanah.*

WADSWORTH, p. 817, ROGER, m. Ann Prior, July 10, 1777.

HORACE, m. Electa Chandler, May 17, 1801.

Lt. TIMOTHY, had [Lucretia, bap. Sept. 16, 1781; ——, bap. Aug. 31, 1783. (Wby. Ch. Rec.)

WAKEFIELD, p. 817, l. 37, ADEN, m. Susanna Barney, March 12, 1794; WARDWELL, p. 818, add " Mariam," bap. Nov. 22, 1775. (Wby. Ch. Rec.)

WARNER, p. 818, l. 20, LOOMIS, had Eli Whitney, bap. March 1, 1798. (W. C. R.)

P. 818, l. 1, *Nathem* read *Nathan.*

Ann (line 5), Mr. Ebenezer (line 6) and Ebenezer, jr. (line 7), should properly come under the head of *Wardwell;* and the name of Abigail Warham belongs at the end of Warham record below. The date of Jane 2d, wife of Rev. Mr. Warham, should be April 23, 1645; Mrs. Abigail Branker was his 3d wife.

From Wby. Ch. Rec.—GEORGE of W. (prob. one mentioned line 21, page 818), m. Nabby Griswold Mills, May 17, 1792; had Abigail, bap. July 3, 1808; George Loomis, bap. Oct. 21, 1810. (W. C. R.)

PLINY (prob. one mentioned line 23, page 818), m. Charlotte Brown, June 17, 1799.

WATERS, JOHN, m. Phebe Roberts, Sept. 29, 1768. JOHN, had Samuel, bap. April 16, 1768. JAMES (father unknown), bap. June 3, 1781. (Wby. Ch. Rec.)

WATSON, p. 819, l. 8, for 1749 read 1747, according to E. W. O.

P. 819, l. 6, for 1730 read 1738, according to E. W. O.; see also Clark.

P. 819, l. 5, Jedidiah d. (not in Dec. 1641) but Dec. 17, 1741, in 76 yr.

P. 819, l. 14, for Aug. 10, read Aug. 19. (Col. Rec.)

P. 819, l. 21, ELIZABETH, was daughter of Joseph Mather, and d. in 30th yr. (E. W. O.)

P. 819, l. 33, JOHN,[6] d. a. LXXV. (E. W. O.) His wife Hannah (see grave-

stone, E. W. O.), d. Dec. v, MDCCCXXVII., æ. LXXVII. Iu the same E.
W. O., are also monument of following children of John ꞏ and Hannah;
Frederic Bliss, b. Sept. 4, 1810, d. Sept. 17, 1810; Mary Alice, b. Oct. 10,
1800, d. Jan. 1. 1809.

ROBERT, d. Nov. 3, 1832, his wife MEHITABLE, d. April 6, 1824, a. 49. (E.
W. O.) SOPHIA, d. March 13, 1811, a. 12. (E. W. O.) EDMUND, d. Dec. 24,
1843, a. 42; his dau. MARIA, by Hannah, his wife, d. Feb. 28, 1840, a. 3
mo. (Sc.)

WAY, p. 820, insert HAMMOND m. Anne Potwine (?) June, 1777.

WEBSTER, p. 821, CYRENUS (line 11). had also child, bap. Feb. 15, 1784;
Warham, bap. Feb. 27, 1791. (E. W. C. R.)

From W by. Ch. Rec.—SAMUEL, had Ashbel, bap. Dec. 17, 1741; d. a few
days old; Elizabeth, bap. Jan. 30, 1743; Ashbel, bap. May 13, 1744; a child
d. Feb. 22, 1746, a few min. old; Ruth, bap. March 8, 1747; Samuel, bap.
April 9, 1749; Micah, bap. March 17, 1751; Aaron, bap. Sept. 1, 1753; Timothy, bap. and d. Aug. 9, 1757; Anne, bap. Nov. 12, 1758; Timothy, bap.
April 26, 1761; Rachel, bap. April 8, 1764.

ASHBEL, had Lucy, bap. April 24, 1774, d. Sept. 2, 1775; Anna, who d.
Sept. 6, 1775, a. about 24; Lucy, bap. May 2, 1779; Eunice, bap. May, 1781;
Ashbel, bap. May 14, 1786.

Sgt. WILLIAM, had James bap. Nov. 16, 1740; Anna, bap. July 20, 1760;
Joseph, bap. Feb. 14, 1762; Hezekiah, bap. March 30, 1766; William, bap.
April 5, 1767; Daniel, bap. April 2, 1768: there were also two (twins) who d.
Sept 6 and 9, 1748, a. a few days.

WILLIAM, Jr. had Asaph, bap. June 5, 1768, d. Sept. 24, 1779; Elijah
Drake, bap. March 18, 1770; Elisha, bap. Aug. 9, 1772; Chloe, bap. April 17,
1774, d. Oct. 2, 1775; Phineas, bap. June 23, 1776; Jehiel, bap. Oct. 10,
1779; Chloe, bap. Nov. 4, 1781.

JAMES, had James, bap. Feb. 7, 1768; Mary, bap. Oct. 15, 1770; John,
bap. May 9, 1773, d. June 23, 1775; John, bap. Nov. 12, 1775; Susanna,
bap. May 9, 1779; Alanson, bap. June 4, 1793.

AARON, m. Mary Sheppard, July 1, 1778; Aaron, bap. June 28, 1779;
Samuel, bap. Aug. 25, 1782; Polly, bap. Aug. 29, 1784; Electi (?) bap. 1786;
Samuel, bap. Nov. 24, 1787; Charles Shepard and Theron, bap. Oct. 14,
1792.

ASAHEL, m. Anna Atwell, July 22, 1778.

Capt. HEZEKIAH, had Anna Harriet, bap. Feb. 23, 1800; Hezekiah Goodwin, bap. Dec. 14, 1800; David Hawley, bap. June 8, 1806; Wealthy Ann,
bap. Oct. 7, 1810; Samuel, bap. Nov. 26, 1815.

JOSEPH, had Joseph Case, bap. Jan. 11, 1801; also Ebenezer, Mehitable,
Nancy, Daniel William.

EBENEZER of W. m. Mary Willis of Farmington, July 5, 1807; had Hiram,
Dwight, Ebenezer Wells, Mary Jane and William Wells, bap. Aug. 4, 1822ꞏ
Sarah Jennette, Milo Merry, Martha Morilla, bap. Oct. 1, 1826.

ASAHEL, jr. m. Esther Bissell, Dec. 2, 1806; Wealthy Ann, m. Thomas Shepard, Jr. Feb. 14, 1802; Nancy, m. Edwin Griswold of Simsbury, April 20, 1825.

WILLIAM'S wife Mary d. May 6, 1754, a. about 44; SAMUEL, d. (at sea), 1772, a. about 2 (?); WILLIAM d. March 21, 1779, a. 76; RUTH, d. Nov. 26, 1785, a. about 38; SAMUEL, d. Nov. 13, 1798, a. 84; HEZEKIAH'S, inf. son a. 6 weeks, d. Nov. 15, 1798; ELIZABETH (wid of Samuel), d. Sept. 24, 1799, in 77; DAVID Hawley of Hezekiah, d. Jan. 29, 1809, a. 3; JOSEPH'S son a. 2, d. Feb. 2, 1809; EBENEZER'S child d. Oct. 1812; WEALTHY ANN of Hezekiah, d. April 11, 1813, a 3; JACOB, d. Dec. 21, 1813, a. 91. JAMES, s. of William (p. 821, l. 3)' should be *William* according to *W by. Ch. Rec.*

WELCH, p. 821, l. 17, JERUSHA, m. William E. Tudor of E. W., June 3, 1819. (W. C. R.)

P. 821, l. 19, CYNTHIA, m. Daniel Barker, June 3, 1819. (W. C. R).

JULIA, m. Stanton Babcock, Jan. 6, 1840. (W. C. R.)

HOPESTILL and Ellis, had Ellis, Vine and Benjamin, all bap. Dec. 25, 1768 (N. S. R.); Sarah, bap. March 24, 1770. (N. S. R.)

WELLER, p. 821, ABNER, m. Mary Griswold, April 1, 1784.

P. 821, l. 27, ANN, wife of Richard, d. July 10, 1655. The date given to Sarah should be of her *bap.* Insert also the name of John, bap. Aug. 10, 1645. (Col. Rec.)

WELLES, p. 821, ELISHA, m. Huldah Clark, Nov. 7, 1784. SILAS (E. W.) m. Anne Denslow, Nov. 10, 1790. URSULA, m. Josiah Corning, Oct. 15, 1834. (W. C. R.) TIMOTHY, m. Huldah Phelps, July 20, 1818. (W. C. R.) THOMAS, had dau. Prudence, bap. Sept. 7, 1799. (W. C. R.)

MOSES, had ——, bap. Nov. 22, 1761; James, bap. Aug. 21, 1763; Silas, bap. June 9, 1765.

SILAS, had Samuel, bap. Nov. 3, 1793; ——, April 9, 1797; Julia, bap. Oct. 6, 1799; Justus Denslow, bap. Nov. 8, 1801; ——, bap. June 17, 1804.

NOAH, had ——, bap. June 23, 1782; ——, Feb. 15, 1784; ——, Nov. 4 1787; ——, Feb. 21, 1790; Frederick, bap. March 18, 1792; Nancy, bap. April 12, 1795. The foregoing from E. W. C. R.

WHALEMAN, p. 822, insert EBENEZER, had a child bap. August, 1776. (E. W. C. R.)

RALPH G. m. Eunice Allyn, Oct. 28, 1829. FLORA, m. Israel J. Palmer of Farmington, Oct. 3, 1828. (Wby. Ch. Rec.)

WESTLAND, p. 822, l. 28, JOSEPH, m. Lucina Rowell, Jan. 5, 1786; same line for *Cota*, read *Catharine*; and for *Grave*, read *Grove*. In addition to these Joseph had Orma, bap. Aug. 14, 1791; Harvey, bap. June 15, 1800. (W. C. R.)

ROBERT, m. Lydia Cook, Sept. 19, 1785. ROBERT, Jr., m. Wid. Chloe Cook, 1818. (W. C. R.) JERUSHA ("adult"), dau. of Robert, bap. March 25, 1792. TRYPHENA (adult), dau. of Robert, bap. Aug. 3, 1794. (W. C. R.) "WARHAM Pease of Tryphena," bap. Aug. 31, 1799. (W. C. R.) HANNAH (see line 27) m. John Alderman, Aug. 23, 1802.

17

OLIVER m. Louise Clement, May 26, 1793.

WESTOVER, p. 822, insert JONAS, had Jonas, b, Sept. 20, 1664. (Col. Rec.)

WHITE, p. 822, OLIVER, m. Lucy Wood, April 10, 1796. HENRY of E. W. m. Jerusha Barber, June 9, 1825. (W. C. R.)

WILLIAMS, p. 823, third line from bottom, I have reason to think that this *Lucinda* should be *Lucretia.*

P. 823, l. 23, ARTHUR, had Zebediah, b. Oct. 29, 1649.

P. 823, l. 24, JOHN was buried April 18, 1681, having been m. 37 yrs.; his wife d. Aug. 3, 1665.

P. 823, l. 27, for *Abiel*, read *Abigail.*

P. 823, l. 28, strike out the word " (Marshall ?)."

P. 823, l. 31, NATHANIEL, m.'Mary Owen, Oct. 3, 1681; their dau. Mary b. 1682. (Col. Rec.)

P. 823, l. 36, should read " the first female child that was *born* in Hartford." (Wind. Town Rec.)

The following from E. W. C. R.—ASHBEL, had Clarissa, bap. July 10, 1796; ——, June 26, 1808; ——, July 14, 1816.

EBENEZER, had ——, bap. May 26, 1799; H—, June 7, 1801; William, Oct. 16, 1803; ——, July 31, 1805; —— July 24, 1808.

JONATHAN, had Sarah, bap. May 1, 1803; Mary Ann, bap. June 7, 1807; Samuel, bap. July 2, 1809; Fa—, bap. July 26, 1812; two children bap. Sept. 9, 1821.

JOSEPH, had Owen D., bap. July 2, 1815; ——, Sept. 19, 1819; ——, June 23, 1811.

WILLIAMSON, p. 823, insert ANN (dau. of Elias), admitted to 1st Church Middletown, Conn., Nov. 19, 1727, by letter from Church in Windsor. (E. S.)

WILLISTON, p. 823, insert WILLIAM, m. Dolly Goodwin McLean, Oct. 27, 1791.

WILSON, p. 824, l. 19, ELI, m. Ruth More, April 8, 1798, for her death see line 34. The words " and his wife who d. a. 62; m. Nov. 3, 1845," in line 19, evidently belongs elsewhere.

P. 824, l. 23, CALVIN, b. in Stafford, Conn., was a Revolutionary soldier, and d. May 20, 1809, a. 54. His wife Submit, d. Dec. 10, 1840, a. 74.

P. 824, l. 28, Dea. PHINEHAS, m. Susannah Giles, Dec. 28, 1785, had Phinehas and Oliver, bap. April 20, 1788. (W. C. R.)

P. 824, l. 31, for Nov. 2, 1829, read Nov. 20, 1827. (W. C. R.)

From Wby. Ch. Rec.—JOEL, Jr. (see line 12, page 824), m. Jan. 24, 1768, Grace Loomis, had Grace, bap. Oct. 1, 1755; Joel and Susannah, bap. March 23, 1774; Susy, bap. Aug. 3, 1777; John, bap. Sept. 16, 1781; Deborah, bap. Aug. 31, 1783.

JOEL, Jr., had Olive, bap. Oct. 10, 1792; Annis, Orson Skinner and Olive bap. Aug. 4, 1822; Olive Cerelia, bap. June 1, 1823.

JOSEPH, m. Candace Barber, March 7, 1811. WARREN, m. Ruth Marshall, March 18, 1811. AMMI, m. Betsy Burr, July 3, 1828.

JOEL, d. Sept. 20, 1797, a. 80. JOSEPH, d. Sept. 28, 1801, a. 64. Wid.
ABIAH, d. April 19, 1813, a. 70. ROXANA, d. Sept. 26, 1826.

HULDAH, m. William Marsh of Hartford, May 9, 1822. (W. C. R.)

P. 824, l. 35, for *No.* 1 read *No.* 2.

WILTON, p. 824, l. 37, for *Stanford* read *Stamford.* (Col. Reo.)

WINCHELL, p. 825, l. 1, for 1638, read 1639. PHEBE, d. May 23, 1662.
(Col. Rec.).

P. 825, l. 3, for *buried* read *died.* (Col. Rec.)

P. 825, l. 4, for *Bruson* read *Brunson.* (Col Rec.)

WING, p. 825, l. 28, SAMUEL, m. Hannah ——; "Aug. 22, 1769, d. Mrs.
JOANNA Wing, wife of Samuel, of a putrid fever after childbearing," a. 30.
(N. S. R.)

MOSES (see line 30), Roger and Martha, children of Samuel and Haunah,
bap. March 19, 1769. (N. S. R.)

SAMUEL and Lydia, had Abigail, bap. Oct. 14, 1771; Samuel, bap. July 9,
1775. (N. S. R.)

P. 825, l. 39, Lt. SAMUEL,[11] " d. at Danbury in the service," July, 1777. (N.
S. R.) There is some confusion in these Samuels, but I consider the date of
the above as less authoritative than the other records.

P. 825, l. 34, ADELINE, m. Oliver Kingsbury of Coventry, April 29, 1805.
PLINY, d. Aug. 5, 1834, a. 39. (W. C. R.)

WITCHFIELD, p. 823, l. 18, Col. Rec. says Elder W.'s wife d. July 27,
1669. (Col. Rec.)

From Col. Rec.—WOLCOTT, P. 826, l. 11, *where,* read *whose*; p. 827, l. 29,
for 7th read 5th.

P. 828, l. 30, for *July,* read *June.* HENRY, Jr., had also son Samuel, b.
April 16, 1656; Hannah, b. March, 7, 1653.

P. 828, l. 37, the name of HENRY's wife was ABIA.

P. 828, l. 38, for *Elizabeth,* read *Abiah.*

P. 828, l. 38, Henry, b. 1667; d. May 14, 1667.

P. 828, l. 42, Samuel, b. 1679; d. 1690.

ELIZABETH, dau. of George, m. Gabriel Cornish of Westfield, Dec. 15,
1686.

P. 829, l. 10, *Curmin,* read *Curwin.*

P. 832, l. 17, ROGER,[8] after the death of his first wife, sued for the hand
of Mrs. Eunice Ely of Springfield, Mass., as will be seen by the following
(now first published), copied from the original in the possession of Mrs. E.
Simmons of Windsor. The lady afterwards m. the Hon. Roger Newbury of
Windsor:

Windsor, Feby. 10, 1759.

Madam:—As I have No other Way of Conversing with you than by Writing I Embraced this opportunity by Mr. Wolcott to Let you know that I am
in helth and must Tel you that when on ye 5 of June Last I committed to ye
Dust the Richest Tresure I had in this World, and a Darkened Gloomy Pros-

pect appeared on Every other Injoyment in Life a sublime Mantel Hung
Round about me, and so it Remained untill I had the Plesur of Waiting
upon you, and then yᵉ Innercens and oblidging Entertainment I met with
Gave me sum Prospect, yᵗ my Dayes might acquire Durence—my sore might
cease, and yᵉ Long Night of affliction be in some mesur att an ende, if I
might be a Partner in yᵉ Pleasurs you Enjoye: it has been yᵉ Greatest Plesur
I ever Enjoyed in Life in Contributing to yᵉ Happiness of her yt is now Removed Beyond my Care.   But shold you smile on my addresses, I hope to
feall yᵉ same Plesure In Doing Every Thing in my Powers to contribute to
your Happiness, there is nothing I more Desier than to Give you full Evidence
of my sincerity in this and Did I Believe this could not be obtained by so
Near and Intimate a Relation with you, I should be farr from Desiring it, But
I should Rather still Remaine in a State of Moping Melancholy.   I now with
Impatiens Waight the Return of the bapy Hour when I hope to have yₑ
Pleasur of Waiting upon you againe.   My Days of Prosperity fly with Raysed
and Impetuous forse, but yᵉ hours of Affliction Especially when I have some
Prospect of Deliverance and Happiness Before me—how slow Do the minits
Roale.

   Time seems to stand still and make a Pause, my fortin is all att you Dys-
pocis, and how Ever you may Dyspose of it I sincerely Wish you a Long,
Prosperous and hapy Life.   I add no more except to answer you, I am your
Affectionate friend and very
Humble Servant,
Mrs. Eunice Ely.   ROGER WOLCOTT.

   P. 832, l. 29, a copy of an acrostic written by Dr. Alexander[8] Wolcott, for
his second wife (Mary Richards), before their marriage :

> Milder than light is my triumphant fair.
> As kind as angels; soft as evening air,
> Rich in her mind, in every state content,
> Young, modest, virtuous, chaste and innocent.
> Religious, pious, meek, sincere and good,
> Iust to her friends, but truer to her God,
> Courteous to all, from affectation free,
> Haughty to none and very kind to me,
> Attached to truth whene'er it does appear,
> Rigid to none, though to herself severe,
> Dear to the world and to the heavenly powers.
> Such is the charmer whom my heart adores.

   The following from E. W. C. R.—ELIHU (mentioned in p. 833, l. 35), son
of Samuel,[12] had Elihu, bap. June 5, 1808; Hannah McClure, bap. Jan. 26,
1812; Samuel (mentioned line 38), bap. Nov. 21, 1813; Arthur, bap. Aug.
27, 1815; ——, bap. Dec. 28, 1817; Nan—, bap. July 18, 1819. ELIHU (perhaps same), had H—, bap. Oct. 10, 1824; ——, bap. Oct. 8, 1826.

   EPHRAIM (prob. the same ment. l. 16, p. 832), had Betsy, bap. March 10,
1793: Ephraim, bap. Feb. 17, 1795.

   " Lt." et " Capt." et " Major " ABIEL (prob. the same ment. l. 15, p. 832), had Ursula, bap. June 27, 1796; Sa--, bap. June 15, 1800; ——, June 17, 1804.

TALCOTT (prob. ment. 1. 31, p. 829), had children bap. April 18, 1798; Aug. 25, 1799; Loyry (?), Dec. 11, 1803.

P. 834, 1. 10, SARAH'S birth according to E. W. C. R., was in 1764.

P. 834, 1. 13, PARMENIO,[15] had a child bap. April 14, 1793.

ALBERT, had children Sept. 24, 1786; March 3, 1793; Laura, Nov. 2, 1794; Oct. 29, 1797.

ARODA, had children, bap. March 31, 1793; Nov. 23, 1796; a dau. Jan. 20, 1799.

P. 834, 1. 23, for 1683, read 1783.

P. 634, 1. 25, to family of Dr. Christopher,[19] add Philip, bap. June 8, 1704; m. Emily Marshall, July 11, 1817 (W. C. R.); Elizabeth, bap, March 18, 1792 (W. C. R.); his son Dr. Christopher, m. Anna Gillet, Sept. 25, 1806.

P. 835, 1. 1, a Guy Wolcott, had Abigail, bap. Sept. 18, 1785. (W. C. R.) Can these two Abigails be the same? Also to Guy,[21] give the following children: Eleazer, bap. Feb. 10, 1793; Henry, bap. Jan. 31, 1796; Anne, bap. Feb. 11, 1798. (All from W. C. R.)

P. 835, 1. 18, MARY, dau. of Roger,[25] was bap. July 17, 1791; add to this family also another dau. Sarah, bap. Sept. 24, 1796.

P. 835, 5th line from bottom, for *discovered*, read *considered*.

FRANCES (perhaps dau. of Alexander [20]), m. Archibald Rolston of Berthier, S. C., May 2, 1840. (W. C. R.)

P. 836, the curious inscription to "B. W." should have been credited to the *Windsor Grave Yard*.

WOOD, p. 836, an Obediah, had child bap. May 7, 1775. (E. W. C. R.)

JAMES,[2] m. S. Elmer both of E. W., Aug. 10, 1780; had child, bap Jan. 6, 1782. (E. W. C. R.)

JONATHAN (last line but one, p. 836), had also child, bap. Dec. 13, 1778; two bap. Nov. 28, 1779.

WOODWARD, p. —, insert Oliver, m. Thankful Brown, 1772, had Wealthy Ann, bap. Oct. 18, 1770; Betty, bap. July 13, 1775; Oliver, bap. Aug. 6, 1780; Eleanor, bap. Aug. 31, 1783; Elihu, bap. June, 1787. (Wby. Ch. Rec.)

WOODWORTH, p. 837, insert JAMES, had Hosea and Pamela, bap. Jan. 14, 1798; ——, Jan. 12, 1800. (E. W. C. R.)

WRIGHT, Moses and Chloe had also children Polly and George, bap. August, 1788; Almira, bap. July 11, 1782; John, bap. Nov. 2, 1783; Jemima, bap. Aug. 21, 1791; Eunice, bap. April 9, 1793; Esther, bap. Aug. 23, 1795.

P. 838, 1. 19, for *Chaptain*, read *Chapman*.

VERSTILLE, p. 842, had child, bap. May 11, 1788; William Henry and another were bap. Aug. 14, 1791; Peter, was bap. (the record says "St." Peter), April 7, 1793; Sheldon, bap. May 29, 1803. (E. W. C. R.)

WILLS, p. 842, JOSHUA, m. Azubah Lamson, May 5, 1670 ; his dau. Hannah was b. Aug. 24, 1682. (Col. Rec.)

P. 842, the heading of Appendix No. 1, should be *Sir Richard Saltonstall's letter*, etc.

P. 854, *Note to Wine and Bread Accounts of the Windsor Church*—It would seem as if the church in Mr. Warham's day (the first communion in the record is dated before his death), in their zeal to imitate that planted by the apostles, may have made a *regular meal* of the communion service, instead of the practice of the present day. The large quantity of bread * and wine used—and the data of calculation in the record (the number of members, the number of communions, and quantities of bread and wine, all being given) are unusually full—would seem to indicate a " love feast " on a more hearty scale than is in accordance with the present custom. Still it may possibly be susceptible of some other explanation.

J. Hammond Trumbull, Esq., of Hartford, Conn., some years ago received letters from England enquiring for evidence of such a practice in the early American churches, and in reply sent to his correspondent a copy of this record.

---

* Supposed to be an average of about two ounces per each member.